COMPANION TO THE
ENGLISH CIVIL WARS

COMPANION TO THE
ENGLISH CIVIL WARS

Peter Newman

Facts On File
New York • Oxford • Sydney

COMPANION TO THE ENGLISH CIVIL WARS

For information contact:

Facts On File Limited
Collins Street
Oxford OX4 1XU
UK

or

Facts On File, Inc.
460 Park Avenue South
New York NY10016
USA

or

Facts On File Pty Ltd
Talavera & Kartoum Rds
North Ryde NSW 2113
Australia

A British CIP catalogue record for this book is available from the British Library

Library of Congress Cataloging-in-Publication Data

Newman, P. R.
    Companion to the English civil wars / Peter Newman.
        p.   cm.
    Includes bibliographical references.
    1. Great Britain—History—Civil War, 1642–1649.—Dictionaries. 2. Great Britain—History—Commonwealth and Protectorate, 1649–1660—Dictionaries. 3. Great Britain—History—Puritan Revolution, 1642–1660—Dictionaries.   I. Title.
DA405.N48   1990
0941'06'033—dc20   90–3114
                                                              CIP

ISBN 0–8160–2237–2 (hc)
ISBN 0–8160–2536–3 (pb)

Australian CIP data available on request from Facts On File

Facts On File books are available at special discounts when purchased in bulk quantities for businesses, associations, institutions or sales promotions. Please contact the Special Sales Department of our Oxford office on 0865 728399 or our New York office on 212/683–2244 (dial 800/322–8755 except in NY, AK or HI).

Photoset in North Wales by
Derek Doyle & Associates, Mold, Clwyd
Printed and bound in Great Britain by
Biddles Ltd, Guildford and King's Lynn

10 9 8 7 6 5 4 3 2 1

This book is printed on acid-free paper.

CONTENTS

Preface   ix

Acknowledgements   xi

Introduction   xiii

A–Z entries   1–165

Chronology   167

Select Bibliography   177

Maps   181

To Captain Helliwell of Heptonstall

Alta Sedent Civilis Vulnera Dextrae

M. Anneus Lucanus, AD 1st century

PREFACE

This *Companion* covers the period of the English Civil Wars – from 1642 to 1641 – in terms of events, personalities and issues that led to or arose from the conflict. In a sense, the expression English Civil Wars is misleading. Wales was caught up in the struggle from its outset, hostilities spilled violently over into Scotland, and the struggle on the mainland transformed that being waged in Ireland between the Catholic rebels who rose in arms in 1641 and the Dublin government. The entries in the *Companion* seek to stress the 'British' aspect of the wars, and to lay stress upon the Irish dimension.

Although some writers have chosen to define the period of the civil wars as 1642 to 1660, that is also misleading. Charles II's attempt to capture the throne became a disastrous failure at the battle of Worcester in 1651. The government of the United Kingdom was thenceforth, perhaps surprisingly, stable in that it met and contained incipient unrest, whether inspired by royalist conspirators or by restless and embittered religious and political radicals. It also sought to resolve the crises of government that had led to the civil wars, and to meet the consequences of the protracted warfare of the 1640s. Although some of the leading figures of the 1650s first emerged in the previous decade – Oliver Cromwell for example – it cannot be argued that the whole period from 1642 to 1660 was one of governmental instability. The last serious armed challenge to the authority of Parliament was in 1651. When Charles II came back to his throne in 1660 it was not by force but by political compromise, itself a measure of the strength of the Republic established following the execution of King Charles I in 1649. Those who put to death the king in that year, must have expected a violent response: they confronted it and defeated the forces of monarchical loyalism. The year 1651 therefore marks a proper terminal date to the period of the civil wars, just as 1642 (the year in which hostilities between king and Parliament broke out) is a self-evident commencement.

None the less, the years from 1642 to 1651 cannot be regarded as if in a vacuum. The *Companion* entries overlap the terminal dates wherever necessary to clarify the events of those years. Oliver Cromwell's importance, for example, must be set against his virtual obscurity prior to the 1640s, and his increasing power in the 1650s alluded to. Similarly, the Bishops' Wars, which began in 1639, contributed to the instability of royal government, and the Irish rebellion of 1641 may be considered to be the major immediate factor in the creation of opposite sides in England in 1642. In terms of doctrines (such as Presbyterianism) and political developments (such as the Solemn League and Covenant of 1643), it is necessary to be aware of earlier developments such as the Scottish National Covenant of the 1630s. The objective has been to relate the events and personalities of the period 1642–51 to causes and consequences beyond those dates.

The criteria for inclusion of individuals as entries raised particular problems. Some – Cromwell, Thomas Fairfax, the king, and Archbishop William Laud, for example – require inclusion. Others are there to provide a link with events and movements, whilst others still reflect or convey the atmosphere of the period, particularly the religious and political radicals, many of whom achieved nothing at all but whose beliefs and ideals illustrate the intellectual and social turmoil of the age. The *Companion* is not, of course, a biographical dictionary: selection and omission is inevitably arbitrary, but the attempt has been made to include those men and women who, if not movers of events, may none the less be held as representative of their time.

In selecting battles for inclusion, the attempt has been made to cite those which had consequences beyond the immediate infliction of maiming and death on the participants, or which tie in with other entries. Military terminology of the period has also been included to elucidate references that the reader might come across in contemporary or specialist works. The structure of the armies is discussed in terms of regimental organization, and the nature of the hardware, such as muskets and other weaponry employed, is discussed. This book seeks to cover the ground between the death of a common soldier in some more-or-less localized combat, and the rarefied atmosphere of political debate and intrigue amongst the movers of the wars.

Clearly, the *Companion* cannot hope to present the many and varied historiographical views of the civil wars and in some instances the attempt to present 'fact' is less easy than might be desired. Everyone, then and now, might agree, for example, that Charles I was physically courageous and fundamentally idealistic, but few, then or now, would agree as to the precise nature of his responsibility for the wars. The present writer has exercised, necessarily, personal judgements, but does not intend them to be prescriptive.

In the following essay, which forms an historical introduction, some of the historiographical issues are touched upon, whilst the bibliography contains a representative selection of historical works that treat the period either as a whole, or approach it from specific, sometimes narrow, perspectives. The *Companion* is an aid to understanding; it does not set out to contribute to the still virile historical debates that focus upon the years 1642–51.

ACKNOWLEDGEMENTS

The author must thank Ronald Hutton of the University of Bristol for suggesting certain entries, and Norman Dore who provided quickly and efficiently some obscure references.

Not a few of the more difficult entries reached finalized format during walks in the peace of the Rosary Way at Hazlewood Castle in Yorkshire, from which place, in 1644, two brothers rode out to die on the field of Marston Moor, an hour's ride from their home.

INTRODUCTION

The study of the period of the English Civil Wars is one of the most contentious in British history. Historians continue to debate, as they debated in the 17th century itself, the causes of the wars, the issues at stake, the nature of allegiance and commitment, and the precise implications of political, economic, social and religious change that England then experienced. For here was a nation, long at peace, entertaining no standing army, that suddenly, in the spring and summer of 1642, divided against itself. Two armed camps emerged, with enough men on either side able and willing to kill to make civil war not just a probability, but a long and protracted and sometimes savage reality. It was a reality from which, short of flight abroad, no individual could escape.

Civil war undermined the security of towns, villages, communities and families. The 1640s were frightening and perplexing: the war intruded into all aspects of the daily routine of life. It came in the guise of marching armies, of soldiers needing to be fed and sheltered. If a man were not marching with some army or other, it was insufficient to protest loyalty to a cause or approval of its proceedings: support was expressed in material donations, in food and money, and if that was not forthcoming voluntarily, it was as often as not seized, not withstanding any orders to the contrary from generals and commanders. The war came in plunder and spoliation, in the burning of barns and houses for devilment or as a warning, for retribution or for precise military reasons. It came in trampled and spoiled crops, and in localized dearth and hunger. It came in the diseases of a besieged town or castle, and in outbreaks of plague. War came in punitive and arbitrary taxation, in heavy duties on certain essential goods, and in exactions called contributions or assessment levied often on a weekly basis. It came in the form of disruption of trade and markets, and it came, too, in the form of press gangs forcing men into the regiments of either side. There was no escape from the war. Those who, for whatever reason, endeavoured to keep aloof found themselves under suspicion from both sides, and plundered by both sides – and plundering armies were no respecters of age or rank or sex. Would-be neutrals were often compelled by the pressure of events to seek shelter within the garrison of one side or of the other. If they were unfortunate enough to choose a royalist garrison, they found themselves treated like any partisan of the king when the time came for a reckoning with the Parliament.

The civil wars were not fought tidily between rival armies under their committed commanders in a pitched battle here or a skirmish or siege there. They were localized and they were everywhere, they were waged in the heart of the realm, and the horror of it all may explain why, when the royalists were defeated in 1646, there was no enthusiasm for subsequent royalist insurrections in 1648 or 1650/51. It was as if, with some exceptions, people were appalled and henceforth reluctant to go the way that so many of them had done in 1642. The civil wars were a failure of government, and any government that gave stability, however it changed the institutions and machinery of power, was inevitably if grudgingly welcomed as a salvation from what had gone before. The success of the Republican experiment lay in that simple fact.

When war began in 1642 both the king and his advisors, and his enemies in Parliament, resorted to simple expedients to legitimize their resort to arms. The king's supporters fought for the king and for his Parliament, as Parliament's supporters fought for the Parliament and the king. Both sides looked to the natural leaders of society – the gentry – to use their influence to raise men and to command them into the field. King and Parliament gave commissions to men who, if England had been threatened by external aggression, would have been recipients of similar commissions to defend the realm. These same men, experienced in government and administration, were able, through influence, familial associations and straightforward persuasion or example, to recruit officers and men to serve under them. In a sense, there was something familiar and reassuring about the developments of 1642, except that men were drilling and training to fight each other and not a foreign enemy. Where all else failed, coercion was resorted to by both sides; landlords expected their tenants to follow their lead, or at least to provide the money to equip men in their place. It was not all straightforward; some tenants reacted against the dictates of their landlords, and whether from true commitment or years of resentment, went against landlord example, but such cases were rare, at least when the war began. The natural leaders of communities, of regions or areas, had the means to raise soldiers, and the civil war was rooted in that reality. In time, the war disrupted and broke down that vertical relationship of obligation and expectation, but in 1642 it mattered and was crucial to the formation of the armies that fought at the battle of Edgehill in October. In essence, given real political and religious divisions within society, putting armies into the field was relatively easy. As the war dragged on, and particularly for the royalists, it became less easy to keep them there. Even the parliamentarians found it necessary to resort to impressment and conscription.

The New Model Army of 1645, which narrowly won the battle of Naseby and so began the defeat of the king, was the ultimate instrument of Parliament's will to win. Its success in a way transformed it; the enthusiasms of 1642 came back in a distinctive and assertive form. By 1648 the New Model was less an intsrument of the Parliament, than it was, in its own eyes at least, of God Almighty, executing the Lord's will and often hamstrung by its erstwhile political masters. The New Model, new in nothing except in its view of itself and its developing cadre of semi-plebeian officers, may be seen as an inevitable product of the civil-war years. It mastered its political masters in Parliament and it made possible the trial and execution of King Charles I, whose servants it had encountered in numerous hard-fought actions. Yet the soldiers of the New Model – drawn for the most part from the old provincial armies – were in much the same position vis-à-vis their commanding generals as the soldiers of the armies of 1642 had been. In the last analysis, the New Model Army was nothing more than a highly polished version of those earlier forces, enhanced by discipline and somewhat muddled political and religious awareness.

Civil war is expressed in the clash of opposing armed forces. Behind those forces, and motivating them, lay conflicting political and religious beliefs entertained by sufficient numbers of activists to provide the personnel and the money for the massive task of organizing for, and sustaining, war. In that context, soldiers and armies are the instruments of politicians and are used to further political causes, the precise definition of which may be elusive or yet to be arrived at. What lay behind the resort to arms in 1642?

Early 17th-century England was, for the most part, self-governed. Central government, based in and around London, was remote in a physical sense, hampered by poor communications, and limited also by the lack of an effective and large bureaucracy. In this sense, heavily wooded Surrey and Sussex were as remote as Cumbria or Cornwall. Effective government depended upon local self-government, and the active support of local leaders in implementing central government policy. To say that the civil wars arose from a crisis within government is certainly true, but the crisis was within its centralized form. The relative efficiency of localized authority is reflected in the way in which the provinces were armed and prepared for war in a very few months.

The gentry (by which is meant those with landed interest, whether mere gentlemen or peers of the realm) were the natural leaders of society. In their capacities as lords and deputy lieutenants, as justices of the peace and as sheriffs, they carried through the policies of central government, and similarly, through Parliament, represented local grievances to that central authority. On their acquiescence or resistance, governmental policies could meet success or failure. When, as gradually happened, these natural leaders of society divided amongst themselves, they offered to whichever side they supported the knowledge and administrative experience of their time, and created fighting armies and the means to pay them. Responsive to them at regional and parish or village level were the high and petty constables, upon whom fell the task, in peace as in war, of collecting taxation. The evidence for the efficiency of the system is shown in the fact of protracted civil wars during this time.

A former royalist general, reflecting upon the events of the 1640s from the new security of Restoration England, gave it as his opinion that the cause of the king had been served wholly by the gentry – his own social peergroup. In terms of organization and the sacrifice of money and possessions for the royalist cause, this was demonstrably true. Yet it was also true for Parliament, too, which looked to the machinery in the established social order to back it in its struggle with the king. The gentry, in short, divided amongst themselves and thereby proved how indispensable they were in the exercise of power. In time, and not exclusively in the forces supporting Parliament, men of humble origins rose to positions of considerable political influence and authority, often by way of military command. The social structure, however, was flexible enough to assimilate them; there was no social revolution in any lasting sense in civil-war England.

It may be felt that resistance to Charles I's government, developing in the course of the 1630s, and revealing itself in the Short and Long Parliaments from 1640, was based upon principle. A good case for this may be made in the issue of Ship Money, an extraordinary tax customarily levied in time of war to finance naval defence of the coast. Charles I imposed it as a regular, nationwide tax in 1636, and overcame the challenge of John Hampden in 1637 with compliant judges. Resistance to this form of arbitrary taxation amongst those responsible for collecting it and paying it and for giving example to others, brought collection of the tax to a virtual halt by 1640. The imposition was denounced in Parliament, but only, it was felt, because of its association with unpopular royal government. For, in the 1640s, Parliament did not balk at utilizing the machinery of Ship Money collection to exact finances for its own war effort, and more effectively and rigorously than Ship Money itself had ever been collected. During the 1640s and 1650s, England was more heavily taxed than it had ever been or would be again for almost 300 years. Clearly, the question of arbitrary taxation centred upon cause and purpose rather than upon any concept of arbitrary taxation as being inimical to the liberty of the subject. When it is considered that many leading figures who had more or less vigorously denounced King Charles's levying of Ship Money, nevertheless championed his cause in 1642, it seems clear that the king's fiscal measures were but a small part in a developing crisis. By 1642 something more fundamental was at stake.

Considerable emphasis has been placed upon the religious issues of the years leading up to civil war as causative factors. In the simplest terms, King Charles and his advisors were regarded by many as 'innovative' in religion, and were accused, more or less unjustly, of seeking to turn the Church of England towards Rome, if not actually to embrace Roman Catholicism. The government-inspired and sustained campaign of hatred towards Catholicism and suspicion of Catholics of the 16th century, had left deep-seated in the English psyche a wholly irrational fear of Popishness. Given that, and the long-postponed further reformation of the English church along Puritan lines advocated by a vociferous and political influential minority, the religious issue was always potentially explosive. The association of the religious policies of William Laud and others with the period of King Charles I's personal rule in the 1630s, successfully combined religious antagonisms with political grievances. Yet it has to be stressed that it was a fusion of the two, rather than emphasis upon one or the other, that galvanized opposition to the king and his government. For, as in the case of Ship Money, many critics of royal religious policy nevertheless found it possible to support the king in 1642 against Parliament.

It is not to be supposed that Laudian innovation in religious observance was necessarily met with uniform hostility. Opposition to the railing off of altars at the east end of churches and the renewed emphasis upon communion came from an articulate few. But that few could, and did, represent these changes as smacking of Popery, and they drew deliberately upon the reservoir of distrust and dislike of Catholics and Catholicism that was endemic in 17th-century England. Religious critics of royal government, whom we tend loosely to label Puritans, were skilful politicians, and they seized upon whatever weapon was at hand to further their cause. Given a Catholic presence at the royal court in the person of Queen Henrietta Maria and her entourage, and the fashionable aspect of court Catholicism, they had an easy target. But throughout the country Roman Catholics who absented themselves from services of the Church of England, still suffered under rigorous, punitive and extraordinary taxation in the form of fines which no one, apart from them, considered unjust or improper. Beyond the royal court, where interpretation of what was happening was open to abuse, there was no sign, nor indication, of any concerted move towards Roman Catholicism. The court's religious enemies, sincerely or otherwise, believed that there was, and that belief fuelled opposition to royal government.

This campaign, when it came to focus upon the role of the bishops and the nature of church government, struck at the roots of royal power itself. A thorough and truly Protestant reformation of the church rquired the abolition episcopacy and of the church courts. In the 1640s the Long Parliament obliged with the necessary legislation. But it is extremely doubtful that the reformers touched upon the feelings of the population at large, except to exploit and manipulate an antipathy towards Catholicism. When King Charles II returned to his throne in 1660, the bishops came back to the church as well, and it has been shown that there was widespread affection and sympathy for the Church of England and its episcopal structure, that survived the reforms of the Long Parliament and the religious turmoil of the civil-war years. As is often the case, the quasi-revolutionary activists of the 1640s represented few other than themselves.

If the attack upon the role of the bishops represented an indirect attack upon royal power and prerogative, the immediate consequence of the Irish rebellion of 1641 was to make that attack more overt. To 17th-century Englishmen, the Irish represented something a good deal less than human: their social structure, their gaelic culture and their unequivocal Catholicism, made them objects of contempt, loathing and fear. The rebellion of 1641, a gaelic and almost nationalist uprising, was seized upon by critics of royal government as a vindication of their claim that the Popish enemy was at the gates. The rebellion gave to critics of the royal government and enemies of monarchical prerogative an additional weapon. Just as religious unrest in Scotland in 1639 had provoked conflict and led to the summoning of Parliament in 1640, so the Irish rebellion gave fresh impetus to the cause of reform. At the same time, however, it also provided the opportunity for the emergence of something like a royalist 'party' both inside the House of Commons and in the country at large. It might reasonably be said that the Irish rebellion precipitated civil war in England, and made it into a real possibility.

Parliament's response to the rebellion struck at the royal prerogative in two important respects. Firstly, in the raising of money to finance the suppression of the rebellion, Parliament took it upon itself to bargain away the lands of the Irish rebels to investors in the struggle. This was an emphatic attack upon the prerogative of the crown in the matter of forfeited property of rebels and traitors. Secondly, in the question of the command of forces raised against the Irish rebels, Parliament challenged the ancient prerogative of the crown to exercise such command, and gave clear warning to the king that he was not trusted. The bill had been first introduced into Parliament in July 1641 – it was, therefore, no new or sudden thing – but the events in Ireland gave it renewed importance from the point of view of the activists in the Commons. It was a proposal to which the king could not assent without signing away a good deal more than his kingly dignity: for it would put into the hands of Parliament an army commanded by a general of Parliament's choice. The issue dragged on until May 1642, when the Parliament took it upon itself to push through an Ordinance embodying the provisions of the Militia Bill. By that time, the issue had polarized political thinking in and outside Parliament. A royalist party, to balance what was left of the Parliament's consensus, had emerged.

The Irish rebellion, it may be argued, helped to create a royalist movement in support of the king, although indirectly. The rebellion certainly emphasized division within Parliament itself, and further alarmed 'moderates' and others who, fearful of royal arbitrary power, were equally as fearful of such power enjoyed by Parliament. Out of this crisis of late 1641 and early 1642 emerged, in the months ahead, the royalist and parliamentarian sides of the civil-war years. Both sides embraced necessary fictions, seeing themselves as the true friends of king and Parliament, but they also embraced divergent religious and political programmes, and made them the touchstone of loyalty.

The split within the House of Commons and the House of Lords mirrored, or was mirrored by, the split in the country at large. Dreadful tales of atrocity and butchery filtering through from Ireland helped to create, in 1642, an atmosphere in which anything was possible and any fearful development likely. Over the issue of the Militia Bill neither the king nor his political opponents would budge, and the royal decision to absent himself from London and to establish his court 200 miles north at York created a physical divide out of which armed conflict could grow. Old political associates found themselves divided in their reactions to developments: MPs steadily abandoned the sittings of the House of Commons, some to associate openly with the king, others to go home and keep their heads down. The sittings of the House gradually became confined to a smaller but more resolute body of men, and their strength and commitment grew commensurately, and increasingly alarmed those who had qualms anyway about what Parliament was doing. Slowly, not without equivocation and resistance, two distinct political groupings were formed, which would, by the late summer of 1642, have at their disposal two military forces to champion their respective causes.

It has been said that the natural leaders of the community of the realm, the gentry, divided amongst themselves. For both king and Parliament their support was essential, their experience was needed, their financial commitment was important. But the division within society was far more than merely a gentry split, and anyway, there were and always would be, degrees of commitment. It is clear from the extant records that all manner of men and women, from the humblest to the highest, took up political positions, however imperfectly they may have understood the issues at stake. That made the task of the political and military leaders of either side, easier to fulfil. For there can be no doubt that, on both sides, there was no lack of willingness in 1642 to contribute in person or by proxy to the war effort.

The issue of allegiance remains a difficult problem. It cannot be ruled out that on both sides there were those with solid and reasoned political loyalties, and they did not exclusively belong to the gentry any more than it would be true to say that only poor men were coerced into taking a stand by dangerous or influential friends and neighbours. Geographical location was an important factor: it was easier to do something for Parliament if you lived in Tower Hamlets near London, than it was to abandon everything and hurry north to associate with the king. Similarly, it was easier to adopt a royalist position if you lived within the protection of one or other of the numerous royalist gentry mansions and castles in and around York. It was, also, commensurately harder to do nothing and to try to keep aloof: for this merely fired the suspicion and animosity of both sides. But in the summer of 1642, with the king firmly established at York and his enemies secure in London, there were whole areas of the country where nothing need happen unless those with authority and influence who lived there allowed it to happen. The king's commissioners of array and the Parliament's commissioners under the Militia Ordinance voluntarily drew their areas into war preparation. The spread of the conflict was the conscious decision of men nationwide, even if some of them regarded their preparations as defensive or exercises in containment. When the king marched towards the Welsh border in the late summer of 1642 he went to meet men armed in his service, and with them he met at Edgehill the soldiers Parliament had drawn preponderantly from the south and east. There were men willing enough to fight and others willing enough to lead them. A profound issue was at stake.

That there were clear differences between the armies of both sides when the civil wars began is as true as that there were clear similarities. In the popular imagination, the differences are summed up in the terms 'Roundhead' and 'Cavalier'. A recent writer has suggested that the term 'Roundhead' conveyed nothing much more to 17th-century men than the term 'skinhead' to the late 20th century. It was a term of opprobrium that the recipients did not care for. 'Cavalier' with its exotic southern European flavour, was likewise a term of opprobium, but one which some royalists assumed voluntarily. The words, common currency now in the English language, convey stereotypes, and colour one's impression of what royalists and parliamentarians were fighting about. But in another sense, the terms accurately portray what must be a necessary assumption: that the bulk of the rank and file were there for pay, the excitement or because they had had very little choice. The rank and file, if they survived to become veterans, probably assumed and clung more or less tenaciously to, the political and religious doctrines of their commanders and their political master, so that it can be argued that the experience of civil war was, for most activists, a schooling in belief and political awareness. An earlier point about the New Model Army of 1648 being a polished version of the armies of 1642 can be understood in this additional sense.

Perhaps a striking difference between the royalist armies and those of Parliament, and one which pamphleteers made much of, was the undoubted importance in the royalist army commands of known Roman Catholics, particularly in the forces raised in northern England by the earl of Newcastle. The presence of men known for their popish beliefs, or long suspected of holding them, in positions of authority played into the hands of the pedlars of the 'Catholic threat' myth which had an ancient, if not respectable, history in political terms. Indeed, for the observers in London, the earl of Newcastle's northern army was 'The Popish Army', but Catholic royalists were widespread throughout England, Wales and even Scotland. Their involvement in the struggle against Parliament still represents one of the most perplexing aspects of the civil-war years, and has variously been explained as either an attempt to ingratiate themselves with the king, or a realization that hard times would be harder in the event of a parliamentarian victory. Neither of those explanations is satisfactory: the important point seems to be that, with one or two exceptions (which appeared in the closing stages of the war as certain royalists abandoned their commands and yielded to Parliament, denouncing belatedly Catholic involvement with the king) the majority of Protestant royalists accepted their Catholic allies easily enough. It may fairly be said that those active gentry royalists were free of the myth of the Catholic plot, recognizing in these adherents of the old religion men who shared their basic loyalty to the crown, and attaching more importance to that than to anything else.

Although Parliament during the war years and afterwards continued to harry and pursue Catholics – whether royalist activists or not – with studied and punitive land seizure and taxation, there can be no doubt that the Catholic-threat mythology offered a good excuse for measures which would help Parliament financially. That did not mean that all parliamentarians implicitly accepted the myth as truth. Indeed, even so godly a soldier as Oliver Cromwell entertained Roman Catholic troopers in his regiment; but, then, there was always a difference of degree between gentry and similar practitioners of Catholicism, and plebeian Catholics. The difference was money and land, and which Catholics could or could not be made milch cows for the state.

That said, the remarkable commitment of Catholics to the royalist cause is an important distinction between the forces of the king and those of the Parliament. In terms of what we might call 'ideology' the differences were theoretically enormous, in practice less so. Some of the royalists were out-and-out supporters of episcopal church government and of the rite of the Anglican church; their counterparts were the extremer forms of Puritan who looked to virtual dis-establishment of the church and to the creation of gathered congregations of believers, rid of priestly and episcopal control. Some royalists were outright supporters of the rights prerogative and privileges of the crown; and there were, in the Parliament's ranks from the outset, men of a determinedly Republican stance who clearly embarrassed and outraged their more moderate colleagues. In time, and certainly after the purge of the House of Commons in 1648 that preceded the trial of the king, the Republicans gained control of the political process, but they were then, as they had always been, a minority, as were the royal absolutists. By no means were all parliamentarian soldiers iconoclasts and all royalists plunderers. The vast majority on either side tempered their allegiance with moderation, unless events drove them to extremes. They were men over whom extremists of one kind or another could achieve a temporary assertion of authority, but that was all.

The similiarities between the two sides will be obvious. The armies were predominantly made up of volunteers, recruited in those areas over which one side or the other had control. As has been said, for many of the fighting men, the war itself was a schooling in politics, the vast majority acting initially less from ideological commitment than from a number of easily imagined and less elevating motives. They were commanded by men of a social background to whom they had deferred, more or less willingly, in time of peace. Both the parliamentarian and royalist army commands underwent changes as the war progressed, gifted, accomplished or just plain dangerous men of humble origins, pushing their way to positions of command and authority on both sides. In the case of Parliament, their progress was virtually legislated for by the Self-Denying Ordinance which cleared all the parliamentarian aristocracy out of army command at one fell swoop in 1645, and theoretically every serving MP as well.

But in less spectacular form, as well, Parliament's war effort encouraged the rise of relatively humble men. The local committees for raising money and for seizing the estates of royalists had to be staffed, and the defection of many obvious committee candidates to the king, opened the way for others who undoubtedly found in their allegiance to the Parliament a useful ladder for their economic and social improvement. But there was no social revolution as such. These men fitted into an existing structure, where they could, and did not, tear it down to build anew. The doctrine of private property and property rights remained sacred to both sides, always in theory, and whenever it was practical to observe it in reality as well. Challenges to it from political radicals were vocal but ineffective. Society contained the civil war and limited its excesses.

It has been suggested that the experience of war and its horrors was one of the reasons for the failure of the population at large to respond when, in 1648 and again in 1650/51, attempts were made to raise royalist insurrection. That of 1648, easily the most dangerous threat to the Parliament subsequent to the conclusion of the civil war in 1646, was suppressed because of its poor nationwide coordination, and because of the lack of positive support in the country. That may be attributable to war-weariness, but it may also be attributed to royalist dismay at the alliance between King Charles and the Scottish Presbyterians which not only seemed, but was, a denial of one of the principal issues for which royalists had taken up arms in 1642. The royalist-presbyterian alliance was, for both parties, a matter of necessity, but that did not make it all that palatable. Indeed, much of the proposed effectiveness of the 1648 attempted insurrection turned upon the armed commitment of men previously staunch parliamentarians, alienated by the religious policies of Parliament, and, many of them, owed large sums of money by their political masters.

The Republican regime established after the execution of the king in 1649 and the subsequent abolition of monarchy by Parliament, together with the abolition of the House of Lords, should have had but a tenuous grip on power. It had many enemies – royalists, presbyterians, even radicals such as the Levellers – and, perhaps most threatening of all, the existence of the dead king's son, now Charles II, with a claim to make and a developing mythology surrounding his dead father to draw upon. Many earlier active royalists, however, had been punished financially for their 'delinquency' and were shy of outright commitment. The attempt of 1650/51 to place Charles II upon his throne rested upon the efforts of a divided and unreliable Scottish presbyterian army with a sprinkling of politically acceptable old royalists, and it was outfought by Cromwell and the Republican army, first in Scotland, and then in England, at Worcester, in September 1651. There can be no denying that the country thereafter settled down under Republican rule, even if it resented aspects of that rule; above all else it offered stability and security, for the most part, and it lifted national pride in its dealings with foreign powers. It was a hard thing for committed royalists to accept, but the realists amongst them did so, that a massive rising against the Republic in favour of ancient monarchy was not at all likely after 1651, and had not even been probable in the immediate wake of the execution of 1649. Life returned to normal for the mast majority of people, and for that majority, whatever their private thoughts and secret hopes, that was more than sufficient.

If the civil wars were fought over the role of the monarchy and the role of Parliament, it is too easy to say that Parliament won. In the end, it won because every attempt to reach agreement with Charles I failed. In the end, the execution of that king was an admission of a kind of defeat, and subsequent government would have to be concerned with filling the vacuum left by the departure of monarchy. In 1660, of course, the vacuum was filled by the restoration of monarchy, a fair indication of the lack of success of the Republican regime, at least in that respect.

Clearly, the royalists were militarily defeated, although that was never a foregone conclusion and at times looked unlikely. The resources of royalism were exhausted, and the survivors of the royalist leadership either fled abroad or were forced into exile, or they accepted the imposition of heavy fines which, whilst benefiting the state financially, curtailed royalist ability to finance revolt and insurrection in the future. But for royalist sentiment, which in some ways is what royalist ideology boiled down to after 1649, the execution of King Charles I, resulting from his wholly intransigent and uncompromising attitude towards his political enemies, proved as beneficial as it was dreadful. The monstrous slaughter of the king, however it was done openly and in the eyes of the world, effectively reunited a disintegrating and fractured party. In the end, for all his compromises of 1647 and 1648, King Charles I had died magnificently and become a martyr, and those of his followers executed before and after him, in their deaths added to the royalist tradition. It survived the Republican years intact, and occasionally burst forth in localized insurrections. Although easily suppressed it was never eradicated, not even by the mass transportation of royalists to the West Indies as slave labour.

To many of the regicides who went to their deaths after the restoration of King Charles II, their executions added lustre to the 'good old cause' they had espoused. To many of the royalists who had likewise suffered under the Republic, their deaths underlined their commitment to the service of their king. It may be that in this distinction between the 'good old cause'and the 'old service' lies the fundamental distinction between royalists and parliamentarians. Of course, royalists claimed that defence of the king and of his prerogatives implied defence of the liberties of the subject. But familiarity with the beliefs of active royalists, insofar as they are ascertainable, vigorously suggests that what motivated them was the sense of 'service', of doing that which their position as subjects of the crown required them to do. Parliamentarians broke with that servitude in the end; indeed, they effectively denied it in 1642. In its place they found and promoted a cause, centred upon the liberties of the subject, guaranteed by the liberty of Parliament. In 1649 they ceased to be the subjects of a king; they became, for eleven years, citizens of a Commonwealth.

A

Aberdeen, Battle of (13 September 1644)

Scottish ROYALIST forces under MONTROSE, chased towards Aberdeen, engaged its garrison, defeated them and occupied the city.

Abjuration, Oath of

An oath imposed upon ROYALIST Catholic DELINQUENTS and upon those ROMAN CATHOLICS whose property had been sequestered (see SEQUESTRATION) for their religious persuasions. It required subscribers to deny papal supremacy, the doctrine of transubstantiation, and the efficacy of images and crucifixes – all items of Catholic belief – before they could be admitted to COMPOSITION.

Acts of Parliament

Written laws of the realm that have received royal consent. From 1642 PARLIAMENT resorted to ORDINANCES, being unable to procure CHARLES I's assent to its measures. Its first Act on its own authority was that of 6 January 1649 setting up the HIGH COURT OF JUSTICE, although as late as 17 January an Ordinance was still resorted to concerning the militia (see TRAINED BANDS) of the city of LONDON.

C.H. Firth and R.S. Rait (eds), *Acts and Ordinances of the Interregnum*, 3 vols (London 1911).

Adams, Mary

An Essex woman and member of the sect of the RANTERS who claimed to be pregnant by the intercession of the Holy Ghost, and who committed suicide in 1652 after the birth of a stillborn child.

Advance of Money, Committee for (Also known as the Committee at Haberdashers Hall)

Committee of PARLIAMENT established 24 November 1642 with an order of Parliament that the public faith of the kingdom be given for the repayment at 8 per cent interest of money advanced for the war effort. Originally a committee of 16 members with salaried officers. Assessments of one fifth of personal estate and one twentieth of real estate were constantly in arrears, and property could be seized if assessments remained unpaid. Property worth £100 or less was exempt. Royalist DELINQUENTS were also required to pay their fifth and twentieth. County-based subcommittees were employed. After undergoing changes in responsibilities in 1650, the committee was terminated in 1655.

Adventurers

Those who subscribed to what was effectively a GOVERNMENT lottery to raise money to suppress the IRISH REBELLION. An ACT OF PARLIAMENT of

19 March 1642 invited subscriptions of £200 upwards for lots of 1,000 acres of land (assessed on the Irish acre of 7,231 square yards – 6,046 square metres) to be confiscated from the rebels. Some 2½ million acres were so earmarked. The Act also effectively deprived the king of the PREROGATIVE right to dispose of the lands of rebels forfeited to the crown. In July 1643 a 'doubling' ORDINANCE doubled land allocation in return for a further subscription, amounting to a quarter of the sum already advanced.

Adwalton Moor, Battle of (30 June 1643)

A comprehensive defeat inflicted upon the Yorkshire PARLIAMENT-ARIANS commanded by FERDINANDO LORD FAIRFAX, by the ROYALIST forces of the EARL OF NEWCASTLE, near BRADFORD in the West Riding of Yorkshire. This battle swept Yorkshire clear of parliamentarian field forces, and gave the royalists a brief but almost absolute ascendancy. The battle also contributed to the pressure for an alliance of the PARLIAMENT with the Scots as a means of turning the tide of war against the king.

Agents

The representatives of five radical cavalry regiments of the NEW MODEL ARMY who endorsed the *AGREEMENT OF THE PEOPLE*. Later, 'new' agents appeared in other regiments in the wake of the PUTNEY DEBATES. They were reckoned to be protégés of the LEVELLERS.

Agitators (Also known as Adjutators)

Representatives of each troop and regiment of the NEW MODEL ARMY elected in April–May 1647 to confer with officers over the presentation to PARLIAMENT of the army's grievances. They first appeared in the regiment of HENRY IRETON. They were removed from the GENERAL COUNCIL OF THE ARMY and sent back to their regiments in November 1647, although an attempt was made in October 1648 to revive their role. Similarities with regimental spokesmen of the Spanish armies in the late 16th century have been remarked by historians.

Agreement (of 1 May 1649)

Issued by JOHN LILBURNE and others then in the Tower for treason. It was a moderate LEVELLER basis for a constitutional settlement, calling for a widely elected assembly to replace the RUMP, and for freedom of conscience. Safeguards for private property were built in.

Agreement of the People

Published 28 October 1647, a written constitutional proposal drafted by civilian LEVELLERS and endorsed by the AGENTS of five NEW MODEL ARMY regiments. 'All power is originally and essentially in the whole body of the people', the proposal stated. This document, and the Leveller–Army alliance, led to the PUTNEY DEBATES. A revised version was imposed by HENRY IRETON, who was denounced by JOHN LILBURNE as 'the cunningest of Machiavellians', and this version appeared in December 1648. For the final version, see *AGREEMENT*. The HOUSE OF COMMONS ignored the proposals. See also *CASE OF THE ARMY TRULY STATED*.

Aldbourne Chase, Battle of (18 September 1643)

A victory by PRINCE RUPERT in Wiltshire over the EARL OF ESSEX, marking the end of the earl's hitherto successful campaign of manoeuvre to get his army back to London unscathed, and enabling CHARLES I to enter NEWBURY. Aldbourne Chase was also the scene of a major ROYALIST army muster on 10 April 1644.

Alford, Battle of (2 July 1645)

Scottish ROYALISTS under MONTROSE defeated a COVENANTER army in a battle that saw 1,500 of the 2,500-strong Covenanter force killed.

Allen, Francis (d. 1659)

A LONDON goldsmith and MP for Cockermouth in Cumberland in the LONG PARLIAMENT, he was treasurer to the NEW MODEL ARMY until 1653. He sat on the HIGH COURT OF JUSTICE to try CHARLES I but refused to sign the death warrant.

Allen, William (d. c. 1667)

AGITATOR in the NEW MODEL ARMY. A BAPTIST from Warwickshire, he represented OLIVER CROMWELL's own regiment of HORSE. In July 1647 he urged Cromwell to march on LONDON and to purge the PARLIAMENT, and was deposed by the influence of JOHN LILBURNE. In the 1650s he became involved in plots against Cromwell and was gaoled in 1660 by the COUNCIL OF STATE.

Alresford, Battle of See Cheriton, Battle of.

Alton, Battles of (22 February and 13 December 1643)

In February parliamentary troops (see PARLIAMENTARIAN) stationed in this Hampshire town fought off a major ROYALIST assault. In December a royalist garrison was attacked by SIR WILLIAM WALLER and slaughtered in the parish church.

Alured, John (1607–51)

MP for Hedon, Yorkshire, in the SHORT and LONG PARLIAMENTS, he served as a commander under SIR THOMAS FAIRFAX and evaded the provisions of the SELF DENYING ORDINANCE. A patron of ANDREW MARVELL. He sat on the HIGH COURT OF JUSTICE to try CHARLES I and signed the death warrant.

Anabaptists

In civil war terms, an abusive label flung at BAPTISTS and, in the 1650s, used against supporters of the REPUBLIC as well. Anabaptism was a religious and social movement that developed in early 16th-century Germany, and was seen as a severe challenge to the social order.

Ancaster Heath, Battle of (11 April 1643)

Scene of the defeat of parliamentary forces in southern Lincolnshire by ROYALISTS pushing south through the county. Captain JOHN HOTHAM was one of the defeated PARLIAMENTARIAN commanders.

Andrews Plot

A plot which centred on the ROYALIST Colonel Eusebius Andrews (1579–1650) and involved SIR JOHN GELL, the former PARLIAMENTARIAN. The objective was to seize the Isle of Ely, but the plot degenerated into a general conspiracy to restore CHARLES II to the throne. An agreement between the conspirators was reached 18 March 1650, Andrews was arrested 25 March, tried before the HIGH COURT OF JUSTICE and executed 22 August. Gell was gaoled. Andrews (like SIR HENRY SLINGSBY) was inveigled into the plot by a GOVERNMENT *agent provocateur*.

Anglesey, Isle of

Off the coast of North Wales, it was secured for the king by the Bulkeley family, whose last fortress of Beaumaris surrendered 14 June 1646. After the battle of Y DALAR HIR in 1648 the isle became a ROYALIST refuge, and was invaded 15 September by PARLIAMENTARIAN forces who won a decisive victory at the Red Hill.

Anticlericalism

A vigorous, rather than a passive, criticism of the established clergy of the CHURCH OF ENGLAND. George Herbert, a contemporary writer and Anglican parish priest, remarked upon the 'general ignominy ... cast upon the profession' of clergyman by the people at large. Anticlericalism underlay popular support for the PURITANS.

Antinomians

An abusive label attached particularly to the RANTERS and others who flew in the face of Calvinist PRESBYTERIANISM by favouring free grace and the doctrine of general salvation (see CALVINISM). Antinomianism was popularly equated with a disregard for moral and statute law.

G. Hyehns, *Antinomianism in English History* (London 1951).

Apologie of the Common Soldiers

The first manifesto of the AGITATORS of the NEW MODEL ARMY, handed in to the HOUSE OF COMMONS 30 April 1647 and published in May. It was signed by 16 soldiers, two from each cavalry regiment, and appears to have reached its final draft 26 March 1647.

Argyle (Argyll), Archibald Campbell Earl of (1598–1661)

The 'arrogant symbol of the covenanting cause' as some have styled him, Argyle was a prominent leader of the SCOTTISH NATIONAL COVENANT and in arms against the king in the BISHOPS' WARS. He was president of an army committee when the SCOTTISH ARMY invaded England in 1644. Upon the execution of CHARLES I he helped engineer the proclamation of CHARLES II as king in EDINBURGH, but opposed military intervention in England. He later served as an MP in the PARLIAMENT in LONDON in 1658. He was executed after the restoration of Charles II.

Armagh, James Ussher Archbishop of (1581–1656)

Ussher was made archbishop of Armagh in Ireland in 1625, but resided primarily in England where, in the crises of 1640–1, he drafted proposals for a modified episcopal structure in the CHURCH OF ENGLAND. He sought to save STRAFFORD, but was nevertheless given a pension by the PARLIAMENT in 1643. He opposed the WESTMINSTER ASSEMBLY on doctrinal grounds.

Arminianism

A respectable, not sectarian, school of theological doctrine rising from the work of Jacob Arminius (1560–1609), a Dutch theologian who emphasized free will above predestination (see CALVINISM). ARCHBISHOP WILLIAM LAUD and others of the High Church party in England were accused of Arminianism by their opponents, and the term LAUDIANISM is interchangeable with it. JOHN PYM claimed that Arminianism was an attempt to 'subvert the state'. Certain Arminian doctrines were embraced by radical religious SECTARIES of the 1650s.

Army, Committee for the

A committee of PARLIAMENT established September 1647 to bring in arrears of ASSESSMENTS to settle the backlog of pay for the NEW MODEL ARMY and the provincial forces. It moved against collectors and assessors rather than those liable to pay. In 1648 payments direct to regiments from the localities were authorized, with the regiments to assist in collection. This meant a decentralization of fund-raising and an overriding of the legal system.

Armyne, Sir William (1593–1651)

An MP of PRESBYTERIAN beliefs but leaning toward RELIGIOUS TOLERATION, who represented Grantham in Lincolnshire in the LONG PARLIAMENT. Involved in the Scottish alliance of 1643 (see SOLEMN LEAGUE AND COVENANT), and a member of the COMMITTEE FOR BOTH KINGDOMS as well as a commissioner attached to the SCOTTISH ARMY, he became disenchanted with the Scots. He refused to serve on the HIGH COURT OF JUSTICE to try CHARLES I.

Army Plots

Two still obscure attempts, originating amongst officers of the army raised to fight the Scots in 1641, to use force against the PARLIAMENT. The first originated at Boroughbridge in Yorkshire, the second was based around the garrison of Portsmouth in Hampshire. Neither succeeded, and both fuelled Parliament's determination: JOHN PYM used them effectively for his political ends.

Arnold, Richard

A soldier in Colonel ROBERT LIL-BURNE's regiment which mutinied at CORKBUSH FIELD 15 November 1647 in support of the *AGREEMENT OF THE PEOPLE*. One of three sentenced to die for mutiny, he alone was shot and became a LEVELLER martyr, occasioning JOHN LILBURNE to write a polemic against the abuses of courts martial.

Arundel Castle

A castle in Sussex, its capture in December 1643 by RALPH HOPTON marked the high point of the ROYAL-IST eastward march from Cornwall. SIR WILLIAM WALLER retook the town and the castle by 6 January 1644.

Ascham, Anthony (1618–50)

Tutor of James Duke of York, the second son of CHARLES I, he sided with PARLIAMENT and helped frame the charges against the king in 1649. ROYALISTS labelled him a regicide, and he was assassinated in Madrid in 1650 where he had gone as representative of the English GOVERNMENT.

His political theoretical writings have Hobbesian (see THOMAS HOBBES) elements.

Assessments

An attempt to provide a regular weekly or monthly income resorted to by both sides. Fixed sums were levied on county or city, and collected at parish or township level by the petty constables (see HIGH AND PETTY CONSTABLES). The ROYALIST assessment system was somewhat hit and miss, but PARLIAMENT based its collection procedures upon those followed in the levying of SHIP MONEY, and these tended to be arbitrary and indifferent to local variations. All paid, but part-time soldiers paid half, and full-time soldiers were excluded. Always in considerable arrears – the Parliament's assessment of February 1645 to September 1646 was 50 per cent behind – the assessments although necessary had a souring effect upon the bulk of the population. These and the EXCISE represented the heaviest direct taxation imposed in England and Wales until the 20th century, and they remained a fundamental source of revenue until 1660. FREE QUARTER was often used against non-payers, and was expressly authorized by the RUMP in 1649.

Assizes

The assizes were a superior court to the QUARTER SESSIONS, and fulfilled as much a political as a judicial role. The judges of assize were called by one contemporary the 'eyes of the kingdom', and represented central

GOVERNMENT to the localities much as they also advised the PRIVY COUNCIL on local matters. By 1642 and the eve of civil war, the judges of assize were virtual spokesmen for royal government and part of the king's propaganda drive to win support from his people.

Astley, Sir Jacob (1579–1651)

Major General of FOOT under CHARLES I, and a man with extensive military experience in Europe. He was raised to the peerage as Baron Astley in November 1644, and took over from CHARLES GERARD in South Wales in 1645. As commander, he surrendered the last ROYALIST field army at STOW-ON-THE-WOLD in 1646.

Aston, Sir Arthur (1590–1649)

Aston had extensive military experience in Europe (particularly in Russia) prior to the civil war when he served under CHARLES I as a cavalry general and governor of READING. This 'testy, froward, imperious and tirannical person' (as a PARLIAMENTARIAN said of him) was killed in cold blood when DROGHEDA fell to CROMWELL in 1649. Aston had been governor of the fortress there.

Aston, Sir Thomas (1600–45)

Aston was a Cheshire gentleman and champion of EPISCOPACY who served as a colonel under CHARLES I. He was instrumental in sending a PETITION to PARLIAMENT in defence of the bishops in 1642, and was a COMMISSIONER OF ARRAY the same year. Sir Thomas was

mortally wounded in action in 1645 and died: an exultant PARLIAMENTARIAN observer delighted in Aston's death following upon the fall of 'his darling episcopacy'.

Atkyns, Richard (1615–77)

Atkyns was a Gloucestershire gentleman who served in the army of CHARLES I and, in 1669, published *Vindication of Richard Atkyns Esqr., as also a Relation of Several Passages in the Western War wherein he was concerned.* His other publications reflect his interest in typography.

Attainder

A purely legislative way of destroying a political enemy or liability; an ACT passed through PARLIAMENT and given the royal assent condemning one accused of high treason to forfeiture of property and goods and the denial of these to his offspring. STRAFFORD was the victim of such an act in 1641. Reversals of attainder might be sanctioned in the case of the heirs of the attainted person.

Aubrey, John (1626–97)

Aubrey is remembered as an antiquary, writer and gossip. His *Brief Lives* contained numerous penportraits and anecdotes of wellknown people, including ROYALIST officers, of the civil war period.,

O.L. Dick (ed.), *Aubrey's Brief Lives* (London 1960).

Auldearn, Battle of (19 May 1645)

Scottish ROYALISTS under MONTROSE routed forces under SIR JOHN URRY in a bitter battle which forced the EARL OF LEVEN, operating in England, to withdraw his army northwards to be nearer developments in Scotland.

Authorized Version of the Bible

A new translation of the Bible authorized in 1604 at the Hampton Court Conference, called by James I to settle differences in the religion of the state. The first edition appeared in 1611. It is known also as the King James Bible, and was 'authorized' because it was appointed to be read in churches to the exclusion of all other translations.

Axtell, Daniel (d. 1660)

A Hertfordshire pedlar who rose to regimental command in the NEW MODEL ARMY and was effective in Kent during the 1648 rising (see SECOND CIVIL WAR). Present at PRIDE'S PURGE, he commanded the guard on CHARLES I during the latter's trial. As Governor of KILKENNY in 1650 he was noted for his savagery towards the Irish. He was executed 15 October 1660 for his part in the death of Charles I.

B

Babylon Hill, Battle of (7 September 1642)

A detachment of the ROYALIST army of the MARQUESS OF HERTFORD was defeated near Yeovil, Somerset, by local PARLIAMENTARIAN forces.

Backs, breasts and pots

Contemporary terms for the basic armour of the cavalryman, the backplate, the breastplate, and the helmet (ordinarily a single- or triple-barred helmet with flexible neck guard).

Baggot-Rath, Battle of (2 August 1649)

Scene in Ireland of the defeat of ROYALIST forces under ORMONDE by MICHAEL JONES, shortly before CROMWELL's arrival at Dublin with reinforcements.

Banbury

A major royalist base in Oxfordshire from its seizure 29 October 1642 until the surrender of the castle 8 May 1646. It endured a three-month siege in 1644.

Baptists

A religious movement apparently established in England c.1600, by John Smyth (d. 1612) who had imbibed Arminian (see ARMINIANISM) influences in Holland. Baptists believed in free grace as against predestination (see CALVINISM), and regarded adult baptism as an entry into the faith of the church. During the civil war years 'Particular Baptists' appeared, more fiercely Calvinist, and against whom the term ANABAPTIST was often used.

Barber, Edward

Author of the TRACTS *To The Kings Most Excellent Majesty* (1641), arguing for RELIGIOUS TOLERATION, and *A small Treatise of Baptisme or Dipping* (1642), which discussed the idea of baptism by total immersion (see BAPTISTS). He sided with the LEVELLERS and was a supporter of the *AGREEMENT OF THE PEOPLE*.

Barkstead, Sir John (d. 1662)

A LONDON goldsmith who became a colonel in the NEW MODEL ARMY and was involved in the SIEGE OF COLCHESTER in 1648. He served on the HIGH COURT OF JUSTICE and signed the king's death warrant in 1649, and in the 1650s worked closely with JOHN THURLOE in intelligence work. He was arrested in Holland in 1662 and executed in London.

Barnstaple

A small North Devon port seized by the ROYALISTS 2 September 1643. In June 1644 its townspeople rose in arms and resisted the royalists until 18 September 1644. It finally surrendered to PARLIAMENT 19 April 1646.

Barthomley

Scene in Cheshire of a notable civil war atrocity at Christmas 1643 when ROYALIST soldiers smoked their opponents from the security of the church and slaughtered them as they emerged, an action usually laid at the feet of JOHN BYRON.

Bascot Heath, Battle of (23 August 1642)

Fought in Warwickshire on the day after the king's standard was raised. PARLIAMENTARIAN troops from WARWICK CASTLE under LORD BROOKE defeated a contingent of local ROYALIST cavalry.

Basing House (Also known as Old Loyalty)

A stronghold in Hampshire of great strategic importance on the roads from LONDON to SALISBURY and the south-west. The ROYALISTS held it from 1642, resisting strenuous sieges in 1643, 1644 and 1645. Basing House fell to OLIVER CROMWELL by storm 14 October 1645, and its fall was marked by a number of atrocities.

W. Emberton, *Love Loyalty. The Close and Perilous Siege of Basing House 1643–45* (London 1972).

Bastwick, John (1593–1654)

Essex physician expelled from the College of Physicians and gaoled by the state in the 1630s for TRACTS attacking EPISCOPACY. In 1637 he, WILLIAM PRYNNE and HENRY BURTON appeared before STAR CHAMBER accused of sedition. His ears were cut off by the common hangman. An influence on JOHN LILBURNE, Bastwick's PRESBYTERIANISM caused a split between them. His beliefs are exemplified by his tracts *Independency Not God's Ordinance* (1645) and *The Storming of the Anabaptists Garrisons* (1647).

Bate, George (1608–69)

The author of *Elenchi Motuum Nuperorum in Anglia* (1649), rendered into English in 1652 as *A Compendius Narrative of the Late Troubles in England*, the first pro-ROYALIST history of the civil wars. Bate acted as physician to OLIVER CROMWELL and then to King CHARLES II.

Batten, William (d. 1667)

Vice-Admiral of the NAVY under the EARL OF WARWICK in 1642, he went over to the ROYALISTS in 1648 from a fit of personal pique and was knighted by CHARLES II, but then defected in the midst of the 1648 rising (see SECOND CIVIL WAR).

Baxter, Richard (1615–91)

Baxter was a PRESBYTERIAN who served during the civil wars as chaplain in the PARLIAMENTARIAN armies. A critic of the INDEPENDENTS, he came to most prominence as a sufferer under CHARLES II after retiring from the CHURCH OF ENGLAND because of his religious principles.

Beacon Hill, Battle of (21 August 1644)

Collective name for three hills near LOSTWITHIEL which the ROYALISTS successfully assaulted, forcing the surrender of the army of the EARL OF ESSEX.

Bedford, Francis Russell Earl of (1593–1641)

A leading opponent of royal policies, Bedford was a patron of JOHN PYM in much the same way as the EARL OF WARWICK was of CROMWELL. Although Bedford's death in 1641 cannot be seen as a major contributory factor in the slide into civil war, some historians have chosen to see him as a possible leader of reformed GOVERNMENT.

Beeston Castle

Believed by contemporaries to be impregnable, this Cheshire castle fell on 13 December 1643 to JOHN BYRON and threw open south Cheshire to the ROYALISTS.

Belasyse, John (1614–94)

Belasyse, despite his CATHOLICISM, was MP for Thirsk (Yorkshire) in the SHORT PARLIAMENT, and in 1642 became a COMMISSIONER OF ARRAY. Defeated at SELBY 11 April 1644, he

was exchanged (see EXCHANGE OF PRISONERS) and commanded in NEWARK-ON-TRENT at the end of the war in 1646. His secretary, Moone, wrote *A Brief Relation of the Life and Memoirs of John Lord Belasyse.*

Historical Manuscripts Commission, *Ormonde Mss.*, New Series, Vol. II (London 1903).

Belton, Battle of (13 May 1643)

Parliamentary forces under OLIVER CROMWELL occupied GRANTHAM in Lincolnshire and then attacked and dispersed ROYALIST forces at Belton.

Benburb, Battle of (5 June 1646)

A thorough defeat inflicted on the Ulster SCOTTISH ARMY of ROBERT MUNRO by the troops of the IRISH CONFEDERACY under OWEN ROE O'NEILL. O'Neill's achievement was dissipiated by his southward march immediately afterwards and his involvement in the political clash in the Supreme Council of the Confederacy.

Benevolences

An almost arbitrary form of taxation originating in the reign of Edward IV (d. 1483) and used with increasing frequency by James I. In 1640, the SHORT PARLIAMENT failing to vote funds, CHARLES I secured a benevolence from CONVOCATION of £20,000. Benevolences were held to be contrary to the PETITION OF RIGHT, but on 31 January 1642 PARLIAMENT

gave statutory authority to a benevolence for assisting Protestants in
Ireland.

Bennet, Robert (1605–83)

Author of the TRACT *King Charles
Triall Iustified* (1649) which stressed
the king's crimes and the SOVER-
EIGNTY of the people in PARLIAMENT.
He was a Cornish 'Particular Baptist'
(see BAPTISTS).

Best, Paul (d. 1657)

A minor Yorkshire gentleman who
became a SOCINIAN while travelling
in Germany, and whose subsequent
writings aroused the anger of the
PRESBYTERIANS. He was condemned
to execution in 1646 but the order
was not implemented, and he was
released in 1647.

H.J. McLachlan, *Socinianism in
Seventeeth-Century England* (London
1951).

Bible   See Authorized Version of the Bible

Biddle, John (d. 1662)

In virtue of his TRACTS *Twelve
Arguments Drawn Out Of The Scriptures* (1647) and *A Confession of Faith*
(1648), in which he denied the
doctrine of the trinity, Biddle is
reckoned the founder of Unitarianism (see SOCINIANISM). A Gloucestershire schoolmaster, he was

gaoled under both CROMWELL and
CHARLES II.

Billeting

The intrusion into civilian households of soldiers who must be given
shelter, bed and board, theoretically
meeting the cost thereof. See also
FREE QUARTER.

Birch, John (1615–91)

A BRISTOL tradesman who, as a
protégé of SIR ARTHUR HASELRIG,
secured command of a regiment in
PARLIAMENT's army. His PRESBYTER-
IANISM estranged Haselrig and made
the NEW MODEL ARMY suspicious of
him, but he became governor of
Bristol in 1645 and took HEREFORD in
the same year. He fought for King
CHARLES II at WORCESTER in 1651 and
found favour after the Restoration.

T.W. Webb (ed.), *A Military Memoir of
Colonel John Birch Written by Roe His
Secretary* (Camden Society 1873).

Birmingham

According to EDWARD HYDE this town
was as 'famed for hearty, wilful,
affected disloyalty to the King as any
place in England'. It was a source of
arms and equipment for the PARLIA-
MENT in 1642. PRINCE RUPERT stormed
and took the town in severe fighting
that led to unrestrained killing.

Bishops' Exclusion Act

A bill to exclude bishops from the
HOUSE OF LORDS was unsuccessful in
June 1641, but after the FIVE MEMBERS

incident a second bill was pushed through, which had the royal assent 13 February 1642. This bill effectively broke the ROYALIST majority in the House of Lords, and the denial of all temporal jurisdictions for bishops paved the way for the suspension of EPISCOPACY 22 September 1642. The Exclusion Act was repealed 30 July 1661.

Bishops' Lands

These lands represented the last temporalities (see CHURCH LANDS) of the church in England. On 9 October 1646 an ORDINANCE of PARLIAMENT abolishing archbishops and bishops *per se* set their lands over to trustees for disposal to the use of the COMMONWEALTH. Isaac Basire's *Deo et Ecclesiae Sacrum* (1646) was a last-ditch protest at this secularization.

Bishops' Wars

Popular generic term for the conflict between England and Scotland of 1639–41, caused by fervent Scottish reaction against CHARLES I's church reforms in that country. Under the umbrella of the SCOTTISH NATIONAL COVENANT, the PRESBYTERIANS abolished EPISCOPACY and raised forces to resist King Charles. The wars ended in Scotland's favour, and the Treaty of Ripon (26 October 1641) ushered in the LONG PARLIAMENT to meet the financial settlement demanded by the Scots.

Black Boy

Nickname coined by Scottish commissioners at THE HAGUE in 1649 and applied to King CHARLES II.

Black Tom

Nickname (it is unclear whether affectionate or otherwise) of SIR THOMAS FAIRFAX.

Black Tom Tyrant

Scurrilous nickname for the EARL OF STRAFFORD.

Black William

Nickname of the ROYALIST colonel William Godolphin, who commanded a regiment in the west of England 1642–6.

Blake, Robert (1598–1657)

From a Somerset trade background, Blake served as an MP in the SHORT and LONG PARLIAMENTS and in 1649 was appointed General at Sea. He destroyed a ROYALIST privateer fleet under PRINCE RUPERT 25 November 1650, and went on to distinguish himself against the Dutch, dying on active service.

J.R. Powell, *Robert Blake, General at Sea* (London 1976).

Blasphemy Act (of 1650)

Aimed at the extreme SECTARIES such as the RANTERS, and at preachers and ministers who represented them.

Bletchingdon House

A ROYALIST strongpoint in Oxfordshire, surrendered to CROMWELL 25 April 1645 without offering resistance. The governor, Colonel FRANCIS WINDEBANK, was court-martialled and shot 3 May at Oxford on the insistence of the king.

Blith (Bligh), Walter

A PARLIAMENTARIAN officer whose 1649 work *The English Improver, or a New System of Husbandry* extolled agriculture as a science and sought to influence national policy. Further editions in 1652 and 1653 were dedicated to PARLIAMENT and to CROMWELL.

Bloody Braggadochio

Nickname coined in the PARLIAMENTARIAN press for JOHN BYRON.

Blundell, William (1620–98)

Blundell was a Lancashire ROYALIST officer who wrote an account of the Isle of Man, and a collection of memoirs and anecdotes.

T.E. Gibson (ed.), *Crosby Records: A Cavalier's Note Book Being Notes Anecdotes & Observations of William Blundell of Crosby, Lancs* (London 1880).

Boldon Hills, Battle of the (6–8 March 1644)

A series of attempts by the EARL OF NEWCASTLE to force the Scottish invasion army to give battle in Durham. They were largely abortive but with tactical advantage to the ROYALISTS.

Bolton

Called derisively the GENEVA OF THE NORTH on account of its fierce PRESBYTERIANISM, this Lancashire town was stormed and taken by PRINCE RUPERT 28 May 1644 with considerable slaughter amongst the inhabitants. In 1651 the EARL OF DERBY was executed here.

Booker, John (1602–67)

Haberdasher and writing master, Booker began to publish almanacks in 1631 and achieved fame as an astrologer. A PURITAN and an inveterate foe of WILLIAM LAUD and of ROMAN CATHOLICISM, from 1643 to 1660 he acted for PARLIAMENT in licensing mathematical books and in censoring almanacks. With the Restoration he shifted his sympathies in line with the GOVERNMENT.

Book of Sports

Two such books were issued with royal approval, in 1617–18 and by CHARLES I in 1633. These books were condemned by PURITANS as the 'Morris Book', an allusion to what they perceived as popish practices reintroduced with government sanction to the observances of the CALENDAR. The *Book of Sports* licensed Whitsun Ales, May Day celebrations and other 'ancient' observances that the Reformation had sought to suppress. On 5 May 1643 PARLIAMENT issued an order for the burning of the *Book of Sports* by the public hangman.

Both Kingdoms, Committee for (Also known as the Derby House Committee)

A committee of Parliament set up February 1644 by ORDINANCE to organize military strategy with the SCOTTISH ARMY. Composed of four Scottish commissioners, seven peers and fourteen MPs, it was given stronger powers 22 May 1644. From October 1646 it was reformed as the Committee for Irish Affairs, a policy-making body influenced by PRESBYTERIANS such as DENZIL HOLLES. Known as the Derby House Committee by January 1648, as the COMMITTEE FOR SAFETY it prosecuted the war effort of 1648 and was responsible for the war effort of the NEW MODEL ARMY.

Bourchier, Sir John (d. 1660)

A country gentleman from Beningborough in Yorkshire, and an enemy of the EARL OF STRAFFORD, Bourchier was a RECRUITER MP in the LONG PARLIAMENT, sat upon the HIGH COURT OF JUSTICE and signed the death warrant of CHARLES I. On his death bed he claimed 'it was a good act ... good men will own it'.

Bovey Tracey, Battle of (9 January 1646)

OLIVER CROMWELL surprised ROYALIST troops in winter quarters in this Devonshire town and defeated them in battle close by.

Braddock Down, Battle of (19 January 1643)

The ROYALISTS attempted to prevent the junction of two parliamentary forces at Launceston in Cornwall, and achieved this by destroying one on Braddock Down. There was fighting there also in August 1644 as the king's forces closed in on the EARL OF ESSEX at LOSTWITHIEL.

Bradford

A clothing town in the West Riding of Yorkshire, taken by the ROYALISTS after ADWALTON MOOR in 1643, and then fought over twice in March 1644 by royalists under JOHN BELASYSE and PARLIAMENTARIANS under JOHN LAMBERT. Both of these last battles were parliamentarian victories. See also JOSEPH LISTER.

Bradford Quarter

On 18 December 1642, during fighting on the outskirts of BRADFORD in Yorkshire, a ROYALIST officer was cut down and killed out of hand when he asked for quarter. In July 1643 after ADWALTON MOOR the citizens of Bradford fled from threats of 'Bradford Quarter' made by the advancing royalists.

Bradshaw, John (1602–59)

A Cheshire lawyer who served as Lord President of the HIGH COURT OF JUSTICE raised to try CHARLES I, and thus he who passed the sentence of death upon the king. On 10 March 1649 he became the first president of the COUNCIL OF STATE, but fell out with CROMWELL. In 1661 his body was exhumed and exhibited in LONDON.

Bramber, Battle of

At this bridging point of the River Adur in Sussex, ROYALIST forces fresh from taking ARUNDEL CASTLE were turned back by PARLIAMENTARIAN troops and their eastward march from Cornwall was stopped.

Brampton Bryan Castle

Major PARLIAMENTARIAN stronghold in the largely ROYALIST county of Herefordshire. The castle was held by LADY BRILLIANA HARLEY until April 1644 when the royalist MICHAEL WOODHOUSE forced its surrender.

Breda

Seat of the court in exile of King CHARLES II in 1650 after abandoning THE HAGUE.

Brentford, Battle of (12 November 1642)

PRINCE RUPERT, in his advance through Middlesex towards LONDON, defeated parliamentary forces under LORD BROOKE and DENZIL HOLLES, only to fall back towards READING within the week.

Brereton, Sir William (1604–61)

One of PARLIAMENT's most able and astute local commanders, Brereton alternately controlled and clung on to Cheshire between 1642 and 1646, escaping the provisions of the SELF DENYING ORDINANCE. A religious INDEPENDENT, he may have been behind JOHN BRADSHAW's appointment as President of the HIGH COURT OF JUSTICE to try CHARLES I in 1649, but did not himself meddle in the business.

Bridgeman, Sir Orlando (1606–74)

Orlando Bridgeman was son to the Bishop of CHESTER (d. 1652) and served as MP for Wigan (see WIGAN LANE), Lancashire, in the LONG PARLIAMENT. He was active for the king in Cheshire and served in the OXFORD PARLIAMENT in 1644. In 1660 he became Lord Chief Justice of the COURT OF COMMON PLEAS and presided over the trials of the REGICIDES.

Bridgnorth

A major ROYALIST base above the River Severn in Shropshire for operations into the West Midlands, it fell 26 April 1646 after the town had been captured and the castle besieged.

Bridgwater

A ROYALIST garrison from 6 June 1643, this Somerset town was taken by parliamentary forces under SIR THOMAS FAIRFAX and CROMWELL 23 July 1645, after three days' bitter street fighting with Colonel Wyndham's royalists.

Bridlington

A small fishing port on the east coast of Yorkshire. On 21 February 1643, QUEEN HENRIETTA MARIA landed here from Holland, pursued by parliamentary naval craft under BATTEN, who bombarded the port in an attempt to kill her.

Bristol

The second city of England, a major port serving Ireland and Wales, Bristol was taken by PRINCE RUPERT 26 July 1643. The magazine of arms and equipment captured armed ROYALIST forces in the south and south-west substantially. On 10 September 1645 forces under SIR THOMAS FAIRFAX forced Rupert to surrender the port, and the munition manufactory established there in 1643 fell into PARLIA-MENTARIAN hands.

Bristol, Thomas Howell, Bishop of (1588–1646)

A former chaplain to CHARLES I, Howell was appointed bishop of BRISTOL in 1644 – a direct defiance of the PARLIAMENT. He died as a result of ill treatment after the fall of Bristol to the PARLIAMENTARIANS.

Brome, Alexander (1620–66)

ROYALIST poet and lawyer, author of *The Royalist*, a play, and, later, translator of the classical Latin poet Horace.

Brooke, Robert Greville Lord (1608–43)

A peer of strict PURITAN leanings and an old antagonist of the king's GOVERNMENT, he was a close associate of JOHN PYM and a member of the COMMITTEE OF SAFETY. His TRACT, *A Discourse Opening the Nature of That Episcopacie Which is Exercised in England* (1642), attacked bishops as low-born dependents of the royal court. Lord Brooke was killed in action 2 March 1643 at LICHFIELD.

Brooke's Plot

A conspiracy, centred on Sir Basil Brooke (1576–1646), who in 1642 had been arrested by order of PARLIAMENT for his involvement with organized Catholic financial support for the king. In January 1644 Brooke was rearrested for endeavouring to create dissension between LONDON and the Parliament, perhaps to disrupt the Scottish invasion.

Brotherly Assistance   See Solemn League and Covenant

Browne, Major General Richard (d. 1669)

Nicknamed derisively by the ROYA-LISTS 'Faggot-Monger', Browne was an extremely active and able PARLIA-MENTARIAN commander 1642–6. In 1647 he received the person of CHARLES I from the Scots, but progressively swung towards support for the king, and was expelled from the HOUSE OF COMMONS and gaoled at the instigation of the army in 1648.

He became involved in plots in favour of CHARLES II and was knighted in 1660.

Browne, Sir Thomas (1605–82)

Noted physician and writer, whose account of his own religious faith, *Religio Medici*, appeared in 1642, to be reissued in 1643. His *Pseudodoxia Epidemica*, an exploration of common errors or folk-beliefs, was published in 1646. For all his urbanity, Browne believed in the reality of WITCHCRAFT.

Bull Inn

An inn in Bishopsgate, LONDON. It was the scene in April 1649 of fighting between soldiers led by ROBERT LOCKYER and other troops loyal to SIR THOMAS FAIRFAX when the former refused to obey orders to suppress LEVELLERS in Essex.

Bulstrode, Sir Richard (1610–75)

ROYALIST diplomatist and Quarter-Master General in the king's armies, Bulstrode is chiefly of importance for his *Memoirs and Reflections Upon the Reign and Government of Charles I and II*, published in 1721.

Bunyan, John (1628–88)

The author of, among other things, *Pilgrim's Progress*, published in 1678, Bunyan was from a poor Bedfordshire family who had once been smallholders. He fought for the PARLIAMENT 1644–7, where he imbibed radical and PURITAN ideas,

emerging as an INDEPENDENT prior to 1651.

Burford

A small town in Oxfordshire. In May 1649 it was the focal point of a LEVELLER-inspired mutiny in the NEW MODEL ARMY, chiefly involving troops from SALISBURY in Wiltshire. On 14 May loyal troops under SIR THOMAS FAIRFAX and CROMWELL attacked and overcame the mutineers, and 350 were sentenced to death. In the event only WILLIAM THOMPSON and two others were shot, in the churchyard.

Burgess, Roger

ROYALIST governor of Faringdon Castle who, in April 1645, refused to surrender to OLIVER CROMWELL, taunted him and decisively beat off his attempted storming.

Burham Heath

Between Rochester and MAIDSTONE in Kent, the scene of the muster of Kentish and other ROYALISTS prior to an advance on LONDON, 29 May 1648.

Burt, Nathaniel

An embittered lawyer gaoled in 1638 for resisting SHIP MONEY. He served in the PARLIAMENTARIAN forces in the civil war and his writings, largely after 1651, attacked the legal profession and argued for law reforms.

Burton, Henry (1578–1648)

A religious INDEPENDENT whose career in the royal household was blocked by his opposition to ARMINIANISM. A prolific TRACT writer, he suffered in the Court of STAR CHAMBER in 1636 with PRYNNE and BASTWICK. The sentence against him was reversed in 1641, and he devoted himself to stringent attacks on PRESBYTERIANISM and denounced secular control of the church. He produced more than fifteen published works, and in 1644 published *Vindication of Churches Commonly Called Independent.*

Burton Upon Trent

Important bridging point over the Trent in Staffordshire. It was stormed by a Yorkshire TRAINED BAND regiment in June 1643 during QUEEN HENRIETTA MARIA's march south from PONTEFRACT to join the king with reinforcements.

Byerley's Bulldogs

A localized nickname for the ROYALIST infantry regiment raised early in 1644 in Durham by Colonel Anthony Byerley to resist the Scottish invasion.

Byron, John (1599–1652)

Byron was a ROYALIST Nottinghamshire gentleman with extensive military experience in Europe, and was made Field Marshal General in North Wales in December 1643, being made Lord Byron at the same time. The 'Bloody Braggadochio', as PARLIAMENTARIANS termed him, Byron was responsible by his impetuosity for the royalist defeat on MARSTON MOOR 1644. In 1646 he went into exile where he died.

C

Calamy, Edmund (1600–66)

Preacher of the first FAST SERMON before PARLIAMENT, and author of *England's Looking-Glasse* (1642) denouncing church ritual. Indicted of high treason in 1643 by CHARLES I for his preaching of a holy war against the ROYALISTS. He sat on the WESTMINSTER ASSEMBLY, but shifted position, criticized the INDEPENDENTS and opposed the TRIAL OF CHARLES I. He later became chaplain to King CHARLES II but declined a bishopric offered him.

Calendar and dating of events

Civil war England still adhered to the ancient Julian calendar, beginning the year not on 1 January but on 25 March. Documents may be dated in strict accordance with that, or in a mixture of Julian (Old Style) and Gregorian (New Style) European practice. Thus in Gregorian terms (which are still observed now) CHARLES I was beheaded 30 January 1649, but according to the Julian calendar his execution took place 30 January 1648. Some writers chose to amalgamate both styles in their dating, and would render it '30 January 1648/9'. England did not officially adopt the European system until 1752, as a result of which it was found necessary to 'lose' 11 days: hence modern calendrical allusions to, for example, Old Christmas Day or Old Michaelmas Day. The Calendar had been shorn of the vast majority of its saints' days during the Reformation. The Protestant liturgical calendar as it was observed in civil-war England was still nevertheless the subject of bitter criticism from PURITANS, who were affronted by the customary usages attached to the celebrations of certain days (such as May Day, and Midsummer Day – 24 June). Curiously, the legal calendar preserved intact much Catholic usage on the grounds of its necessity for the proper ordering of court business. Yet it was the 'reformed' liturgical calendar which attracted hostility far more than the legal calendar. THE BOOK OF SPORTS concentrated attention upon the liturgical calendar by its endorsement of, allegedly popish, practices such as Whitsun Ales.

Callan

A town in County Kilkenny, Ireland. It was stormed by troops of the NEW MODEL ARMY 8 February 1650, the defenders of two of three fortified points being slaughtered in cold blood.

Callendar, Battle of (13 February 1646)

Scottish ROYALIST troops defeated COVENANTER forces.

Cal to all the souldiers of the Army, A

TRACT disseminated 29 October 1647 and written by JOHN WILDMAN, accusing CROMWELL and IRETON of treachery and collaboration with the king. It was seen as an incitement to mutiny in the NEW MODEL ARMY.

Calvinism

A framework of religious belief based upon the expositions of John Calvin (d. 1564). The fundamental tenet is the doctrine of predestination – that salvation or damnation is predetermined by God. PRESBYTERIANISM was a Calvinist theology and church structure.

Cambridge Platonists

A group of Anglican Protestant thinkers, the most important being Ralph Cudworth (1617–88), Benjamin Whichcote (1609–83) and Henry Moore (1614–87). Cudworth adopted the concept of a rational system of knowledge based upon innate ideas, influenced by the writings of Plato, Philo and other Greek philosophers. Their views represented an intellectual reaction to PURITAN fundamentalism.

Cannon

Civil war cannon can be divided into three groups of weapons: (a) siege pieces – the cannon royal at 63 lb (28.6 kg) shot, the cannon at 47 lb (21.3 kg) and the demi-cannon at 27 lb (12.2 kg); (b) heavy field guns – the culverin at 15 lb (6.8 kg) and the demi-culverin at 9 lb (4 kg); (c) light field guns – the saker at 5¼ lb (2.4 kg), the minion at 4 lb (1.8 kg) the falcon at 2½ lb (1 kg), the falconet at 1½ lb (0.6 kg) and the robinet at ¾ lb (0.3 kg). There was also a light gun called a drake. These cannon fired iron balls, grape shot or canister. Roaring Meg, a ROYALIST gun used at HOPTON HEATH, fired a 29-lb (13.2-kg) ball. Gog and Magog, also called the Queen's Pocket Pistols, were of similar size and were used at ADWALTON MOOR by the royalists. Basiliske of Hull, firing a 32-lb (19.5-kg) ball serves to indicate the degree of variation from prescribed or desired calibres.

Cansfield, John (d. c.1648)

A leading Lancashire Catholic, Cansfield was prominent in arming his co-religionists for the king in 1642. As Colonel of the Lifeguard of QUEEN HENRIETTA MARIA he distinguished himself in battle, and saved the king's life at NEWBURY in October 1644. Cansfield failed to secure the governorship of OXFORD because of his religion, and died in prison.

Canterbury

A town in Kent. On 25 December 1647 a localized ROYALIST rising seized the town, but surrendered it in January 1648. Indictments against the instigators were thrown out at the May ASSIZES, but this encouraged further royalist activity which became part of the SECOND CIVIL WAR of that year. Retreating royalists fleeing MAIDSTONE surrendered to SIR

THOMAS FAIRFAX at Canterbury 9 June 1648.

remained acquiescent following the king's execution.

Canterbury, William Laud Archbishop of   See William Laud

Capel, Arthur Lord (1610–49)

Capel was a rich Hertfordshire gentleman, MP for his county in the LONG PARLIAMENT, later condemned as 'atheisticall Lord Capel' by the PARLIAMENTARIANS. To the ROYALISTS he was 'a man of incomparable honour'. Unsuccessful as Lieutenant General in North Wales in 1643, he nevertheless served elsewhere with distinction. Captured at COLCHESTER Castle in 1648, he was tried before the HIGH COURT OF JUSTICE and executed in 1649.

Historical Manuscripts Commission, 12th Report, Appendix Pt. IX, *Beaufort Mss*, pp. 38–45, for an account of him by a contemporary comrade in arms.

Carbery, Richard Vaughan Earl of (1600–86)

Carbery was a powerful Carmarthenshire ROYALIST and former MP, castigated by one PARLIAMENTARIAN writer as a man of 'pride and menacing insolencies'. Lieutenant General in South Wales from March 1643, Carbery was outfought by ROWLAND LAUGHARNE and his command had ceased to exist by 1644. His influence obliged PARLIAMENT to be lenient towards him. He kept clear of the Laugharne rising of 1648, and

Carbisdale, Battle of (27 April 1650)

Scene of the defeat of the MARQUIS OF MONTROSE by COVENANTER troops under Archibald Strachan. Montrose had invaded Scotland as Lieutenant General to King CHARLES II, and Carbisdale marked the end of his campaign.

Carisbrooke Castle

King CHARLES I arrived at Carisbrooke Castle on the Isle of Wight 14 November 1647, in his flight from Hampton Court Palace, Middlesex, occasioned by fear of assassination. Although the king was confined in the castle, his flight had left the NEW MODEL ARMY in an isolated position in their dealings with the LONG PARLIAMENT by denying to them the possession of his person.

Carlisle

A city in Cumberland. It was a ROYALIST stronghold from 1642, but its strategic importance postdated the fall of YORK in July 1644 and the arrival in Carlisle of York's former governor SIR THOMAS GLEMHAM. It was under siege from October 1644 to its surrender on 25 June 1645, when it was handed over to the Scots. On 29 April 1648 it was seized again for the king, but fell to the NEW MODEL ARMY 1 October. See also ISAAC TULLIE.

Carlisle Sands, Battle of (24 October 1645) (Also known as the Battle of Burgh by Sands)

This was the last engagement of the NORTHERN HORSE and saw their complete overthrow by local, Cumbrian, PARLIAMENTARIAN forces.

Cary, Mary

Fifth Monarchist whose TRACT *The Resurrection of the Witnesses* (1648) saw the victory of the NEW MODEL ARMY as the first stage in the coming millennium (see MILLENARIANISM). She foresaw the New Jerusalem as coming in 1701, and was more concerned with the practical matters of state power than with spiritual values.

Case of the Army Truly Stated, The

A document, drawn up at Guildford, Surrey, in October 1647 by army AGITATORS, which preceded the *AGREEMENT OF THE PEOPLE*. Its main theme was the diminution of royal power, and the meeting of biennial PARLIAMENTS with extended suffrage. SIR THOMAS FAIRFAX laid it before the GENERAL COUNCIL OF THE ARMY, which condemned it as an attack on the competence of the Council and an effort by the LEVELLERS to control the army's political manoeuvres.

Cashel

On 12 September 1647 pro-PARLIAMENTARIAN troops under LORD INCHIQUIN stormed Cashel, County Tipperary (Ireland), and slaughtered the Catholic garrison.

Castle Cary

On 2 June 1645 more than 5,000 CLUBMEN of Somersetshire gathered at Castle Cary to challenge the ROYALIST garrison of LANGPORT. After the NEW MODEL ARMY's decisive victory at Langport 10 July, the Somersetshire Clubmen hunted down and killed hundreds of royalist fugitives.

Castle Chamber, Court of

Established in Dublin, comparable with the COUNCIL OF THE NORTH, and used by the EARL OF STRAFFORD to hound his political opponents in Ireland during his time as Lord Deputy.

Castle Dore, Battle of (31 August 1644)

Part of the general action around LOSTWITHIEL, the action at Castle Dore forced the EARL OF ESSEX to abandon his army, which surrendered to the king.

Catholic Confederacy   See Irish Catholic Confederacy

Catholic Recusants

Those who, adhering to the doctrines of the Roman Catholic church, chose not to attend the services of the CHURCH OF ENGLAND. Recusancy fines were levied upon them by the state. In 1642 it was claimed that many Recusants resorted to their local churches in order to qualify them to serve in the armies of the king, but whether this was widespread or not is difficult to assess. Certainly by late 1642 the king entertained no misgivings about commissioning thorough-going Catholic Recusants into his officer corps. See also PAPISTS AND CHURCH PAPISTS.

Cavalier Poets

As the term suggests, poets who were ROYALISTS (or royalists who were also poets), the common theme of their work being a use of colloquial language, often lightly casual in expression. They form part of the lyrical tradition of English verse, their work being a marked contrast to the laboured intensity of MILTON, for example. Some of the best known are RICHARD LOVELACE, SIR JOHN SUCKLING and JOHN CLEVELAND.

Cavaliers

Originally a term of opprobrium used against those whom PARLIAMENT accused of misleading the king, it came to be regarded as a mark of honour by many ROYALISTS serving the king during the civil wars. Edward Symmons in a 'Militarie Sermon' of 1644 said 'a complete cavalier is a child of honour ... the only reserve of English gentility and ancient valour', but cavaliers may also be seen as royalist hard men and warlords. Certainly to their enemies

the term 'cavalier' remained one of abuse throughout the wars.

Caversham Court

A house in Berkshire where, in July 1647, CHARLES I spent three weeks as a prisoner of the NEW MODEL ARMY.

Censorship

Censorship of publications collapsed with the disappearance of episocopal temporal power and the COURT OF STAR CHAMBER in 1641. On 14 June 1643 an ORDINANCE was passed by PARLIAMENT to suppress 'false, scandalous, seditious and libellous' works, and authorized the destruction of presses not licensed by the London Stationers Company. JOHN MILTON's *Areopagitica* of 1644 was an attack on censorship laws, but Parliament consistently asserted its condemnation of 'odious and abominable ... schismatical and seditious sermons and pamphlets'.

Chagford, Battle of (8 February 1643)

An action notable for the death of SYDNEY GODOLPHIN, a ROYALIST, during the royalist advance on PLYMOUTH. Otherwise an inconclusive encounter.

Chalgrove Field, Battle of (18 June 1643)

ROYALIST forces under PRINCE RUPERT, moving towards OXFORD, turned to confront PARLIAMENTARIAN pursuers commanded by JOHN HAMPDEN. In the battle Hampden was killed and his forces scattered.

Challoner, Thomas (1595–1661)

MP for Richmond, Yorkshire, in the LONG PARLIAMENT and a witness in the trial of ARCHBISHOP LAUD, Challoner was a religious INDEPENDENT and friend of CROMWELL in 1648 and opposed to negotiations with the king. He served on the HIGH COURT OF JUSTICE and signed the death warrant, but in 1653 as a member of the COUNCIL OF STATE he was denounced by Cromwell as a drunkard. He died in exile in Holland.

Chamberlen, Peter (1601–83)

Physician attendant upon James I and CHARLES I, and a noted reformer of his profession as well as, in later life, a FIFTH MONARCHIST. Expelled from the College of Physicians for his pains, his TRACT of 1649, *Poore Mans Advocate*, advanced the idea of public employment by an expansion of trade and commerce, to be financed by the confiscations of property resulting from the civil war. JOHN LILBURNE favoured him. In 1661 he became court physician to CHARLES II.

Chancery, Court of

Part of the central GOVERNMENT, headed by the Lord Chancellor and including the Master of the Rolls in its senior officers, the Master being legal advisor of the crown. It became overloaded with business following the abolition of the COURTS OF STAR CHAMBER, HIGH COMMISSION and REQUESTS and the COUNCIL OF THE NORTH.

Charles I (1600–49)

Second son but heir to King James I, and king from 1625. His failure to win the civil wars of 1642–6 and 1648 led to his arraignment for treason against his people and to his execution 30 January 1649. He was tried as a reigning monarch, not having been deposed, and monarchy was officially abolished in England on 17 March 1649. His death created a cult around him which served the ROYALIST cause more effectively than he in his lifetime had done. Although conscious of the dignity of kingship, conspicuously brave in battle and no mean general, Charles I generated severe mistrust, a crucial element in creating an atmosphere for civil war.

Charles II (1630–85)

Eldest son of King CHARLES I and QUEEN HENRIETTA MARIA, his youth was spent in the vicissitudes of civil war. Proclaimed king in succession to his father, in Scotland on 5 February 1649, his attempts to regain the throne culminated in disaster at WORCESTER in 1651. He narrowly escaped to France. From the court in exile, plagued as it was by dissensions and rivalries, he endeavoured to restore himself to the throne. His return in 1660, however, was the result of a compromise between old enemies and ROYALISTS.

Charles, Prince of Wales

The title and designation of King CHARLES II during his father's lifetime.

Charles Stuart

The forename and surname of both King CHARLES I and King CHARLES II, used in a demeaning manner against Charles I at his trial and, after the abolition of monarchy in March 1649, used by Charles II's enemies to convey his lack of right to any title of honour.

Chepstow Castle

In Monmouthshire in the spring of 1648 Sir NICHOLAS KEMYS seized this former ROYALIST garrison of 1642–5 and held it for the king. On May 11 CROMWELL laid siege to the castle, which was ultimately stormed and Colonel Kemys shot out of hand. From 1660 to 1680 it was to be the prison of HENRY MARTEN the republican (see REPUBLIC), whose place of incarceration can still be seen.

Cheriton, Battle of (29 March 1644)

The PARLIAMENTARIAN army of SIR WILLIAM WALLER clashed with the ROYALISTS of LORDS FORTH and HOPTON between Cheriton and Alresford in Hampshire and defeated them, destroying the southern army of the king and effectively lifting the blockade of GLOUCESTER.

Chester

A key ROYALIST stronghold on the edge of North Wales. It was intensively besieged for the first time in 1645, by SIR WILLIAM BRERETON. Chester held out, latterly under JOHN BYRON, until 3 February 1646.

Chewton Mendip, Battle of (10 June 1643)

A ROYALIST victory in Somerset by PRINCE MAURICE over SIR WILLIAM WALLER. It was marred for the royalists by the fall of darkness and the wounding and capture of Prince Maurice.

Chidley, Katherine

A religious INDEPENDENT out of Shropshire. In 1641 her TRACT *The Justification of the Independent Churches of Christ* called upon ministers to earn their livings by labour. In 1649 she may have been behind the women's petition in support of JOHN LILBURNE, the LEVELLER, and in 1653 she led several thousand women to Parliament to support Lilburne in his trial that year. Her son Samuel, a prominent Leveller, argued for the destruction of all churches as places defiled and unfit for worship.

Childerley Hall

A house in Cambridgeshire. It was the residence, 5–7 June 1647, of King CHARLES I under the guard of the NEW MODEL ARMY, and the scene of discussions between the king and SIR

THOMAS FAIRFAX, CROMWELL and IRETON.

Chinnor, Battle of (18 June 1643)

In an action preliminary to CHAL-GROVE FIELD, PRINCE RUPERT routed the dragoons of SIR SAMUEL LUKE and then fired the town.

Cholmeley, Sir Hugh (1600–57)

MP for Scarborough, Yorkshire, in the SHORT and LONG PARLIAMENTS. He garrisoned the town and SCAR-BOROUGH CASTLE for the PARLIAMENT in late 1642. Upon the arrival of QUEEN HENRIETTA MARIA at BRIDLING-TON in February 1643, Cholmeley went over to the king and did not surrender Scarborough until 1645, after siege. *The Memoirs of Sir Hugh Cholmeley* were first published in 1787.

C.H. Firth (ed.), 'Sir Hugh Chol-meley's Memorials Touching the Battle of York', *English Historical Review*, V, London 1890.

Church Lands

By this term was meant the secular property, the temporalities, of the post-Reformation CHURCH OF ENG-LAND. By the time of the civil war, the lands of the bishops were under particular threat (see BISHOPS' EXCLU-SION ACT and BISHOPS' LANDS. The church lands were largely sold off by PARLIAMENT during the 1640s.

Church of England

The state church, established in 1534 by Henry VIII's assertion of his own supremacy against that of the Pope. The legal standing of the monarch as head of the Church of England was considered a guarantee of its ortho-doxy and Protestantism. The Book of Common Prayer (see PRAYER BOOK) was published in 1549 and revised in 1559. The Thirty-Nine Articles of faith, published in 1563, were fun-damentally CALVINIST in doctrine. An AUTHORIZED VERSION OF THE BIBLE appeared in 1611.

Cirencester

Strategically important Glouces-tershire town on the route to the south-west from the midlands. It was captured 2 February 1643 by PRINCE RUPERT.

Civic Elites

An historiographical term to denote the leaders of urban society, the merchants, aldermen and others who effectively controlled cities and towns in GOVERNMENT by oligarchy. Civic elites often divided along pre-civil wars lines of tension and political divergence, as for example at NEWCASTLE UPON TYNE, where a group of local dignitaries led by Sir John Marley sided with the king and ousted their old opponents.

Civil War, First (1642–6)

Officially commenced 22 August 1642 with the raising of the king's stand-ard at NOTTINGHAM and concluded 13

July 1646 (although some garrisons continued to hold out). It was fought between the king and his adherents, the ROYALISTS, on the one side, and PARLIAMENT and its supporters (from 1644 helped by the Scots) on the other.

Civil War, Second (1648)

Began 23 March 1648 with a revolt in Pembrokeshire, a patchy and localized uprising that petered out during the summer and autumn of that year. It was fought between the RUMP PARLIAMENT and its military arm, the NEW MODEL ARMY, and a loose alliance of ROYALISTS, ex-PARLIAMENTARIANS, and the Scots. The insurrection suffered from lack of coordination, and was effectively and often brutally suppressed.

Clanricarde, Ulrick Bourke Earl of (1604–57)

An Irish Catholic peer, he commanded in Connaught for ORMONDE and then replaced him as Lord Deputy in December 1650. Defeated at Meelick Island in the Shannon, 25 October 1650, he surrendered 28 June 1652 at Carrick after a brilliantly executed raid into Donegal.

Clarendon, Earl of   See Edward Hyde

Clarkson, Lawrence (1615–67)

One of the RANTERS. His pamphlet *A Generall Charge or Impeachment of High Treason* (1647) adopted a neo-LEVELLER stance in urging the SOVEREIGNTY of the people. By 1649–50 he

was 'Captain of the Rant' and head of the MY ONE FLESH Ranter group in LONDON, from which derived the 'Claxtonians', who looked to his leadership. He denied the existence of sin and evil except in the human imagination.

Act of Classes

Passed in 1649 by the COMMITTEE OF THE ESTATES in Scotland to exclude MALIGNANTS, enemies of the Covenant (see SCOTTISH NATIONAL COVENANT), Engagers (see *ENGAGEMENT*) and immoral people from public office. The Act effectively deprived DAVID LESLIE of good commanders in 1650 against CROMWELL and was repealed in January 1651 after the coronation of King CHARLES II in Scotland.

Clement, Gregory

MP for Fowey, Cornwall, he attended the HIGH COURT OF JUSTICE and signed the king's death warrant, but in May 1652 his name was scratched out after he fell from favour and was expelled from the HOUSE OF COMMONS. He was tried and executed in October 1660.

Cleveland, John (1615–58)

Cleveland was one of the CAVALIER POETS and, in 1640, a noted opponent of CROMWELL in the elections for Cambridge. He served in the garrison of NEWARK-ON-TRENT, and was later gaoled under Cromwell (1655). His *Poems* were published in 1656.

Clonmacnoise

On 13 December 1649 the Irish ROMAN CATHOLIC bishops met here and issued a declaration supporting ORMONDE against CROMWELL. On 12 August 1650 at Jamestown, County Antrim, they withdrew that declaration and proclaimed against Ormonde's struggle.

Clonmel

A town in County Tipperary. It was defended by HUGH O'NEILL against the NEW MODEL ARMY from 27 April 1650. An attempted storm was repulsed 9 May, and a second 17 May. O'Neill slipped away with his men and the town fell 18 May.

Clubmen

A descriptive term found as early as 1642, and technically meaning irregular troops armed with all manner of weapons. A quite specific usage developed from December 1644 to describe armed resisters to the military authority of either side. They first appeared December 1644 in Worcestershire, in opposition to the MARCHER ASSOCIATION, and showing marked anti-Catholicism. The 'Clubmen' phenomenon spread throughout the Welsh borders and, in 1645, appeared in Dorset, Wiltshire and neighbouring counties. Some Clubmen tended to favour whichever was the stronger side, some were more demonstrably partisan, but the essence of the movement was war-weariness and a desire to drive the war away from the areas represented by the Clubmen. In 1648 the term was applied to grain rioters in Gloucestershire incensed by high prices for bread.

Coat and conduct money

A form of taxation levied heavily in 1639/40 during the BISHOPS' WARS to finance movement of soldiers. In conjunction with SHIP MONEY it created resentment and resistance to payment.

Cobbet, John (Also known as Honest Major Cobbet)

An officer of the NEW MODEL ARMY and an AGITATOR, in 1647 at the PUTNEY DEBATES he voted against the resolution that the HOUSE OF COMMONS must have final say in changes in the law. Involved in the mutiny at Ware (see CORKBUSH FIELD), as late as May 1649 he was an outspoken supporter of the LEVELLERS, but was never cashiered.

Colby Moor, Battle of (1 August 1645)

Fought near Haverfordwest in Pembrokeshire. A ROYALIST column on a punitive expedition was defeated by ROWLAND LAUGHARNE in two actions, the second centred on an earthwork called the Rath. The royalists fell back on Haverfordwest which surrendered shortly afterwards.

Colchester, Siege of

The Essex rising (part of the SECOND CIVIL WAR) began 8 June 1648, and Colchester was fixed on as a port town able to service the ROYALIST fleet. Colchester was occupied 13 June, and became the general resort for royalists fleeing from Kent after the MAIDSTONE action. A bitter siege led by SIR THOMAS FAIRFAX forced the town and castle to surrender 27 August 1648.

Coleford, Battle of (20 February 1643)

ROYALIST forces under Edward Lord Herbert (see EARL OF GLAMORGAN), advancing on GLOUCESTER, collided with PARLIAMENTARIAN garrison troops here.

Coleman, Thomas (1598–1647)

Nicknamed 'Rabbi Coleman' for his Hebraic scholarship, a supporter of PARLIAMENT whose ERASTIANISM brought about difficulties with the HOUSE OF COMMONS. His obstructiveness towards PRESBYTERIANISM in the WESTMINSTER ASSEMBLY was cut short by his death in 1647.

Colepeper, Sir John (d. 1660)

MP for Kent in the LONG PARLIAMENT and, although opposed to STRAFFORD, a powerful supporter of the EPISCOPACY and opponent of the GRAND REMONSTRANCE. A Privy Councillor (see PRIVY COUNCIL) and advisor to the king from 1642, he fell foul of PRINCE RUPERT, and as early as 1645 advocated a ROYALIST alliance with the Scots. Raised to the peerage by CHARLES I, he remained an advocate of the Scottish alliance and a prime mover of CHARLES II's rapprochement with the COVENANTERS.

Collier, Thomas

A BAPTIST and unofficial chaplain to the NEW MODEL ARMY, whose actions in 1648 he wholly supported in his TRACT *Vindication of the Army Remonstrance.*

Commissions and Commissioners of Array

The Commission of Array (obsolete since 1557, but used in 1640 – see BISHOPS' WARS) was the means of raising fighting men by the king's direct summons sent to named gentry in every country. It empowered them to raise all men aged from 15 to 60, from whose number fit candidates would be chosen. The Commissions of Array (written in Latin on vellum) bypassed the LORDS LIEUTENANT and the MILITIA ORDINANCE to get to the TRAINED BANDS and POSSE COMITATUS. The earliest was that for Warwickshire, 6 June 1642; others followed on 11 June and thereafter. The Commissioners of Array became the basis of ROYALIST county administration, although in practice they were later subordinate to military commanders, and were named to implement the Commissions. Their duties were wide, and could be subsumed under the title of Commissioners of Array and of the Peace, or of Commissioners for guarding counties or for public safety.

Commission for the Propagation of the Gospel in Wales

An ACT OF PARLIAMENT 'For the Better Propagating and Preaching of the Gospel in Wales' was passed 22 February 1650. It sanctioned seizure of church livings and their conversion for use by a secular commission to fund missionary work. The Commission thus set up became the seat of power in Wales, considered as a 'dark corner of the land' where the Anglican (see CHURCH OF ENGLAND) clergy had been instrumental in raising support for the king.

Commissioners of Trust

Twelve representatives of the IRISH CATHOLIC CONFEDERACY appointed to assist ORMONDE in the autumn of 1648 after the dissolution of the Confederacy.

Committee of Parliament

See under name of individual committee, as follows: ADVANCE OF MONEY; ARMY; BOTH KINGDOMS; COMPOUNDING WITH DELINQUENTS; DEFENCE; DERBY HOUSE (see BOTH KINGDOMS); GOLDSMITHS HALL (see SCOTTISH AFFAIRS); HABERDASHERS HALL (see ADVANCE OF MONEY); INDEMNITY; IRISH AFFAIRS (see BOTH KINGDOMS); NAVY (see NAVY COMMISSIONERS); PLUNDERED MINISTERS; SAFETY; SCOTTTISH AFFAIRS; SEQUESTRATIONS; TAKING THE ACCOUNTS OF THE KINGDOM.

Common Pleas, Court of

A common-law court, part of the central GOVERNMENT, headed by the Chief Justice of the Common Pleas assisted by three Puisne Justices.

Commonwealth

A term generally applied to England between 30 January 1649 (execution of CHARLES I) and 8 May 1660 (restoration of CHARLES II), but more accurately the period from 19 May 1649 to 16 December 1653, from the declaration of the REPUBLIC to the establishment of the Protectorate of CROMWELL. It was a preferred term to that of 'Republic' and was rooted in the declaration by the RUMP that the English people were a 'free state'.

Commonwealthsmen

A group of INDEPENDENTS emerging in the HOUSE OF COMMONS in 1646, led by HENRY MARTEN, SIR ARTHUR HASELRIG and EDMUND LUDLOW. The name is a euphemism for 'Republicans' (see COMMONWEALTH).

Composition

The system whereby a ROYALIST might atone for his misdeeds by paying a punitive fine levied upon his property by the GOVERNMENT. See also COMMITTEE FOR COMPOUNDING WITH DELINQUENTS.

Compounding with Delinquents, Committee for (Also known as the Goldsmiths Hall Committee)

Centralized attempt to regularize the

activities of county-based committees charged with seizure of the property and revenues of ROYALISTS and CATHOLIC RECUSANTS which were entering into localized bargains with the owners for their recovery. The Committee (of PARLIAMENT) diverted funds from the localities to central GOVERNMENT. From July 1644 the Committee at Goldsmiths Hall took over all such negotiations with DELINQUENTS. A graduated scale for COMPOSITION was introduced, with subsequent amendments. One third or one half of estates of major royalists were to be compounded for, going as low as one sixth or one tenth for lesser delinquents. All those worth less than £200 were to be discharged without compounding. Time was allowed for payment, usually in two halves six weeks apart, often forcing sales of property to raise the money. On 16 March 1648 Roman Catholic royalists were permitted to compound as well. Between 1644 and 1652 over £1,300,000 was gathered in by the committee, exclusive of all property seized and not compounded for.

Confiscation Acts

The first Confiscation Act, of 16 July 1651, was a measure to facilitate the sale of the estates of 70 leading ROYALISTS, the sums accruing to go to the GOVERNMENT. On 17 July an act for the sale of the goods of the late king, the queen and the PRINCE OF WALES was also passed. Another Confiscation Act was passed 4 August 1652.

Congregationalists   See
Independents

Conscription   See Impressment

Conservatism, custom and deference

Historiographical terms or concepts intended to summarize the fundamental features of a hierarchically structured society such as that of civil-war England. The social structure was seen as patriarchal, a familial structure on a grand scale. 'As the Father over one family so the King over many families' as ROBERT FILMER described it. This structure created and enforced mutual obligations, duties and responsibilities rather than 'rights'. The Tudor idea of four sorts – nobility, gentry, burgesses and yeomen, and those 'that do not rule' (servants, cottagers and others) still had validity. But there was a wide gap between the fourth sort and those 'MASTERLESS MEN' who might be 'vagabonds and wanderers' and who can be seen as outcasts whose very existence was a reminder of the potential anarchy upon which society teetered, and against which the system of obligations and deference was seen as a guarantee. English society in the 17th century was imbued with concepts of customary usage 'whereof the memory of man runs not to the contrary', and this has been seen as a source of much support for the King: just as perceived infringements of customary rights and hard-won privileges by the king might account for support for PARLIAMENT. Customary usage and economic development frequently clashed, particularly in the case of ENCLOSURES, and this view of society should not be taken as indicating something rigidly imposed and acquiesced in by the people at large. Conservatism, custom and deference were part of the collective attitude of mind; in a sense they militated against extremism in religion and politics, but could also underlie violent assertions of perceived interests as well.

Constable, Sir William (1582–1655)

MP for Knaresborough,Yorkshire, in the LONG PARLIAMENT, he fought at EDGEHILL in 1642 and then in Yorkshire under LORD FAIRFAX. An INDEPENDENT deprived of command by the SELF DENYING ORDINANCE, he was active in PARLIAMENT. He sat on the HIGH COURT OF JUSTICE to try the king in 1649, signed the death warrant and served on the COUNCIL OF STATE. His body was exhumed in 1660 and displayed in LONDON.

Constitutional royalists

A historiographical term applied to men like HYDE and FALKLAND who abandoned PARLIAMENT for the king in 1641/2. They were seen as exerting a moderating influence in royal counsels.

Convocation

Assembly of the clergy, either of the archdiocese of CANTERBURY or of that of YORK, comprising an upper house of bishops and a lower house. In 1533 it was required that royal permission be obtained for such meetings. In 1640 King CHARLES I secured £20,000 from Convocation towards his war effort (see BISHOPS' WARS). The Convocation of Canterbury, sitting after dissolution of the SHORT PARLIAMENT, passed several strong LAUDIAN canons (church decrees).

Conway Castle

The North Wales stronghold fortified for the king in 1642 by ARCHBISHOP WILLIAMS OF YORK. Town and castle fell to PARLIAMENT 9 August 1644 and 18 November 1646 respectively.

Cook(e), John (1608–60)

A supporter of the EARL OF STRAFFORD who by 1646 defended JOHN LILBURNE before the HOUSE OF LORDS. As GOVERNMENT solicitor he prepared the charges against CHARLES I in 1649, and acted as prosecutor at the trial. Chief Justice in Munster, Ireland, from 1650, he was executed in 1660.

Coote, Sir Charles (d. 1661)

Coote was one of the most violent of the GOVERNMENT's commanders against the IRISH REBELLION, and served the cause of PARLIAMENT against the Irish ROYALISTS as well. He served as President of Connaught from 1645.

Coppe, Abiezer (1619–72)

Street orator and RANTER, considered by some a LEVELLER but distinguished by an insistence upon the extinction of private property. His TRACT *A Fiery Flying Roll* was condemned as blasphemous in 1650 and

Coppe withrew it. Coppe denied the existence of God and the sinfulness of fornication and adultery.

Coppin, Richard

Author of *Divine Teachings* (1649), used by the RANTERS as their text, although Coppin distanced himself from them. His publications began to grow less frequent by 1660.

Corbet, Miles (1595–1662)

MP for Yarmouth, Norfolk, in the LONG PARLIAMENT and part founder of the EASTERN ASSOCIATION. PARLIAMENT sent him to inform the king of his forthcoming trial in 1649 (see TRIAL OF CHARLES I), and Corbet signed the death warrant. He was seized in Holland in 1662, returned to England and executed.

Corbridge, Battle of (19 February 1644)

Brought on by ROYALIST attempts to dispute the crossings of the River Tyne in Northumberland with the Scottish invasion army. A royalist victory, but with no advantageous consequences.

Corkbush Field

Scene in Hertfordshire of the final defeat of NEW MODEL ARMY radicals by SIR THOMAS FAIRFAX and the officers. It was the first army rendezvous after the PUTNEY DEBATES, marred by arrival of regiments sporting the *AGREEMENT OF THE PEOPLE* in

their hats. The leaders of the mutiny were forced to dice for their lives and RICHARD ARNOLD was shot on the spot.

Council in the Marches of Wales

Originally founded in 1471 by King Edward IV, and reconstituted 1501, it was the chief court of Wales and the administrative centre of GOVERNMENT there. Its head was the Clerk of Council, a court sinecure. It was abolished in 1641 by the LONG PARLIAMENT, but revived 1661–89.

Council of Officers (of the New Model Army)

The usual title for the General Council of Officers, it emerged 29 August 1647 to replace the COUNCIL OF WAR. This body negotiated with the king from November 1647, offering its own terms for a settlement after being alarmed by IRETON and his Remonstrance (see REMONSTRANCES OF THE NEW MODEL ARMY), but CHARLES I rejected their terms, which included biennial PARLIAMENTS and control of the armed forces for 10 years by a COUNCIL OF STATE nominated by Parliament.

Council of State

The executive arm of the RUMP which first met 17 February 1649, with CROMWELL as president, to direct the army, conduct foreign affairs and generally carry out the orders of PARLIAMENT. Forty councillors were elected by a group of MPs, but compromise produced 41, of whom nine were nobles. It may be seen as heir to the royal PRIVY COUNCIL.

Council of the North

Originally founded by King Edward IV, it was revitalized in 1537 following unrest against King Henry VIII's religious policies, and covered the northernmost counties of England excluding Lancashire. Associated with the EARL OF STRAFFORD, it was abolished by the LONG PARLIAMENT at the instigation of EDWARD HYDE. In the 1650s JOHN LAMBERT toyed with plans to revive it.

Council of the West

Founded by CHARLES I in February 1645 and centred on his son CHARLES, PRINCE OF WALES, it was more or less a COUNCIL OF WAR comparable to that held by the EARL OF NEWCASTLE prior to July 1644.

Council of War

The Councils of War of the armies of king and PARLIAMENT were essentially directive bodies composed of military and civilian personnel advising the king (in the case of the ROYALISTS) or the Lord General (in the case of the PARLIAMENTARIANS). The EARL OF NEWCASTLE had his own Council of War in the north which acted on its own initiative.

County Associations

County associations were formed by both sides in the civil war to counter the effects of LOCALISM. The cooperation of leading gentry was crucial, for example, in 1642 when Shropshire, Cheshire, Flint and Denbighshire arranged regular weekly meetings of their representatives to finance the war effort of the ROYALISTS in those counties. On 15 December 1642 PARLIAMENT's Midland Association was formed by ORDINANCE; Warwick and Staffordshire were associated 31 December, and the basis of the EASTERN ASSOCIATION was laid in an Ordinance of 20 December 1642. Associations might undergo change, as when Parliament joined Shropshire to Warwick and Staffordshire in April 1643. Both sides, clearly, associated the same counties: the effectiveness of the associations depended upon military control.

County Committees

Set up by both sides in the civil war to deal with matters as diverse as military forces, SEQUESTRATION of the property of enemies, taxation (see ASSESSMENTS) and regulation of the clergy. Sometimes a single large committee devolved into separate subcommittees for various tasks.

Court and Country

A term descriptive of a division within English society that contributed to the outbreak of civil war. Historiographically its meaning is critical of the court (characterized as corrupt, effeminate, popish and tyrannical) compared with the country (virtuous, patriotic, Protestant and free). To courtiers, the country equated with 'factionalism' (see FAC-TION). In 1645 the term 'country' was applied to CLUBMEN resisting ROYA-LIST soldiers in Dorset. After 1646 it could be applied to, or adopted by, critics of the central GOVERNMENT howsoever it was composed.

Courts (of law)

See under name of individual court, as follows: CASTLE CHAMBER; CHAN-CERY; COMMON PLEAS; HIGH COMMIS-SION; HIGH COURT OF JUSTICE; KING'S BENCH; REQUESTS; STAR CHAMBER; WARDS AND LIVERIES.

Covenant

See particularly SCOTTISH NATIONAL COVENANT. The term was also used in an ORDINANCE of PARLIAMENT of 9 June 1643 towards the revelation of plots and conspiracies against the Parliament.

Covenanters

Supporters of the SCOTTISH NATIONAL COVENANT of 1638, drawn up to unify resistance to church innovation. The Covenanters may be compared with another Scottish movement, the Lords of the Congregation of 1581, who took a covenant to protect Protestantism. The immediate ancestry of the Covenanters was the Supplicant movement of 1637 which petitioned against the imposition of the new Prayer Book. In civil war terms, the name was applied generally to Scottish PRESBYTERIAN soldiers and their supporters.

Crawford, Major General Lawrence (1611–45)

A Scottish professional soldier who, as Major General of the Infantry in the EASTERN ASSOCIATION, outranked CROMWELL. Mutual hostility between them was terminated by Crawford's death in action at HEREFORD in 1645.

Cromwell, Oliver (1599–1658)

Cromwell was of yeoman status in his native Huntingdonshire, and probably not even a freeholder. He served in the SHORT and LONG PARLIAMENTS for Cambridge, and appears to have been favoured by the EARL OF WARWICK, upon whom he depended for his rapid advancement, politically and militarily. His genuine belief in serving God's will in what he did, dated back to a religious conversion in the early 1630s. A competent, occasionally brilliant, military commander (MARSTON MOOR was won largely by his skill), his implacable determination may be seen in his brutal treatment of the Irish (see DROGHEDA), and his facing down of the LEVELLERS. ROYALIST writers saw him as a religious fanatic and desecrator of churches: but his religious fervour was kept in check by a natural conservatism. He replaced SIR THOMAS FAIRFAX as commander of the army in 1650, having already eclipsed the other, and became Lord Protector of the Realm from 1653, although he declined to assume a crown.

Sir Charles Firth, *Oliver Cromwell* (London 1900).
W.C. Abbot (ed.), *The Writings and Speeches of Oliver Cromwell*, 4 vols. (London 1937–47).

Cropredy Bridge, Battle of (29 June 1644)

A striking victory in Oxfordshire by a ROYALIST army commanded in person by the king, over a PARLIAMENTARIAN force under SIR WILLIAM WALLER.

P. Young and M. Toynbee, *Cropredy Bridge 1644* (Kineton 1970).

Crowland (Croyland)

A town in Lincolnshire, seized 23 March 1643 by ROYALISTS. It was taken by CROMWELL with heavy bombardment 28 April. Refortified again by royalists October 1644, it surrendered in December.

Crown Lands

Those possessions belonging to the crown, the revenues of which accrued to the crown. In February 1649 PARLIAMENT set up a committee to survey the lands of the crown and of the Duchy of Lancaster as a preliminary to sale. CROMWELL served on this committee. On 18 April £600,000 assessed as due from EXCISE was shifted to the crown lands as a debt due from them, forcing the process of sale, and on 16 July an ACT OF PARLIAMENT was passed to enable the sale of crown lands to go ahead. Later acts followed.

Cuirassiers

Mounted troops clad in three-quarter length armour of a type almost obsolete by 1642, but a few troops appeared so armed during the civil wars. They carried swords and pistols, and were essentially heavy cavalry.

Culmer, Richard (d. 1662)

A PURITAN minister who clashed with ARCHBISHOP LAUD in 1635 over *THE BOOK OF SPORTS*. In 1643, as Rector of Chartham near CANTERBURY, he supervised the destruction of glass and images in Canterbury Cathedral and had to be saved from a hostile crowd of townspeople. He was a virulent witness against Laud at the latter's trial. He was universally disliked by his parishioners, who nicknamed him 'Blue Dick'.

Cumberland, Henry Clifford Earl of (1591–1643)

The single most powerful nobleman resident in Yorkshire. He was given command of the county in 1642 by CHARLES I. He proved incapable of opposing the PARLIAMENTARIANS, and was forced to step down in favour of the EARL OF NEWCASTLE.

D

Dangan Hill, Battle of (8 August 1647)

Defeat of an IRISH CONFEDERATE army by MICHAEL JONES in an action near Trim.

Dartmouth

Crucial south-coast Devonshire port taken by PRINCE MAURICE 4–5 October 1643. It was captured by SIR THOMAS FAIRFAX 18 January 1646 in a combined sea and land operation.

Davenant, Sir William (1606–68)

Davenant was criticized in 1645 by one PARLIAMENTARIAN as 'the great pirate – the agent in projecting and bringing up the northern army [of the EARL OF NEWCASTLE]' in 1642. More famous as a writer, and perhaps as a dissolute, Davenant was General of the Ordnance under the Earl of Newcastle until June 1643. He was condemned for trial before the HIGH COURT OF JUSTICE in 1650, but was spared.

A. Clark (ed.), *Brief Lives, Chiefly of Contemporaries set down by John Aubrey* (Oxford 1898).

Davies, Lady Eleanor (1590–1652)

This nobly born woman, the daughter of the Earl of Castlehaven, believed herself to be a prophetess. As fortune-teller to QUEEN HENRIETTA MARIA, she was hauled before the COURT OF HIGH COMMISSION for her published writings. Clearly insane, she nevertheless continued to prophesy and is reputed to have foreseen the death of CHARLES I.

Deane, Richard (1610–53)

General of the artillery in the army of the EARL OF ESSEX and of the NEW MODEL ARMY, then Comptroller of the Ordnance. He sat on the HIGH COURT OF JUSTICE to try CHARLES I and signed the death warrant. He was killed when a General at Sea, fighting the Dutch in 1653.

Debauched Cavalleer, The

A TRACT of 1642 co-written by the PURITAN George Lawrence and Christopher Love, demanding the exile and SEQUESTRATION of those about the king and urging a 'holy war'.

Declaration of Dislike, The

Drafted 29 March 1647 by DENZIL HOLLES and passed by the HOUSE OF COMMONS. It denounced the *PETITION OF THE OFFICERS AND SOLDIERS OF THE ARMY* and cited its instigators as enemies of the state. It was repealed in June 1647.

Declaration of Fears and Jealousies

A draft version of the NINETEEN PROPOSITIONS and drawn up between 15 and 24 January 1642 in the HOUSE OF COMMONS. It did not pass the HOUSE OF LORDS.

Declaration (of June 14th 1647), The

Issued by the NEW MODEL ARMY in the role of defenders of liberty calling for the purge of PARLIAMENT and reapportionment of seats. The COUNCIL OF WAR advising SIR THOMAS FAIRFAX was responsible, as against the GENERAL COUNCIL OF THE ARMY, and it followed the ENGAGEMENT of the army not to disband. Its declaration that 'All authority is fundamentally seated in the office, and but ministerially in the person [of the king]' rehearsed arguments of 1642. PARLIAMENT rejected the declaration 25 June, and a more conciliatory Manifesto followed.

Declaration of the General Council of the New Model Army

The last meeting of the GENERAL COUNCIL 9 January 1648 gave rise to this document, co-written by CROMWELL and IRETON. It supported the FOUR BILLS as the minimal basis for talks with the king and resolved to preserve the kingdom 'without the king and against him' if necessary.

Defence, Committee for

Appeared September 1641 to consider the question of authority over the TRAINED BANDS and other future military forces in the light of the IRISH REBELLION. In July 1642 a revitalized committee of five peers and ten MPs was set up 'to oppose any force that may be raised against PARLIAMENT'. It planned an army of 10,000 men, and on 11 July declared the nation to be in a state of war. It appointed the EARL OF ESSEX Lord General. Members of the committee included PYM, HOLLES and LORD SAYE AND SELE.

Delinquents

A term applied to active and passive supporters of King CHARLES I before and during the civil war. The surrender of such persons was demanded by PARLIAMENT as part and parcel of any settlement. On 6 September 1642 Parliament declared it would not disband its troops until the king abandoned 'delinquents' and 'MALIGNANTS'.

Denbigh

A town in North Wales, garrisoned for the king from 1642. On 1 November 1645 ROYALISTS under Sir WILLIAM VAUGHAN were routed on Denbigh Green as they marched for CHESTER. Denbigh Castle was besieged November 1645 to October 1646, and was used in 1648 to imprison SIR JOHN OWEN, leader of the North Wales rising.

Denbigh, Basil Fielding, Earl of (d. 1674)

The earl succeeded his ROYALIST father in 1643, and became PARLIAMENTARIAN Commander-in-Chief in Warwickshire, Staffordshire, Worcestershire and Shropshire 12 June.

He acted with others for the PARLIA-
MENT in negotiations at UXBRIDGE in
1645. Although he distanced himself
from the trial (see TRIAL OF CHARLES I)
and execution of the king in 1649, he
served on the COUNCIL OF STATE.

Derby, Charlotte Stanley Countess of (1599–1664)

Lady Derby commanded the ROYA-
LIST garrison of her house of LATHOM,
Lancashire, from 1643 and during the
siege of February 1644 to May 1644,
after which she retired to the Isle of
Man with her husband, the EARL OF
DERBY.

Derby House Committee   See
Committee for Both Kingdoms

Derby, James Stanley Earl of (1607–51)

The earl was the mover of the
ROYALIST war effort in Lancashire
from the summer of 1642, but lost
control of the county at the BATTLE OF
WHALLEY. In 1644 he fled to the Isle of
Man, returning to England to take
part in CHARLES II's invasion plans.
Captured at WIGAN LANE, he was
tried and executed at BOLTON. See
also RICHARD PERCEVAL.

B. Coward, *The Stanleys, Lord Stanley
and Earls of Derby* (London 1983).

Dering, Sir Edward (1599–1644)

CROMWELL considered Dering a man
'full of impertinences'. He was MP
for Kent in the LONG PARLIAMENT

and introduced the ROOT AND BRANCH
bill into the HOUSE OF COMMONS, but
emerged shortly afterwards as a
champion of EPISCOPACY. He promoted the KENTISH PETITION of 25
March 1642, which was an indictment
of PARLIAMENT's proceedings. Hostility towards him died down after his
surrender in 1644 and taking of the
Covenant (see SOLEMN LEAGUE AND
COVENANT).

Devil of Shrawardine

Nickname for SIR WILLIAM VAUGHAN,
the ROYALIST. SHRAWARDINE CASTLE
on the Welsh border was held by him
for the king.

Devizes

ROYALIST garrison in Wiltshire from
February 1643 but besieged by SIR
WILLIAM WALLER in July. His defeat on
ROUNDWAY DOWN obliged him to lift
the siege. Town and castle fell to
CROMWELL September 1645.

D'Ewes, Sir Simond(s) (1602–50)

D'Ewes was MP for Sudbury, Suffolk, in the LONG PARLIAMENT and a
noted 'moderate', whose brother was
killed fighting for the king in 1643.
His published journals are too
restrained and self-praising to be as
informative as they might have been.
His moderation and PRESBYTERIANISM
led to his expulsion during PRIDE'S
PURGE.

W.H. Coates (ed.), *The Journal of Sir
Simonds D'Ewes* (London 1942).

W. Notestein (ed.), *The Journal of Sir Simonds D'Ewes* (London 1923).

Digby, George Lord (1612–77)

Digby sat as MP for Dorset in the LONG PARLIAMENT and, from 1641, as Lord Digby in the HOUSE OF LORDS. A courtier and a close advisor of CHARLES I, reporting on events in PARLIAMENT to the monarch, he was one of those against whom Parliament developed a pronounced animus. His personal feud with PRINCE RUPERT did not weaken his standing with the king, but his period as a general in 1645 was disastrous. Parliament banished him as a traitor in 1649.

Diggers

Popular name for a group which termed itself 'the true LEVELLERS', was led by GERRARD WINSTANLEY and established a commune on waste land at St George's Hill near KINGSTON UPON THAMES 1 April 1649. The execution of the king was hailed by them as the throwing off of the 'Norman yoke'. SIR THOMAS FAIRFAX regarded them as harmless cranks, but local opposition dispersed them during March 1650. The term 'diggers' was applied to anti-ENCLOSURE rioters in Northamptonshire in 1607.

Digges, Dudley (1613–43)

Digges was probably the most outstanding ROYALIST polemicist of the civil wars. He was author of *The Unlawfulness of Subjects taking up Armes against their Soveraigne* (which may be said to be a forerunner of the work of HOBBES), and he tackled HENRY PARKER, the PARLIAMENTARIAN, in *An Answer to a Printed Book*.

Directory of Public Worship (of God in the Three Kingdoms)

The *Directory* was the product of the deliberations of the WESTMINSTER ASSEMBLY OF DIVINES and was prepared as an alternative to the PRAYER BOOK of the CHURCH OF ENGLAND, as the ORDINANCE of 4 January 1645 making possible the *Directory* expressly stated.

Dissenting Brethren

A group of five INDEPENDENTS in the WESTMINSTER ASSEMBLY led by THOMAS GOODWIN. The others were PHILIP NYE, John Archer, Jeremiah Burroughs and William Bridge.

Diurnals

Contemporary spelling of 'journals', and meaning newspapers and newssheets appearing on a regular (weekly, bi-weekly or monthly) basis during the civil war years, which saw a great expansion in the publication of newspapers.

Divine Right of Government

Book written by Michael Hudson, a clergyman and officer in the army of the EARL OF NEWCASTLE, and published in 1647. It condemned 'polarchy' or GOVERNMENT by the many. Hudson saw order in society as reflective of order in the universe, and denied to the mass any role in government.

Divine Right of Kings

A doctrine largely European, and especially French, in origin and application, arguing for direct inheritance of a throne as signifying divine right, and treating rebellion as therefore a sin against God. Its first appearance in England as a doctrine was in 1569, but LAUDIANISM, especially in the canons of 1640 (see CONVOCATION), pushed home the doctrine vigorously. It was unsuited to concepts of monarchy in England, and it is doubtful that CHARLES I himself accepted this doctrine.

Dobson, William (1610–46)

A portrait painter attached to the royal court at OXFORD, where he portrayed not only prominent courtiers of CHARLES I but also field commanders of the ROYALIST armies.

Doncaster

A town in Yorkshire where, 29 October 1648, ROYALIST raiders from PONTEFRACT located and killed Colonel RAINSBOROUGH.

Donnington Castle

Strategic fortress in Berkshire controlling the LONDON–Bath road and the OXFORD–south coast route, and held by the ROYALISTS from 1642 to April 1646. Governor Boys repulsed two sieges in 1644, and only surrendered after an arduous three-month siege in 1646.

Dorislaus, Isaac (1595–1649)

A Dutchman, lecturer in history at Cambridge University and protégé of LORD BROOKE. He was dismissed from Cambridge for lecturing on the SOVEREIGNTY of the people. Judge Advocate in the army of the EARL OF ESSEX from 1642, in 1649 he helped draft the charges against the king. As Special Envoy from England to the States General of his native Holland, he was assassinated by ROYALIST agents at THE HAGUE 12 May 1649.

Downes, John (d. 1666)

MP for ARUNDEL, Sussex, in the LONG PARLIAMENT, and a signatory of the death warrant of the king in 1649. He claimed at his own trial in 1660 that CROMWELL had forced him to sign, but he had nevertheless served on the COUNCIL OF STATE 1651–2 and accepted reappointment in 1659. He died in prison.

Draconic Ordinance

The anti-heresy law of 2 May 1648 aimed at the proliferation of sects and SECTARIES.

Dragoons

Lightly armed, mounted infantry units common to both sides in the civil war, and usually organized in a regimental structure, although occasionally met with as troops attached to cavalry regiments.

Drake, Nathan

Drake was a clergyman and gentleman volunteer who served in the defence of PONTEFRACT Castle 1644–5, and was later vicar of Pontefract. His *Journal of the First and Second Sieges of Pontefract Castle* has been published in editions of varying quality. The best was that of the *Surtees Society*, No. 37, 1861.

Drogheda

Fortress town on the mouth of the River Boyne in County Louth, Ireland. On 2 September 1649 CROMWELL led 12,000 of the NEW MODEL ARMY against the garrisoned town, which controlled the route north into Ulster. It was held by SIR ARTHUR ASTON and 3,000 men. In the storm of the walls, 11 September, more than 2,000 of the garrison were slaughtered. 'Our men were ordered by me to put them all to the sword', Cromwell reported. St Peter's Church was burned with all inside it. Governor Aston was beaten to death for the money concealed about him.

Duckenfield, Robert (1619–89)

Governor of CHESTER and convenor of the court martial which, October 1651, sentenced to death the EARL OF DERBY. He subsequently captured the Isle of Man from the earl's widow (see COUNTESS OF DERBY).

Dudley Castle

A ROYALIST stronghold in Worcestershire from 1642 to its surrender 14 May 1646, despite siege by the EARL OF DENBIGH in May 1644. A royalist relief attempt was beaten at nearby Tipton Green 12 June 1644. The royalist governor was the war-hardened Thomas Leveson.

Dugdale, Sir William (1605–86)

In his own time a prominent antiquary and historian (his works include the 1656 *Antiquities of Warwickshire*), Dugdale was a royal herald and Garter king-of-arms (from 1677). He attended upon CHARLES I at OXFORD. Among his other works are *Monasticon Anglicanum* (1655–73) and *Origines Juridiciales* (1666).

W. Hampner (ed.), *The Diary of Sir William Dugdale* (London 1821).

Dunbar, Battle of (3 September 1650)

The major victory of CROMWELL over the Scots (commanded by DAVID LESLIE) after steady retreat south. In a night assault Cromwell retrieved the initiative, destroyed Leslie's army, and secured access to EDINBURGH.

Dundee

On 4 April 1645 MONTROSE and 750

men stormed and took the town, but withdrew before a COVENANTER army could catch them. On 1 September 1651 GEORGE MONCK with forces of the NEW MODEL ARMY stormed and took Dundee and slew 500 civilians.

Dunfermline Declaration

On 16 August 1650 King CHARLES II, under pressure from the Scots, denounced all alliance with the Irish. ORMONDE summoned the COMMISSIONERS OF TRUST in Ireland 23 October 1650, and again 15 November, before abandoning his command and quitting Ireland 11 December.

Dury, John (1596–1680)

A Scottish PRESBYTERIAN minister working in Germany who became an Anglican (see CHURCH OF ENGLAND) clergyman with the favour of ARCHBISHOP LAUD, and was favoured also by PYM and SIR WILLIAM WALLER for his ceaseless work against Rome. He sat on the WESTMINSTER ASSEMBLY, advocating educational policies as a means of unification of the people, which CROMWELL approved. He died in exile in Germany.

Dymock, Cressy

A ROYALIST cavalry officer who, in 1651, published *An Essay For the Advancement of Husbandry Learning*, which proposed a college of agriculture for farmers. Further reforming tracts followed, but Dymock was in dire financial straits by 1670.

E

Earle, Sir Walter (1586–1665)

Prominent PURITAN opponent of the court as early as the 1620s and leading figure behind the PETITION OF RIGHT. He sat as MP for Lyme (Regis) in the SHORT and LONG PARLIAMENTS and was an active supporter of PYM. Vehement against STRAFFORD and instrumental in the GRAND REMONSTRANCE, he served in arms until 1649 despite the SELF DENYING ORDINANCE. He was gaoled after PRIDE'S PURGE because of his PRESBYTERIANISM. One ROYALIST described him as 'a rogue and a roundheaded rogue … chief raiser of these combustions'.

Eastern Association

PARLIAMENTARIAN association of Norfolk, Suffolk, Essex, Hertfordshire and Cambridgeshire formed 20 December 1642, to which were later added Huntingdonshire and Lincolnshire (see COUNTY ASSOCIATIONS). The Eastern Association was crucial to the parliamentarian war effort. On 25 July 1643 an ORDINANCE of PARLIAMENT sought to raise 5,000 cavalry from the Association under the command of the EARL OF MANCHESTER, who on 9 August became general of an Association-based army, which that month was to be expanded to 20,000 men. The Association army at MARSTON MOOR in July 1644 was 8,000 strong, half cavalry.

Clive Holmes, *The Eastern Association in the English Civil War* (Cambridge 1974).

East Farleigh

Important bridge over the Medway in Kent where, 1 June 1648, ROYALIST troops were defeated by SIR THOMAS FAIRFAX while advancing on MAIDSTONE during the Kentish rising.

Eaton, John (1575–1642)

Influential ANTINOMIAN writer whose most important works, *The Discovery of the Most Dangerous Dead Faith* and *The Honey-Combe of Free Justification*, were published posthumously. In his denial of human corruption and sinfulness he challenged a broad range of Protestant theology.

Ecclesia Anglicana

Strictly, the Anglican Church (see CHURCH OF ENGLAND); but as a concept, indicative of a middle way between PURITANISM and LAUDIANISM, but loyal to the episcopal church structure which was under threat from the ROOT AND BRANCH MOVEMENT.

Ecclesiastical courts

These were: the Court of Delegates, with jurisdiction over the provinces of YORK and CANTERBURY and headed by a Registrar; the Court of the Arches, with jurisdiction in the province of Canterbury; the Court of Audience, headed by a judge; the Prerogative Court of Canterbury; and the Court of the Archbishop's Vicar-general. See also COURT OF HIGH COMMISSION.

Edgehill, Battle of (23 October 1642)

The first major battle of the civil wars, at Edgehill in Warwickshire, concerning the outcome of which historians remain divided. Since the EARL OF ESSEX failed to block the advance of the king upon LONDON and withdrew after the engagement, it would seem clear that it was a ROYALIST victory. Lack of a successful follow-up deprived the victory of its usefulness, however: the royalists wasted their advantage.

P. Young, *Edgehill 1642. The Campaign and the Battle* (Kineton 1967).

Edinburgh

The Scottish capital and, in 1650, base of DAVID LESLIE's army, which from July into August evaded attempts by CROMWELL to force a battle. Edinburgh was thrown open to the English and occupied by JOHN LAMBERT after the disastrous encounter at DUNBAR, 3 September.

Edwards, Humphrey (d. 1658)

In 1642 Edwards attended upon CHARLES I during the attempt on the FIVE MEMBERS, but he changed sides, sat as MP for Shropshire in the RECRUITER elections of the LONG PARLIAMENT, and supported PRIDE'S PURGE. He sat on the HIGH COURT OF JUSTICE and signed Charles I's death warrant.

Edwards, Thomas

Author of *Gangraena or a Catalogue and Discovery of Many of the Errours, Heresies and Blasphemies and Pernicious Practices*, published in three parts in 1646. Part three was aimed at the SECTARIES and INDEPENDENTS in or associated with the NEW MODEL ARMY, denouncing them as a vociferous minority. *Gangraena* reflected the growing unease at the proliferation of beliefs and sects, and although not necessarily accurate in its depictions, it is a good guide to the complexity of heresies.

Eikon Basilike

A book purportedly compiled by CHARLES I himself, the first printing of which was 8 February 1649. Its title translates as 'The Royal Image'. Actually more or less written by Dr JOHN GAUDEN, but based extensively upon royal papers, it presented the dead king as a martyr and victim of tyranny, and went into numerous editions. It was the basis of subsequent sentimental attachment to the king's memory even among former enemies. MILTON wrote *Eikonoklastes* ('The Image Breaker') as a counterattack.

Eleven Members

On 16 June 1647 the NEW MODEL ARMY

introduced into the HOUSE OF COMMONS the 'heads of charges' against HOLLES and ten other MPs of PRESBYTERIAN leanings, seeking to impeach them. AGITATORS tried to add LORD SAYE AND SELE to the list but failed. The Commons deliberated and then the members named withdrew. The action, part of the army's 'rescuing' of the PARLIAMENT from the LONDON mob, exacerbated feelings further.

Enclosures (inclosures)

The fencing in and dividing up into severalty of common fields and pastures, or the abandonment of arable in favour of less labour-intensive grassland and animal husbandry. Enclosures also trampled upon and extinguished common rights and struck at the fabric of customary land usage (see CONSERVATISM, CUSTOM AND DEFERENCE). Enclosures provoked riots all over England in the 1630s, and were coupled in the popular mind with fen drainage, which had undermined wetland occupations and the local economy. Serious localized rioting occurred in 1642 in the Forest of Dean area and in eastern England, and continued through the civil war years; for example, at Gillingham Forest in 1643 and again in 1645. Proprietors, whether ROYALIST or PARLIAMENTARIAN, suffered at the hands of mobs, often led by women or men disguised as women in a ritual inversion of the social order which enclosures threatened.

Engagement, The

The first such document was that of 26 December 1647 forming an alliance between CHARLES I and the Scots. The king acceded to the SOLEMN LEAGUE AND COVENANT of 1643 and accepted PRESBYTERIANISM for a three-year period. Scottish COVENANTERS were split by the alliance, which foundered anyway at PRESTON, Lancashire. The second *Engagement* was an oath of allegiance to the REPUBLIC or COMMONWEALTH of England, imposed in 1650 on all men aged 18 or over, and expressly ordered by PARLIAMENT. The term 'Engagers' ordinarily refers to those who subscribed to the *Engagement* of 1647.

Engagement, The Solemn (of the New Model Army)

Drafted by IRETON 5 June 1647, it preceded by a week or so the army's attempt on the ELEVEN MEMBERS. It was a military COVENANT comparable with the SCOTTISH NATIONAL COVENANT, and ushered in the GENERAL COUNCIL OF THE NEW MODEL ARMY.

England's New Chains Discovered

The published version of a PETITION presented to the RUMP PARLIAMENT by JOHN LILBURNE 26 February 1649, denouncing the unrepresentative nature of the PARLIAMENT and the arbitrary powers of the HIGH COURT OF JUSTICE. *The Second Part of England's New Chains Discovered* attacked the NEW MODEL ARMY officer corps as betrayers of the people, and the COUNCIL OF STATE, which sent Lilburne to prison, as exercising the bankrupt powers of the Rump. In April 1649 a mutiny in the New

Model Army was largely influenced by this LEVELLER argument.

English Revolution

An historiographical view of the events of the years 1642–60 which sees them as the total overthrow of established order and the creation of an entirely new system of GOVERNMENT, the REPUBLIC. Not the same thing as the GREAT REBELLION, which was EDWARD HYDE's interpretation of the events of those years.

Episcopacy

Government of the church by bishops, sanctioned by Queen Elizabeth I, and a link with the pre-Reformation church. Bishops were abolished in Scotland in 1638 (see BISHOPS' WARS), and in England by the LONG PARLIAMENT 9 October 1646. They were restored in 1660.

Erastianism

A theory which holds that the state may determine the religion of its people, allegedly based upon the doctrines of Thomas Erastus (d. 1583). By the time of the civil war the term was used pejoratively. The LAUDIANS adopted Erastianism to support their church reforms, but it may also be seen in the anti-EPISCOPACY of the ROOT AND BRANCH MOVEMENT.

Essex, Robert Devereux Earl of (1591–1646)

From July 1642 Lord General of the army of the PARLIAMENT, because of his long military experience and his hostility towards the court. His bitter enmity towards STRAFFORD may have recommended him as well. Subjected to much unfounded criticism in the HOUSE OF COMMONS, he was denied military command in 1645 by the SELF DENYING ORDINANCE.

Committee of the Estates

Appointed by the Scottish PARLIAMENT in 1640 and abolished in 1648. On 5 April 1649 King CHARLES II was recognized by this revived committee but, under the leadership of ARGYLE, it required him to subscribe to the SCOTTISH NATIONAL COVENANT. The committee was captured to a man at Alyth 28 August 1651 and sent into England.

Evelyn, John (1620–1706)

Famous diarist and writer (and civil servant). He initially supported the king in the civil wars, but went to Europe in 1644 to escape the SOLEMN LEAGUE AND COVENANT imposed by PARLIAMENT. The bulk of his work, and therefore the basis of his fame, belongs to 1649 and later.

Everard, William

AGITATOR and DIGGER and a promoter of the *AGREEMENT OF THE PEOPLE*, gaoled for involvement at CORKBUSH FIELD and thought to be involved in a plot to murder CHARLES I. He saw the Diggers as the Jews come to rid

England of the Norman yoke. Abandoning them, he wandered England until committed as insane.

Ewer, Isaac (d. 1650)

A member of the COUNCIL OF OFFICERS OF THE NEW MODEL ARMY with a distinguished war record, who delivered the REMONSTRANCE OF THE ARMY to PARLIAMENT in November 1648. Ewer's men removed CHARLES I from CARISBROOKE CASTLE to HURST CASTLE, and he himself sat on the HIGH COURT OF JUSTICE and signed the king's death warrant.

Exact militia

Attempt by CHARLES I to improve the ability and quality of the TRAINED BANDS by bringing experienced officers over from Europe on tours of duty. They were paid from local funds but had responsibility to the PRIVY COUNCIL. From 1635 trained band weaponry and equipment approached standardization.

Exchange of prisoners

With very few exceptions, prisoners taken in arms by either side in the civil wars rarely endured long detention. Common soldiers might be freed on their paroles not to fight again, non-commissioned and other officers might be exchanged (following a formal and universal procedure) for those held by the other side. For example, in January 1646 BYRON in CHESTER confirmed to BRERETON by letter that Brereton's officers would be handed over 'midway between our fort and your next guard' at 2 p.m. on the following day, in return for ROYALIST captives. Values were ordinarily established (for example, four troopers for a single sergeant), and fees were sometimes payable to the provost-marshal or whoever arranged the exchanges.

Excise and excise riots

In July 1643 PARLIAMENT introduced a 'new Impost' or tax, the excise, upon luxury goods and alcohol, a system gradually copied by the ROYALISTS. There were suggestions that the Excise might eventually supersede ASSESSMENTS but in fact they were levied together. Such a tax had been expressly denounced in the GRAND REMONSTRANCE. The excise occasioned widespread violent reaction against whichever side was levying it. In CHESTER a royalist alderman named Gamull was voted out on the platform of 'No Gamull No Excise', and in 1646 and later anti-excise riots suppressed by troops were attributed, misleadingly, to royalist incendiaries.

Exeter

An important port town in Devonshire which fell to PRINCE MAURICE 7 September 1643 and was taken by SIR THOMAS FAIRFAX 9 April 1646.

F

Faction

ROYALIST polemical term for the leaders of the Country (see COURT AND COUNTRY) in the HOUSE OF COMMONS. Their policies were parodied and displayed in the TRACT *A Complaint to the House of Commons* (1643).

Faggot-Monger Brown(e)   See
Major General Richard Brown(e).

Fairfax, Ferdinando Lord (1584–1648)

Lord Fairfax held a Scottish peerage, and thus was enabled to sit in the HOUSE OF COMMONS as MP for Yorkshire in the LONG PARLIAMENT. He commanded the army of PARLIAMENT's NORTHERN ASSOCIATION against the EARL OF NEWCASTLE from 1642, and was governor of YORK 1644–5. He gave up his appointments in the latter year. His activities have been overshadowed by those of his son, SIR THOMAS FAIRFAX.

Fairfax, Sir Thomas (1612–71)

Son of FERDINANDO LORD FAIRFAX and second in command to him in Yorkshire from 1642. His forces were badly mauled at MARSTON MOOR in 1644. On 21 January he was appointed Captain General of the NEW MODEL ARMY, an appointment approved by radical elements. In July 1647 he was made Commander-in-Chief of all armed forces. Out of touch with radical pressures in the army by late 1648, he was eclipsed by CROMWELL. He was said to have opposed the TRIAL OF CHARLES I but did nothing to prevent it. He served on the COUNCIL OF STATE and sat as MP for CIRENCESTER. He threw up his army command in 1650 in favour of Cromwell, withdrew from public life, and emerged to favour the restoration of CHARLES II.

M.A. Gibb, *The Lord General, A Life of Sir Thomas Fairfax* (London 1938).

Falkland, Lucius Cary Viscount (1610–43)

Lord Falkland, centre of a literary and philosophical circle attached to the royal court, served as MP for Newport, Isle of Wight, in the LONG PARLIAMENT, where he opposed STRAFFORD but favoured EPISCOPACY. Secretary of State to CHARLES I from 1642, he is reputed to have deliberately courted his own death at NEWBURY September 1643. His most important work was probably his 1630s attack on Catholicism, *Discourse of Infallibility*.

Fantom, Captain Carlo

A PARLIAMENTARIAN cavalry officer of Croatian extraction, who fought at EDGEHILL under the EARL OF ESSEX.

53

This 'admirable horse officer' developed a mysterious and exotic persona, leading to the development of legends about him.

Faringdon Castle   See Roger Burgess

Farnham

A PARLIAMENTARIAN garrison in Surrey from 1642, captured briefly by GEORGE GORING 28 January 1645. It was the original base for the army of SIR WILLIAM WALLER. CHARLES I lodged in the castle 19 December 1648 on his way to his trial in LONDON.

Fast sermons

On 8 January 1642 CHARLES I proclaimed that a public fast be held upon the last Wednesday of every month until the crushing of the IRISH REBELLION. From 23 February 1642 these became occasions for political sermons in LONDON attended by MPs and peers, and the sermons' contents were published and disseminated.

Featherstonhaugh, Sir Timothy (1601–51)

A ROYALIST soldier and commander from Cumberland, Featherstonhaugh was one of those few singled out for judicial execution after the abortive royalist invasion of 1651.

Ferne, Henry

ROYALIST political theorist and writer. His TRACT of 1643, *A Reply unto Severall Treatises*, was a response to the seminal *A TREATISE OF MONARCHY*, and argued that although the king is bound by the law he is also the ultimate judge of it.

Fiennes, Nathaniel (1608–69)

Son of LORD SAYE AND SELE, MP for BANBURY, Oxfordshire, in the SHORT and LONG PARLIAMENTS, and a vigorous committee man. In July 1643 he surrendered BRISTOL to PRINCE RUPERT and was condemned to death for cowardice by a COUNCIL OF WAR, but was spared. By late 1648, although an INDEPENDENT, he favoured negotiations with the king, and was excluded and gaoled at PRIDE'S PURGE. By 1654 he was serving on the COUNCIL OF STATE.

Fifth and Twentieth   See Committee for Advance of Money

Fifth Monarchists

Predominantly a phenomenon of the 1650s, they were a sect (see SECTARIANS AND SEPARATISTS) who foretold the imminence of the fifth monarchy, that of Christ, based upon a text in Daniel 2:44. They believed in using violent means to bring this monarchy about.

Filmer, Sir Robert (d. 1653)

ROYALIST polemicist and defender of the DIVINE RIGHT OF KINGS in his 1642 work *Patriarcha* (published in 1680), in which he argued against PARLIAMENT's claim to be guardian of some common good. Filmer's *Observations*

Upon Mr. Hunton's Treatise of Monarchy or, the Anarchy of a Limited or Mixed Monarchy (see *A TREATISE OF MONARCHY*) appeared in 1648. It long remained influential in royalist thinking.

P. Laslett (ed.), *Patriarcha and Other Political Works* (Oxford 1949).

Firelock

Contemporary term for an early form of flintlock firing mechanism on a musket, in which the powder is ignited by a flint striking upon steel at the depression of the trigger. Firelocks were more reliable than matchlocks, which required the application of a burning tallow cord to the powder pan. Companies of firelocks were established to guard vulnerable munition waggons and trains.

Five Members

CHARLES I tried to seize five leading MPs on 4 January 1642 from the body of the HOUSE OF COMMONS. They were JOHN PYM, JOHN HAMPDEN, DENZIL HOLLES, SIR ARTHUR HASELRIG and WILLIAM STRODE. Forewarned, they fled the chamber and hid in LONDON. He had also planned to seize Lord Kimbolton. This attempt to demoralize the Commons was a signal failure, and the members returned to their duties within a week.

Fleetwood, Charles (1618–92)

Colonel of a regiment in the EASTERN ASSOCIATION and then in the NEW MODEL ARMY, where he adopted a radical position. RECRUITER MP for Marlborough, Wiltshire, from 1646, he was absent from all proceedings against the king in 1649, but became commander of the cavalry under CROMWELL in 1651, and then served as Commander-in-Chief in Ireland from 1652. He was a close confidant of Cromwell.

Foot

Contemporary term for the infantry. Civil war foot regiments were set at 1,200 men, divided into companies commanded by captains, the regimental field officers being the Colonel, Lieutenant Colonel and (Sergeant) Major. Regiments of foot might be brigaded together in 'tertias' in battle. The rank and file were musketeers and pikemen, the role of the pikeman being considered the more gentlemanly because it was an ancient calling.

Forced loans

In principle levied only in times of crisis and subject to repayment: BENEVOLENCES were forced loans that were not repaid. Forced loans in 1626–7 met resistance and were denounced in the PETITION OF RIGHT, and after reappearing in 1640, were never again resorted to.

Foreign aid

King and PARLIAMENT employed individual foreign (European) soldiers in their armies. Financial aid from abroad went largely to the king.

Frederick Henry, Prince of Orange (whose son married King CHARLES I's daughter Mary in 1641), facilitated the supply of men and money to the king, borrowing extensively and arousing the antagonism of Parliament. France also contributed after the death of Cardinal Richelieu, who as principal minister had preserved a form of neutrality.

Forlorn hope

A body of soldiers, not necessarily volunteers, so positioned in anticipation of a battle or other engagement that they bore the full initial brunt of an attack.

Fortescue, Faithful (1581–1666)

Fortescue, who had military experience in Ireland, came over to England to support PARLIAMENT in 1642. He and his regiment defected to the king at the BATTLE OF EDGEHILL, seriously weakening the PARLIAMENTARIAN cavalry there. JOHN VICARS called him 'Faithlesse Fortescue'.

Forth, Patrick Ruthven Earl of (1573–1651)

A soldier in the Swedish armies in Europe, ennobled by the Swedish king Gustavus Adolphus. Ruthven fought for CHARLES I in the BISHOPS' WARS, and in 1642 became General in Chief of the ROYALIST armies, a rank he relinquished because of age and injury in 1644. He remained on the PRIVY COUNCIL and was created, as well as Earl of Forth (1642), Earl of

Brentford (1644). He served CHARLES II in his native Scotland.

Four Bills

On 14 December 1647, in an attempt to create agreement between king, PARLIAMENT and the Scots, Parliament passed Four Bills initiated in the HOUSE OF LORDS for approval by the king. Under these bills, Parliament was to control the army for 20 years, with no royal veto in military matters after that; proceedings against the Parliament and its supporters were to be stopped; peerages created since 1642 were to be void; EPISCOPACY was to remain abolished and the sale of BISHOPS' LANDS was to continue. CHARLES I rejected these terms 28 December.

Fowey

On 2 September 1644 some 6,000 men of the army of the EARL OF ESSEX surrendered to the king at Fowey in Cornwall. Some 5,000 weapons and 42 CANNON fell into the king's hands. See also LOSTWITHIEL.

Fowke, John (d. 1662)

LONDON merchant and political radical gaoled by the PRIVY COUNCIL in 1627. He organized the London PETITION of 1641 demanding the removal of EPISCOPACY, and served on the COMMITTEE OF SAFETY in 1642. He was proscribed by the king for high treason in January 1643. A bitter critic of the EARL OF ESSEX, his role was crucial in London's failure to resist the occupation of the NEW MODEL ARMY in 1647.

Franklin, William

An extreme SECTARY leading a group expressing a fusion of RANTER and FIFTH MONARCHIST ideas. Proclaimed himself to be Christ and built up a following at Southampton, but was arrested and tried, and recanted.

Freeborn John

Nickname of JOHN LILBURNE.

Free quarter

Ideally soldiers paid cash for board and lodging, but in the absence of money 'free quarter' applied. House-holders boarding soldiers were given tickets to be redeemed for cash at a later date. The PETITION OF RIGHT deemed such tickets or vouchers to be illegal, but the necessity of the civil war years made them common. Aware of the hostility towards free quarter, PRINCE RUPERT forbade it in February 1644, conditional upon organization of regular income from the ASSESSMENTS, in those areas where he commanded.

Frieze, James

Law reformer supported by JOHN LILBURNE. In 1646 he published *Everyman's Right*, calling for prison visitations to remove injustices. A LEVELLER, his TRACT *The Levellers Vindication* appeared in 1649. In it he condemned the use of any language other than English in the courts.

Frightfulness

A policy advocated and implemented by PARLIAMENT's representatives in Dublin, aimed at the IRISH CATHOLIC CONFEDERACY and its supporters. It prescribed military reprisals against the civilian population.

Fuller, Thomas (1608–61)

Fuller was a clergyman and chaplain in the ROYALIST army of Lord Hopton (see SIR RALPH HOPTON). Fuller's Anglican (see CHURCH OF ENGLAND) moderation, manifested in his *Church History* (1655), was criticized by royalists. In his *Worthies of England* (1662), written when he was chaplain to CHARLES II, he referred to many leading figures of the civil war years.

G

Gadbury, Mary

RANTER and Virginal 'Bride of the Lamb' to WILLIAM FRANKLIN, who believed himself to be Christ. Franklin abandoned her when he recanted, and she was tried for blasphemy at WINCHESTER.

Gage, Sir Henry   See Jesuit

Gainsborough

Prosperous port in Lincolnshire occupied by the ROYALISTS January 1643, but retaken in July by parliamentary troops. Besieged by fresh royalist forces, the port was relieved by CROMWELL and MELDRUM in a fierce battle 28 July, but advancing royalists took the port 31 July nevertheless. It fell to Meldrum in December but was abandoned in March 1644 after PRINCE RUPERT's relief of NEWARK.

Gangraena   See Thomas Edwards

Gathered churches

Virtually autonomous churches and communities united by shared belief, including the rejection of a state church. See also INDEPENDENTS.

Gauden, John (1605–62)

Although chaplain to the EARL OF WARWICK in 1640 and a member of the WESTMINSTER ASSEMBLY OF DIVINES, Gauden was a supporter of EPISCOPACY and an opponent of PRESBYTERIANISM and the SOLEMN LEAGUE AND COVENANT. He has been credited with authorship of EIKON BASILIKE (1649), the fundamental ROYALIST text for the view of CHARLES I as a martyr.

Gell, Sir John (1593–1671)

Gell was the PARLIAMENTARIAN governor of Derby, whose troops were notorious for their rapacity. During 1645 this effective local commander began to shift towards the king. He was tried and gaoled in 1650 for plotting against the new regime, but released in 1652.

General Committee of Officers of the New Model Army   See Council of Officers of the New Model Army

General Council of the (New Model) Army

Constituted June 1647 at KENTFORD HEATH near Newmarket and made up of general officers plus two junior officers and two private soldiers of each regiment of the army. Their task was to coordinate and present the soldiers' grievances. The General Council organized the PUTNEY DEBATES and exerted control over the AGITATORS. The *ENGAGEMENT* of the army (June 1647) shows the General Council still existed then.

Geneva of the North

Nickname for BOLTON, Lancashire, and an allusion to the town's prevalent and fierce PRESBYTERIANISM, because the first Presbyterian government had been established in Geneva.

Geography of loyalties

Historiographical theory that certain areas of the country were inclined generally towards either king or PARLIAMENT. In its simplest form, the theory is that the north, west and south-west were pro-ROYALIST, the midlands, east and south-east pro-PARLIAMENT. Within these broad distinctions, some historians identify certain socio-economic conditions as influencing allegiance. The concept of north and west as backward, and south and east as progressive, is generally discounted now.

Gerard, Charles (1618–94)

Gerard, 'the grand PAPIST', took over command in South Wales in 1644 from the EARL OF CARBERY. His ruthless pursuit of the king's war aims aroused local antagonisms from the CLUBMEN and jealousy from LORD DIGBY. Gerard abandoned his commands not long after the dismissal of

PRINCE RUPERT in 1645. His supposed Catholicism notwithstanding (although like many Catholics in exile he favoured the alliance with the Scots), his politics became more radical after 1660.

Glae-Eyed Marquess

Literary (rather than widespread) nickname for the MARQUESS OF ARGYLE, arising from his squint.

Glamorgan, Edward Somerset Earl of (1603–67)

As Lord Herbert of Raglan (see RAGLAN CASTLE), Somerset fought for the king from 1642. He was a devout ROMAN CATHOLIC and son to the MARQUESS OF WORCESTER. In January 1645 he was made Earl of Glamorgan and empowered to treat with the IRISH CATHOLIC CONFEDERACY for a cessation (see GLAMORGAN'S TREATIES). His unsuccessful endeavours were disowned by the crown, and he fled abroad.

Glamorgan's Treaties

The accession of Pope Innocent X in 1644 encouraged the king and his advisors to seek an agreement with the IRISH CATHOLIC CONFEDERACY. The EARL OF GLAMORGAN was commissioned 12 March 1645 to negotiate the treaty of 25 August, which conceded to the Irish their own PARLIAMENT and RELIGIOUS TOLERATION. RINUCCINI denounced the treaty, and a second in December failed also. Glamorgan was then arrested for (cosmetic) political reasons, to make it appear that the king had not been involved in treating with Irish rebels.

Glemham, Sir Thomas (d. 1649)

A professional soldier from Suffolk and a former MP, Glemham was successively ROYALIST governor of YORK, of CARLISLE and of OXFORD, in all of which he distinguished himself. The surrender of Oxford, May 1646, was forced upon him by royal order. He fought during the SECOND CIVIL WAR and died in exile.

Gloucester

A strategically important city controlling the crossing of the River Severn at its lowest point and thus road routes into Wales. Held for the PARLIAMENT from 1642 by EDWARD MASSEY, it was besieged August 1643, but the siege was raised in September by the EARL OF ESSEX. After BRISTOL fell into ROYALIST hands, Gloucester had the same importance to Parliament as NEWARK to the royalists, both places being key fortresses controlling converging routeways.

Godolphin, Sydney (1610–43)

A far from prolific ROYALIST poet, and MP for Helston, Cornwall, in the LONG PARLIAMENT, Godolphin was killed in arms for the king at CHAGFORD.

Goffe, William (d. c.1680)

Nicknamed 'Praying William' at the PUTNEY DEBATES (1647). He was one of the NEW MODEL ARMY officers sent to PARLIAMENT to demand the surrender of the ELEVEN MEMBERS. He sat on the HIGH COURT OF JUSTICE to try the king in 1649 and signed the death warrant, and later fought at DUNBAR and at WORCESTER. He fled to America in 1660 where he died.

Goldsmiths Hall Committee   See Committee for Scottish Affairs

Goodwin, John (1593–1665)

INDEPENDENT minister who fell foul of the BISHOP OF LONDON in 1638. His TRACTS of 1642, *Anti-Cavalierisme* and *The Butcher's Blessing*, fiercely promoted the parliamentary war effort. His ARMINIANISM precluded him from attending the WESTMINSTER ASSEMBLY. Goodwin's tract *Theomachi* denounced the coercion of PRESBYTERIANISM. Goodwin was a champion of JOHN LILBURNE and of the LEVELLERS.

Goodwin, Thomas (1600–80)

INDEPENDENT minister whose TRACT of 1641, *A Glimpse of Syon's Glory*, displayed PARLIAMENT as ushering in the reign of Christ. He was the Leader of the DISSENTING BRETHREN at the WESTMINSTER ASSEMBLY from which he resigned in 1645.

Goring, George (1608–57)

Of Goring, EDWARD HYDE said, 'he had wit and courage, and understanding, and ambition, uncontrolled by fear of God or man'. Goring was MP for PORTSMOUTH in the LONG PARLIAMENT but abandoned his governorship there and went to Europe, returning as Lieutenant General of the HORSE under the EARL OF NEW-CASTLE. Captured in 1643 and exchanged (see EXCHANGE OF PRISONERS), he subsequently held an independent command in the west country (see GORING'S CREW). From 1646 he was in Europe, as a commander for the Dutch and then the Spanish. He died in Spain.

Goring's Crew

Contemporary term of abuse, arising among the common people subject to their depredations, for the undisciplined troops led by GEORGE GORING in the west country in 1645.

Government

England had a central legislative authority (see PARLIAMENT) and a central executive authority (the king), but the basic unit of regulation was the parish or township. Each of these controlled its own affairs and elected its parochial or township officers (see HIGH AND PETTY CONSTABLES) who were responsible to the JUSTICES OF THE PEACE and so, through them, to the executive. The Justices of the Peace were the crucial element between executive decision and its implementation. In the case of SHIP MONEY, the SHERIFF was preferred by the executive, but in its collection the system relied again upon the self-taxing and self-regulating parish or township.

Gowran

A town in County Kilkenny, Ireland,

captured by the NEW MODEL ARMY 21 March 1650. CROMWELL ordered the officers of the garrison shot.

Grandees

A term applied, around 1647/8, to the generals and senior officers of the NEW MODEL ARMY, usually pejoratively. The term could also be applied to ROYALIST generals, such as the EARL OF NEWCASTLE or the EARL OF CARBERY, of no military experience but appointed for their social standing.

Grand Juries

Empanelled at QUARTER SESSIONS or special sessions to present matters of importance to the county community. Both sides used the grand jury system, with its influential social makeup, for their political ends. It was used both to denounce and to enforce obedience to the COMMISSION OF ARRAY. The association (see COUNTY ASSOCIATIONS) of 11 January 1645 of Worcestershire, Shropshire, Staffordshire and Herefordshire was at the initiative of the Worcestershire grand jury.

Grand Remonstrance

The demands put by PARLIAMENT before the king in 1641, rehearsing the reforms of the LONG PARLIAMENT and demanding further concessions of the ROYAL PREROGATIVE. It passed the HOUSE OF COMMONS by a mere 11 votes and alienated moderate opinion, which managed to delay its publication. It was presented to the king 1 December 1641; he rejected its provisions 23 December. It was purely the manifesto of an alliance of interests amongst MPs.

Grantham, Battle of (13 May 1643)

An engagement in Lincolnshire following the one at BELTON during CROMWELL's advance on NEWARK, which he abandoned despite the victory at Grantham.

Great Rebellion

A view of the civil wars first given wide currency by EDWARD HYDE. It sees the struggle as the rebellion of PARLIAMENT against the crown, described in contemporary terms as like the Biblical revolt of Absalom against his father King David. The term denies absolutely any inherent legality or justification in the Parliament's proceedings, and equates their actions with those of any earlier 'rebels' against royal authority.

Great Seal

This authenticated all documents to which it was affixed, and thus symbolized ultimate authority in the state. The Lord Keeper of the Great Seal took it secretly to CHARLES I at YORK 1 June 1642, obliging PARLIAMENT, in an ORDINANCE of 10 November 1643, to provide its own Great Seal and, at the same time, to annul all acts authorized by the former Great Seal since the May of 1642. The COMMISSION OF ARRAY had carried the Great Seal to authenticate it.

Grenville, Sir Bevil (1596–1643)

Sir Bevil Grenville was MP for Cornwall in the LONG PARLIAMENT and one of the committee of 1640 set up to enquire into SHIP MONEY. COMMISSIONER OF ARRAY in 1642, he rapidly became colonel of a regiment in his native county – 'I cannot contain myself when the King of England's standard waves in the field upon so just an occasion', he declared – and was killed at LANSDOWN, where his example led to a ROYALIST victory.

John Stucley, *Sir Bevil Grenville and His Times* (Chichester 1983).

Grenville, Sir Richard (1600–58)

Sir Richard Grenville was the younger brother of SIR BEVIL GRENVILLE and served against the Irish 1641–3, where he acquired a reputation for atrocities. Becoming a ROYALIST in that year – he claimed to be appalled by PARLIAMENT's hypocrisy – and later as Lieutenant General of the HORSE to HOPTON, he employed his 'Irish' policies against PARLIAMENTARIANS. In consequence he was banished in 1649, and died in exile, an isolated and embittered figure.

Amos C. Miller, *Sir Richard Grenville of the Civil War* (London 1979).

Grey of Groby, Thomas Lord (1623–57)

MP for LEICESTER in the LONG PARLIA-

MENT and commander of cavalry to the EARL OF ESSEX. Grey's feud with the Hastings family (see HENRY HASTINGS) rapidly polarized opinion in Leicestershire in 1642. He cooperated actively with PRIDE'S PURGE by identifying those MPs to be excluded from the HOUSE OF COMMONS. He sat on the HIGH COURT OF JUSTICE and signed the death warrant of the king. He fell from favour with CROMWELL and was suspected of LEVELLER beliefs.

Gurdon, Brampton (1608–69)

Colonel of HORSE in the NEW MODEL ARMY and a RECRUITER MP for Sudbury in Suffolk from 1645. He sat on the court martial at COLCHESTER in 1648, which sentenced to execution the ROYALISTS SIR CHARLES LUCAS and SIR GEORGE LISLE.

Gurney, Sir Richard (1577–1647)

Lord Mayor of LONDON in 1642 when CHARLES I sought to arrest the FIVE MEMBERS, but took no steps to raise the TRAINED BANDS in defence of PARLIAMENT. He was gaoled after countenancing the publication of royal proclamations in the city.

H

Haak, Theodore (1605–90)

German linguist and translator of Calvinist (see CALVINISM) theological works, and an associate of SAMUEL HARTLIB. He was emissary for the PARLIAMENT to Holland, where he translated for publication the SOLEMN LEAGUE AND COVENANT. The WESTMINSTER ASSEMBLY authorized him to set the Dutch Bible into English, which he completed in 1657. He was a friend and colleague of JOHN MILTON.

Haberdashers Hall Committee   See Committee for Advance of Money

Hacker, Francis (d. 1660)

PARLIAMENTARIAN commander and brother of a ROYALIST officer. He and Hercules Huncks commanded the guard over CHARLES I at his trial in 1649, and he was responsible for the formalities of the actual execution. He was executed 19 October 1660.

Hague, The

The court in exile of CHARLES II was established here in 1649. In April emissaries from the COMMITTEE OF THE ESTATES in Scotland arrived here for consultations.

Hailstone Tracts

A large collection of civil war TRACTS similar in nature if not in scale to the THOMASON collection, and held in YORK Minster Library. The collection holds most of those tracts published in York by the royal printers in the summer of 1642.

Hall, Joseph   See Norwich, Bishop of

Hambledon Hill

On 4 August 1645 some 2,000 CLUBMEN were attacked on this hill in Dorset by NEW MODEL ARMY forces under CROMWELL, after attempts to disperse them by negotiation failed. The Dorset clubmen were pro-ROYALIST.

Hambleton Boys

A unit of parliamentary troops commanded by RICHARD NORTON, engaged against BASING HOUSE in 1645.

Hamilton, James Duke of (1606–49)

Hamilton served on the PRIVY COUNCIL of CHARLES I in England and in Scotland (his dukedom was in the Scottish peerage), and from at least

1634 was a close personal advisor to the king on Scottish affairs. In 1638 he endeavoured to persuade the king to give way to the COVENANTERS, but succeeded only in alienating the Covenanters, particularly MONTROSE, who regarded Hamilton as a double-dealer. Gaoled in 1644 by order of Charles I, Hamilton was set free in 1646, and in 1647 led the Scottish PARLIAMENT in entering alliance with the king, against the wishes of ARGYLE. Taken prisoner in August 1648, Hamilton was tried and executed by the English Parliament.

Hammond, Robert (1621–54)

Governor of CARISBROOKE CASTLE on the Isle of Wight, where CHARLES I sought refuge in 1647. He was a cousin of CROMWELL and son-in-law of HAMPDEN. His brother was a prominent ROYALIST cleric. A PRESBYTERIAN, unsympathetic to the political manoeuvres of the NEW MODEL ARMY, he was dismissed from Carisbrooke 21 November 1647 and replaced by ISAAC EWER, and was briefly gaoled.

Hammond, Thomas (d. 1652)

General of the artillery in the EASTERN ASSOCIATION army and an associate of CROMWELL in the latter's denunciations of their commander, the EARL OF MANCHESTER. He served on the HIGH COURT OF JUSTICE which tried the king but did not sign the death warrant. A prominent GRANDEE of the NEW MODEL ARMY, and the uncle of ROBERT HAMMOND.

Hampden, John (1594–1643)

Defendant in HAMPDEN'S CASE and MP for Buckinghamshire in the SHORT and LONG PARLIAMENTS. He shared his fierce anti-Catholicism with JOHN PYM, whose close associate he became. SIMOND D'EWES, a fellow MP, called him a man of 'serpentine subtlety'. One of the FIVE MEMBERS whose arrest the king attempted in 1642, Hampden was killed in action at CHALGROVE FIELD in 1643.

J. Adair, *A Life of John Hampden* (London 1976).

Hampden's Case

A law case which arose from the refusal of JOHN HAMPDEN to pay the SHIP MONEY levy in Buckinghamshire. Hampden, as far as the GOVERNMENT was concerned, was an easier target than LORD SAYE AND SELE, who was also a defaulter, and the case went against Hampden.

Hampton Propositions

Negotiations at Hampton Court Palace, Middlesex, from August to September 1647, based on the king's ignoring of the HEADS OF THE PROPOSALS and reversion to the terms of the NEWCASTLE PROPOSITIONS of 1646.

Hare, John

Law reformer and pamphleteer who believed that all the evils of English society arose from the Norman Conquest. He advocated depriving the nobility of their property, was suspicious of PARLIAMENT as a

Norman institution, and held LEVEL-LER sympathies. His works included *St Edward's Ghost or Anti-Normanism* (1647).

Harlech Castle

ROYALIST garrison in North Wales from 1642 until its surrender 15 March 1647, making it the last of the king's garrisons to yield to the PARLIAMENT.

Harley, Lady Brilliana (1600–43)

Wife of the PARLIAMENTARIAN activist Sir Robert Harley, Lady Brilliana defended the castle of BRAMPTON BRYAN in Herefordshire to her death in 1643. Her letters to her husband and others survive.

Harris, John (d. 1660)

LEVELLER writer and commentator whose *The Grand Designe* and *The Royal Quarrell* (1647) championed JOHN LILBURNE. In 1649 he was commissioned to hunt down seditious works and their printers. He claimed to have been on the scaffold when CHARLES I was beheaded. He was hanged in 1660 for larceny.

Harrison, Thomas (1616–60)

Army officer and from 1646 RECRUITER MP for Wendover, Buckinghamshire. At the PUTNEY DEBATES he demanded the trial of the king, and in 1648 was actively seeking to unite the army and the LEVELLERS. He was CHARLES I's guard

on his way to LONDON for his trial, and from 1650 President of the COMMIS-SION FOR THE PROPAGATION OF THE GOSPEL IN WALES. He was a FIFTH MON-ARCHIST, and was executed in 1660.

C.H. Simpkinson, *Thomas Harrison – Regicide and Major General* (London (1905).

Hartlib, Samuel (1600–62)

Hartlib was a German reformer whose life work evolved around a commitment to Protestant unity. Described by a contemporary as 'the Great Intelligencer of Europe', he kept MPs informed of events during the break between the SHORT and LONG PARLIAMENTS. During the 1640s he sought to introduce an OFFICE OF ADDRESSES to disseminate new ideas and new technology nationwide. Disappointed in GOVERNMENT support, he pursued his ideas privately.

C. Webster (ed.), *Samuel Hartlib and the Advancement of Learning* (London 1970).

Harvey, William (1578–1657)

Harvey, a noteworthy physician and discoverer of the circulation of the blood (described in his *Exercitatio Anatomica de Motu Cordis et Sanguinis in Animalibus*) in 1628, was physician to CHARLES I in 1633. He sided with the king, resided at OXFORD from 1642, and produced a revised version of *Exercitatio* in 1649. An edition in English was issued in 1653.

Haselrig(g), Sir Arthur (1601–61)

MP for LEICESTER in the SHORT and

LONG PARLIAMENTS, with a history of clashes with the PRIVY COUNCIL and COURT OF HIGH COMMISSION. He introduced both the bill for the ATTAINDER of STRAFFORD and the MILITIA BILL into the HOUSE OF COMMONS in 1641, and was one of the FIVE MEMBERS. He served under SIR WILLIAM WALLER in 1643, played a critical role at CHERITON in 1644 and was an original member of the COMMITTEE FOR BOTH KINGDOMS. An INDEPENDENT in religion, he moved the NULL AND VOID ORDINANCE and the VOTE OF NO ADDRESSES, and was described by the EARL OF MANCHESTER as 'a bloody fellow'. Although he opposed PRIDE'S PURGE and the king's trial and execution, he became a Councillor of State (see COUNCIL OF STATE).

Hastings, Henry (1610–67)

ROYALIST commander against whom the PARLIAMENTARIAN writers of TRACTS in LONDON developed a particular animus, nicknaming him 'ROB-CARRIER'. He was in arms for the king in Leicestershire in 1642, and became Colonel General, but contributed to the royalist defeat at SELBY in April 1644 by his slowness in obeying orders. His war effort degenerated into a series of feuds with other royalist commanders. He was an inveterate conspirator from 1648 against the GOVERNMENT.

Heads of the Proposals

Propositions drawn up by the NEW MODEL ARMY and submitted to the king as the basis for negotiation 23 July 1647. Some historians regard them as the work largely of CROMWELL and IRETON, but as drafted by Ireton and JOHN LAMBERT. The terms offered, regarded as generous, called for biennial elections for PARLIAMENT, control of the army for 10 years by a COUNCIL OF STATE, and retention of EPISCOPACY alongside guaranteed toleration of dissent. CHARLES I rejected these out of hand, looking towards an alliance with the Scots.

Heligoland, Treaty of

This treaty, dated 11 June 1650, represented the alliance between CHARLES II and the Scots. Charles subscribed to the SCOTTISH NATIONAL COVENANT 23 June.

Hell

Tavern or inn close to Westminster where more than 40 MPs excluded at PRIDE'S PURGE were temporarily imprisoned.

Helmsley Castle

ROYALIST garrison in Yorkshire from 1642 commanded by Jordan Crossland. It was besieged from August 1644 by SIR THOMAS FAIRFAX, who was wounded, almost fatally, by a garrison marksman. JOHN LAMBERT took the castle's surrender 22 November 1644.

Henderson, Alexander (1583–1646)

Prominent Scottish PRESBYTERIAN minister, and instrumental in drafting the SCOTTISH NATIONAL COVENANT. At the outbreak of civil war, as chaplain to CHARLES I, he endeavoured to have the king summon the Scottish PARLIAMENT. He prepared the SOLEMN LEAGUE AND COVENANT and was involved in the *DIRECTORY OF PUBLIC WORSHIP*. He seems to have believed that peace with the king could be reached on a Presbyterian-based church structure, and was pressing for such at UXBRIDGE in 1645.

Henrietta Maria, Queen of England (1609–69)

Daughter of Henry IV of France, she married CHARLES I in 1625. Their relationship developed into a love match, which enabled her to influence royal policy. Although she attracted PURITAN supporters in the 1630s, critics of royal GOVERNMENT associated her with LAUDIAN innovations and ROMAN CATHOLICISM. She raised men, money and arms in Europe in 1642, and returned to England in February 1643. PARLIAMENT impeached (see IMPEACHMENT) her in May. She returned to France in 1644 to try to negotiate foreign help for the king. After Charles I's execution (1649), her influence at the court in exile of CHARLES II was immense, but created factionalism. She has been seen as a strong element in Charles I's determination to pursue the war with Parliament, and her influence with him never waned.

Herbert of Cherbury (Chirbury), Edward Lord (1583–1648)

Philosopher and friend of the great writers John Donne and Ben Jonson, with experience of soldiering in Europe prior to 1617. He was a Deist, and author of the philosophical works *De Veritate* and *De Causis Errorum*, as well as poetry (see CAVALIER POETS) and an autobiography. Unable to win the favour of CHARLES I, Lord Herbert went over to the PARLIAMENT early in the civil war.

J.M. Shuttleworth (ed.), *The Life of Lord Herbert of Cherbury* (Oxford 1971).

Hereford, City of

Changed hands two or three times before the ROYALISTS garrisoned it properly in mid 1643. Besieged by the SCOTTISH ARMY July–August 1645; the siege was then abandoned, and Colonel JOHN BIRCH finally took the city 18 December.

Herle, Charles (1598–1659)

PRESBYTERIAN and tutor of the EARL OF DERBY, he served on the WESTMINSTER ASSEMBLY; he became Prolocutor of the Assembly in 1646 and chaplain to the HOUSE OF COMMONS. He drafted the *DIRECTORY OF PUBLIC WORSHIP* and indulged in a polemical dispute with the royalist HENRY FERNE, in which he claimed that PARLIAMENT by its very nature was less likely to err than a single person in the shape of a king.

Hertford, William Seymour Marquess of (1587–1660)

Long out of favour at court because of a clandestine marriage with a cousin of King James I, he became a member of the PRIVY COUNCIL of

CHARLES I in 1641, when he was made a marquess. Sent from YORK to the west country in 1642 to raise troops for the king, he fought unspectacularly, and was more of a courtier and advisor than a soldier. He was present at the UXBRIDGE talks in 1645. Almost until the summer of 1642, it seems, PARLIAMENT regarded him as a possible friend and supporter.

Hewson, John (d. 1662)

Proclaimed himself the 'child of wrath', champion of INDEPENDENCY and officer of the NEW MODEL ARMY. He was an enemy of the LEVELLERS, and on 28 November 1648 was appointed one of five officers to draft a formal justification of the army's march upon LONDON. He served on the HIGH COURT OF JUSTICE and signed the king's death warrant. He died in exile in Holland.

Heylyn, Peter (1600–62)

Leading churchman largely responsible for the grant of money by CONVOCATION to CHARLES I in 1640, and a vigorous defender of EPISCOPACY. He edited MERCURIUS AULICUS. In later life he produced a study of ARCHBISHIP LAUD (1668), and wrote against the PRESBYTERIANS and PURITANS. His 1656 work, *Observations on the Historie of the Reigne of King Charles*, represents both an attack on Hamon L'Estrange's biography of the king and, more importantly, a definition of high ROYALIST attitudes.

High and petty constables

The office of constable was of considerable antiquity by 1642. The high constable was appointed by the JUSTICES OF THE PEACE for a specific area of a county, effectively to oversee the petty (or parish or township) constables, who were chosen by rote or election. In the civil war, high constables were crucial to the execution of warrants from either side, particularly in collecting ASSESSMENTS and the EXCISE.

High Commission, Court of

An ecclesiastical court established in 1534 to enforce the Acts of Supremacy and Authority which underlay the assertion that the monarch was head of the CHURCH OF ENGLAND. Headed by a Chief Registrar, it was used by the LAUDIAN reformers to coerce their enemies in the 1630s, and its abolition by the LONG PARLIAMENT occurred in 1641 (although it has been suggested that the 1686 Ecclesiastical Commission was a revival).

High Court of Justice

From January 1649 the RUMP PARLIAMENT declared that its decrees and ORDINANCES would henceforth be ACTS OF PARLIAMENT, and the first of these established a High Court of Justice of 135 commissioners to try the king. The HOUSE OF LORDS initially rejected the measure, but the assumption of full legislative power by the HOUSE OF COMMONS 4 January 1649 facilitated the enactment. The court tried CHARLES I for levying war against his people and for high treason. A subcommittee of seven members or commissioners drew up the death sentence. The same court tried the DUKE OF HAMILTON, the EARL OF HOLLAND and LORD CAPEL between 10 February and 6 March 1649 and sentenced them to death also. Another High Court of Justice was established 26 March 1650 for further trials.

Highnam, Battle of (23 March 1643)

ROYALIST forces under Lord Herbert of Raglan (see EARL OF GLAMORGAN) were attacked at Highnam House in Gloucestershire by units under SIR WILLIAM WALLER and EDWARD MASSEY in a running fight that saw a rearguard engagement at Tibberton. Waller pursued the fleeing royalists into Wales but achieved little of consequence and withdrew.

Hill of Crofty

Near DROGHEDA in Ireland, and the meeting place 3 December 1641 of the OLD ENGLISH from the PALE of Dublin and the Ulster Catholic rebels led by RORY O'MORE, which resulted in a united front against the GOVERNMENT in Dublin.

Hilton, Battle of (23 March 1644)

Engagement in Durham between the EARL OF NEWCASTLE and the SCOTTISH ARMY based around Sunderland, induced by Newcastle's attempts to draw the Scots into battle. The Scots avoided a full-scale encounter but sustained heavy losses.

Hobbes, Thomas (1588–1679)

Political philosopher who observed the civil war from exile in Paris. Contemporaries regarded him as an atheist, but Hobbes merely considered religious disputes and divisions as destructive of the SOVEREIGNTY of the state. His book *Leviathan* (1651) portrayed mankind as existing in a state of natural antagonisms. His important TRACT 'Behemoth' (1668) explained the civil wars as a consequence of the expansion of radical, divisive religious beliefs. Some of his other observations lie beneath the historiographical 'Crisis of the Aristocracy' theory. He was a monarchical absolutist.

J.W.N. Watkins, *Hobbes' System of Ideas* (London 1965).

Hobson, Paul (d. 1666)

Officer of the NEW MODEL ARMY and a man of separatist (see SECTARIES AND SEPARATISTS) principles. He was arrested for preaching in 1645, and was involved in the CORKBUSH FIELD mutiny of 1647. In 1650, as commander of a column of Scottish prisoners marching from DUNBAR to Durham, his excessive cruelty led to the deaths of more than 1,500 of them. Certainly considered an ANTINOMIAN, his activism led him into plots against CHARLES II and he died in prison.

Hodgson, (Captain) John (1617–84)

Halifax weaver who left detailed memoirs of his military service under SIR THOMAS FAIRFAX and JOHN LAMBERT. In the course of doing 'the

Lord's work' he fought at SEACROFT MOOR and ADWALTON MOOR in 1643, at PONTEFRACT in 1645, at PRESTON in 1648 and at DUNBAR and WORCESTER.

Holbourne, Sir Robert (d. 1648)

Radical lawyer, defender of JOHN HAMPDEN, opponent of SHIP MONEY and strenuous advocate of the sanctity of private property, Holbourne was MP for Southwark in the SHORT PARLIAMENT and for St Michael Cornhill, LONDON, in the LONG PARLIAMENT. He opposed the ATTAINDER of STRAFFORD and defended EPISCOPACY, positions not inconsistent with his earlier radicalism. He became attorney general to CHARLES, PRINCE OF WALES, on the outbreak of war and was present at the UXBRIDGE negotiations in 1645.

Holdenby House

King CHARLES I was lodged at Holdenby in Northamptonshire in the spring of 1647. On 3 June Cornet GEORGE JOYCE, acting with the connivance of CROMWELL, removed the king and took him to the army rendezvous at NEWMARKET.

Holland, Cornelius (1600–61)

MP for New Windsor, Berkshire, in the LONG PARLIAMENT, he helped to list the MPs to be excluded from the HOUSE OF COMMONS at PRIDE'S PURGE. He had already drawn attention to himself as a leading spokesman of those calling for the trial of the king. Although appointed to the HIGH COURT OF JUSTICE he neither attended nor signed the death warrant.

Holland, Henry Rich Earl of (1590–1649)

Holland's behaviour in the FIRST CIVIL WAR was erratic. His position in the household of the Queen, HENRIETTA MARIA, prior to the war was ambiguous – he was a PURITAN peer with strong associations in anti-court circles (see EARL OF WARWICK). In 1643 his attempt to ingratiate himself with CHARLES I was rebuffed and he thereafter served PARLIAMENT. In 1648 he took up arms against the Parliament, was captured, brought before the HIGH COURT OF JUSTICE and executed in 1649.

Holles, Denzil (1598–1680)

MP for Dorchester in the SHORT and LONG PARLIAMENTS, but with a political career established by 1629. Holles was one of the FIVE MEMBERS the king sought to arrest in 1642. He fought at EDGEHILL but gave up arms after that in pursuit of an accommodation between PARLIAMENT and the king. Mistrusted increasingly by his former allies by 1645, he was one of the leading PRESBYTERIANS against whom the NEW MODEL ARMY proceeded in 1647. He fled to France where he wrote his quite remarkably uninformative memoirs, notable for their hostility towards the INDEPENDENTS. His cousin Gervase Holles, a ROYALIST compiled the *Memorials of the Holles Family 1493–1656*.

Holt Castle

Controlling a bridge across the River Dee into North Wales and garrisoned for the king in 1642. SIR WILLIAM BRERETON captured the bridge, but could not dislodge the garrison, in November 1643.

Honest John

Nickname for JOHN LILBURNE.

Hopkins, Matthew (d. 1647)

Hopkins styled himself the 'Witchfinder-General' (see WITCH-CRAFT), operating in Essex and East Anglia between 1644 and 1647, during which time probably 100 or more women were put to death for sorcery. He was himself hanged for the same offence in 1647.

Hopton Castle

PARLIAMENTARIAN garrison in Shropshire which was besieged by MICHAEL WOODHOUSE in February 1644 and then stormed 13 March. The 31 defenders surrendered and were immediately slaughtered.

Hopton Heath, Battle of (19 March 1643)

PARLIAMENTARIAN forces under BRERETON and GELL, advancing on Stafford, were routed by ROYALISTS under the Earl of Northampton and HENRY HASTINGS, the earl being killed in action.

Hopton, Sir Ralph (1596–1651)

MP for Wells, Somerset, in the SHORT and LONG PARLIAMENTS, and one of those who presented the GRAND REMONSTRANCE to the king in 1641. Gaoled by the HOUSE OF COMMONS for protesting at the MILITIA ORDINANCE, upon his release he went over to the king and commanded for him in the west country, initially under the MARQUESS OF HERTFORD. He was made Lord Hopton in 1643. Victor at BRADDOCK DOWN and STRATTON, he finally surrendered at TORRINGTON in 1646 and went into exile. His memoirs, *Bellum Civile*, are important.

F.T.R. Edgar, *Sir Ralph Hopton* (Oxford 1968).
C. Chadwyck-Healey, Bellum Civile, *Somerset Record Society*, 18, 1902.

Horse

Contemporary term for the cavalry. At the time of the civil war they were ordinarily grouped in regiments of 500 men divided into six troops. Cavalry tactics usually involved either the headlong charge or the charge halted for exchange of pistol fire followed by sword play, the latter a development of the European wars and introduced effectively into England by PRINCE RUPERT. The PARLIAMENTARIAN cavalry field commanders were the regimental colonel and the (sergeant) major; the ROYALISTS had lieutenant colonels as in their FOOT regiments.

Hotham, John (1622–45)

Son and heir of SIR JOHN HOTHAM, whose actions in 1642 John (called 'Captain John') supported. The memoirs of SIR HENRY SLINGSBY show that John Hotham was the most active PARLIAMENTARIAN commander in Yorkshire in the summer and autumn of 1642. His subsequent subordination to the Fairfaxes (see FERDINANDO LORD FAIRFAX) may have determined him to change sides with his father. He was arrested in 1643 and executed in LONDON 1 January 1645.

Hotham, Sir John (d. 1645)

PARLIAMENT's man in the governorship of the port of HULL, which he closed against CHARLES I in 1642 to safeguard the magazine there. SIR HENRY SLINGSBY, who knew Sir John Hotham well, said of him 'he was manly for the defence of the liberty of the subject & privilege of Parliament but was not at all for their new opinions in Church government'. Hotham's half-heartedness turned into disillusion in 1643, but he was arrested before he could defect to the ROYALISTS, and was eventually executed in LONDON, 2 January 1645. See also JOHN HOTHAM.

House of Commons

The lower house of PARLIAMENT, all members of which were elected by franchise. The power to originate taxation here was established by the early 15th century. During the period 1640–2 the committee system (see COMMITTEES OF PARLIAMENT) evolved under the guidance of JOHN PYM and his associates. The parliamentary war effort was directed by MPs – members of the House of Commons – sitting in various committees. See also HIGH COURT OF JUSTICE.

House of Lords

The upper house of PARLIAMENT, attended by right of rank by all peers of the realm and bishops of the CHURCH OF ENGLAND, with effective power of veto over legislation passed to them from the HOUSE OF COMMONS. By mid 1642 the House of Lords was so depleted – bishops had been excluded from sitting 5 February 1642 (see BISHOPS' EXCLUSION ACT) and many peers had abandoned the House – that it was no more than a 'Rump', as the Commons was to be from 1648 (see THE RUMP). On 6 February 1649 the House of Commons voted to lay aside the House of Lords as 'useless and dangerous', and the upper house was abolished 19 March, two days after the abolition of monarchy.

Howell, Thomas See Bristol, Bishop of

Howley Hall

Fortified Tudor mansion in Yorkshire, between Leeds and BRADFORD. On 22 June 1643 the EARL OF NEWCASTLE ordered the storm of the house after the garrison refused to surrender, and issued a warning that all inside would be killed. The life of the governor was saved only by Newcastle's intervention.

Hull

(Properly Kingston upon Hull) A port in Yorkshire which housed a large magazine of weapons and equipment. CHARLES I was refused admission to the port by its governor, SIR JOHN HOTHAM, 23 April 1642. A blockade proved fruitless – the magazine was removed by sea to LONDON – and a siege lasting 3–27 July 1642 was abandoned. On 2 September 1643 the EARL OF NEWCASTLE laid further siege, but gave up 12 October.

B.N. Reckitt, *Charles the First and Hull* (London 1952).

Humble Petition, The

A LEVELLER document presented to the HOUSE OF COMMONS and much in the developing spirit of the times, demanding the abolition of the HOUSE OF LORDS and of monarchy, dated 11 September 1648.

Humble Remonstrance, The

Short title of *The Humble Representation of the General Council of the NEW MODEL ARMY*, which followed upon the suppression of the CORKBUSH FIELD mutiny. The army asserted itself almost as a fourth estate of the realm, and tabled proposals for the maintenance of itself. The HOUSE OF COMMONS ignored the document and

so precipitated the army's occupation of LONDON early in December 1647.

Humble Representation of the Dissatisfaction of the Army

Dated 4 June 1647, this schedule of army grievances focused on the problem of prosecutions of soldiers for acts performed in war time, which the ORDINANCES of INDEMNITY had been intended to prevent.

Hunting of the Foxes, The

A TRACT published 21 March 1649 by LEVELLERS and aimed at CROMWELL and IRETON, GRANDEES who, it claimed, had betrayed the people's cause. Probably written by RICHARD OVERTON, it rehearsed the death of the Leveller RICHARD ARNOLD in 1647.

Huntly, George Gordon Marquess of (d. 1649)

Huntly was one of the few Scottish noblemen to defy and oppose the SCOTTISH NATIONAL COVENANT, for which his lands were harried by MONTROSE in 1638 and he himself arrested. In 1642 Huntly declared for the king, and was involved with Montrose in the war against the COVENANTERS in Scotland. Arrested in 1647, Huntly was executed in 1649.

Hunton, Philip (1604–82)

Author of the important *A TREATISE OF MONARCHY*. A clergyman of the CHURCH OF ENGLAND who accepted the religious changes of the civil war, he became provost of the University of Durham under CROMWELL.

Hurst Castle

King CHARLES I was held at Hurst Castle in Hampshire in November 1648 after his removal from the Isle of Wight (see CARISBROOKE CASTLE) by the NEW MODEL ARMY. The HOUSE OF COMMONS voted his removal illegal.

Hutchinson, Mrs Lucy

Wife of PARLIAMENT's governor of NOTTINGHAM. She set down a snobbish account of his actions both there and as MP and a member of the COUNCIL OF STATE under CROMWELL. Colonel Hutchinson served on the HIGH COURT OF JUSTICE and signed the king's death warrant. He and his wife leaned towards BAPTIST beliefs and seem to have flirted with those of the LEVELLERS, but Mrs Hutchinson had a nice sense of social distinctions.

C.H. Firth (ed.), *Memoirs of the Life of Colonel Hutchinson* (London 1906).

Hyde, Edward (1609–74)

MP for Saltash in the LONG PARLIA-MENT, where he was implicated in the IMPEACHMENT of STRAFFORD but opposed ROOT AND BRANCH and the GRAND REMONSTRANCE. He became the most famous (if not the most influential) of CHARLES I's advisors. This is largely due to his influential history of the wars, which reveal his immense intellect, and which remain fundamental to historical work on the period. The first books of his history were written on Jersey in 1646–8; the remainder were completed after 1660. His ministerial importance and his rank as Earl of Clarendon date from 1661, but from 1641 until 1645 he was constantly at the king's side, and was largely responsible for the calling of the OXFORD PARLIAMENT.

W.D. Macray (ed.), *Clarendon's History of the Rebellion and Civil Wars*, 6 vols (Oxford 1888).

I

Iconoclasm

The defacing and destruction of images, stained glass and other decorative detail in churches, and the pulling down of market and wayside crosses. This was done only by PARLIAMENTARIAN forces during the civil war: CROMWELL first attracted notice by appearing to countenance it. In many cases iconoclasm had less to do with religious fervour than with deliberate affronts to local sensitivities, evidenced by the wrecking of funeral monuments.

Idle Dick

Nickname for RICHARD NORTON.

Impeachment

The arraignment before PARLIAMENT of persons charged with serious offences against the state. Moves for impeachment began in the HOUSE OF COMMONS; trial took place in the HOUSE OF LORDS. Both STRAFFORD and LAUD were impeached.

C.G.C. Tite, *Impeachment and Parliamentary Judicature in Early Stuart England* (London 1974).

Impressment

The forcible drafting of men into the armies of king or PARLIAMENT to make losses good or to arrive at prescribed strengths. Theoretically, the king would grant permission to specific commanders to 'impress', but as often as not it was done arbitrarily. It was stated that 'Single men, mechanics rather than husbandmen [i.e. farmers]' were preferred. Parish officers (see HIGH AND PETTY CONSTABLES) did most of the selection (see also MASTERLESS MEN). On 22 February 1645 SIR THOMAS FAIRFAX was empowered by ORDINANCE of Parliament to impress men in rebel areas over a nine-month period, and on 11 June the powers were extended to cover any area through which Fairfax might march.

Inchiquin, Murrough O'Brien Earl of (1614–74)

Nicknamed Murchdah na Atoithean – Murrough of the Burnings – for his brutality at CASHEL 12 September 1647. He afterwards went over to the king, having served PARLIAMENT since 1644, and conquered Ulster, defeating GEORGE MONCK and capturing DROGHEDA. He was defeated 1 November 1649 at Arklow in an engagement with the NEW MODEL ARMY.

Incident

A mysterious plot of 1641, contrived whilst king CHARLES I was in EDINBURGH, to assassinate the EARLS OF HAMILTON and ARGYLE.

Inclosures   See Enclosures

Indemnity

A major issue in the grievances of the NEW MODEL ARMY. On 21 May 1647 an ORDINANCE of Indemnity passed through PARLIAMENT to safeguard its soldiers against criminal prosecution for acts committed in time of war. This was reinforced 7 June. A central committee of 52 MPs and 26 peers was charged with reversing verdicts already obtained. The TRACT *Vox Militaris* (August 1647) denounced the measures as inadequate. (See also *HUMBLE REPRESENTATION OF THE DIS-SATISFACTION OF THE ARMY*). The 1660 Act of Oblivion and Indemnity pardoned all those involved in the civil wars except the 50 REGICIDES, of whom 13 were executed. See also COMMITTEE FOR INDEMNITY.

Indemnity, Committee for

The Committee for Indemnity of 1649–56 was established to protect from prosecution in the courts all those who, in service of the PARLIA-MENT, had seized goods and property, taken FREE QUARTER or caused damage. Proceedings could be suspended or merely set aside. It also protected the purchasers of estates taken by SEQUESTRATION. See also INDEMNITY.

Independents

A broad term embracing many sects (see SECTARIES AND SEPARATISTS) including BAPTISTS, the common denominator of them all being their rejection of state-regulated worship (see, especially, PRESBYTERIANISM) in favour of autonomous congregations or gatherings of believers. CROMWELL is considered a leading Independent although he was suspicious of sepa-ratist tendencies. The Independents' political leanings were towards con-frontation with the king and the need for outright victory as the civil war progressed. The LEVELLERS regarded Independents as men without prin-ciple, 'the broken reeds of Egypt'.

G. Yule, *The Independents in the English Civil War* (London 1958).

Ingoldsby, Sir Richard (1617–85)

Colonel in the NEW MODEL ARMY whose regiment in September 1649 was markedly LEVELLER in sympa-thies and mutinied, taking Ingoldsby prisoner. He later put down the mutiny. He sat on the HIGH COURT OF JUSTICE to try the king, but claimed CROMWELL physically forced him to sign the death warrant. He also served on the COUNCIL OF STATE, but made early contacts with CHARLES II and escaped punishment.

Interregnum

That period between the execution of King CHARLES I, 30 January 1649, and the Restoration of King CHARLES II, 8 May 1660.

Inverkeithing, Battle of (20 July 1651)

Fought between Scottish troops under DAVID LESLIE and NEW MODEL ARMY units under JOHN LAMBERT and JOHN OKEY, in an attempt by Leslie to forestall an advance on his base at

Stirling. The Scots were routed and 2,000 killed.

Inverlochy, Battle of (1–2 February 1645)

The COVENANTER army of ARGYLE was surprised and attacked by MONTROSE. Argyle fled, his army was destroyed, and Inverlochy Castle fell to the ROYALISTS.

Ireton, Henry (1611–51)

Second in command of the HORSE of the NEW MODEL ARMY under CROMWELL, whose son-in-law he was. RECRUITER MP for Appleby, Westmoreland, from 1645, he drafted THE ENGAGEMENT of 1647 and the HEADS OF THE PROPOSALS. He opposed the LEVELLERS at the PUTNEY DEBATES, declaring 'No person hath a right to an interest or share in the disposing of the affairs of the kingdom ... that hath not a permanent fixed interest'. He was a staunch defender of private property, which he regarded as fundamental to true liberty. 'That chief of Machiavellians', as JOHN LILBURNE described him, Ireton was effectively directing the political moves of the New Model Army from 1648. He died on active service in Ireland; his body was exhumed in 1660 and displayed.

Irish Affairs, Committee of   See
Committee for Both Kingdoms

Irish Brigade

A military force that existed only on paper in the plans of the ROYALIST northern forces of the EARL OF NEWCASTLE. SIR MARMADUKE LANGDALE was to be effective commander of this accession of strength, to be composed of cavalry units brought over from the army in Ireland.

Irish Catholic Confederacy

Formed at KILKENNY late in 1642 as an alternative GOVERNMENT of Ireland, under the slogan 'Pro Deo, rege et patria Hiberni unanimes' – 'Irishmen united for God, King and Country'. Its first General Assembly met 24 October 1642. The third General Assembly (November–December 1643) sent seven delegates to OXFORD to discuss peace with the king. The Confederacy was dissolved in September 1648 by ORMONDE.

Irish Cessation

On 23 April 1643 CHARLES I ordered his deputy in Ireland, ORMONDE, to negotiate a cessation of hostilities with the IRISH CATHOLIC CONFEDERACY to free troops for service in England. On 15 September 1643 a one-year truce was signed, preceding peace talks scheduled for the winter. The papal envoy Scarampi, advising the Irish rebels, denounced it, even though it left them in control of all Ireland except Cork, Belfast and Dublin and the coastal communications between them. A second cessation was agreed 25 August 1645 (see GLAMORGAN'S TREATIES). On 28 March 1646 the Supreme Council of the Irish Confederacy formulated with Ormonde a peace treaty that was also denounced by the Irish clergy, who laid an interdict (exclusion from some of the sacraments) upon its supporters.

Irish Guard

Eight warships and 13 armed merchantmen established in 1643 by PARLIAMENT to cruise the Irish Sea against Spanish and Irish privateers operating out of Wexford and ports in Brittany, and to preserve the Welsh port of Milford Haven.

Irish Rebellion

Broke out in Ulster 23 October 1641, and officially declared to be at an end by PARLIAMENT 27 September 1653. A war of national liberation launched by native Gaelic ROMAN CATHOLICS, but soon attracting the active support of the OLD ENGLISH of the same religious persuasion. King CHARLES I appointed ORMONDE as his commander against the rebels; Dublin was occupied by Parliamentary forces under Lord Lisle; a Scottish COVENANTER army was operating in Ulster under ROBERT MONRO. There was little cooperation between them. As the rebellion in Ireland and the civil war in England progressed, Ormonde allied with the Irish rebels (1646) against the PARLIAMENTARIANS,

and in 1648 Monro joined them in support of the Scottish–royalist alliance. The rebellion was finally brought to an end by the NEW MODEL ARMY between 1649 and 1653.

Irish troops

Between September 1643 and March 1644 some 12,000 troops from ORMONDE's army, which had been fighting against the Irish rebels (see IRISH REBELLION), came into England to serve the king. Contemporary propaganda and later historiography have confused the matter of fact, and conveyed the impression the troops were native Irish, when in fact they were of English extraction. On 24 October 1644, PARLIAMENT, anticipating the arrival of native Irish, passed an ORDINANCE denying quarter to any such taken in arms in England. The king's efforts to import native Irish soldiery (see GLAMORGAN'S TREATIES) came to nothing, although some fought in Scotland under MONTROSE and were handled barbarously by the COVENANTERS.

Ironsides

Nickname of CROMWELL, applied also to his cavalry forces and specifically to his own regiment.

J

Jenkyns, David (1582–1663)

A presiding judge in Carmarthenshire, Pembrokeshire and Cardiganshire in 1643, and a convinced ROYALIST. He aroused parliamentary condemnation by his ruthless indictments of PARLIAMENTARIAN supporters, and was gaoled from 1645 until 1660. He denied the authority of PARLIAMENT to try him, and issued TRACTS and treatises during his imprisonment.

Jermyn, Henry (1604–84)

Jermyn was said to be 'the Queen's great favourite, a man looked upon by the whole Court' by the time civil war broke out. Jermyn was with QUEEN HENRIETTA MARIA in Europe in 1642, and in 1643 commanded her Lifeguard of HORSE. The PARLIAMENTARIANS termed him 'Butcherly Jermyn'. Raised to the peerage in 1644, he went to France with the queen in that year and remained influential in exile politics thereafter, as a great advocate of an alliance between ROYALISTS and PRESBYTERIANS.

Jesuit

Nickname applied by SIR ARTHUR ASTON to his comrade in arms Colonel Sir Henry Gage, a ROMAN CATHOLIC (as Aston was). Gage was 'a compleat Soulgier and a wise man', according to SIR HENRY SLINGSBY. He

was mortally wounded in 1645. 'Scarce any Prince had a worthier servant', noted SIR EDWARD WALKER.

Jones, Inigo (1573–1652)

Considered to have been the greatest architect and designer of the Jacobean age, Jones, a ROMAN CATHOLIC, designed the banqueting house at WHITEHALL, where CHARLES I was later executed. A ROYALIST, Jones was in the garrison of BASING HOUSE at its surrender in 1645, and was permitted to compound (see COMPOSITION) for his property.

Jones, Michael (d. 1649)

Described by OLIVER CROMWELL as his 'noble friend', Jones was a PARLIAMENTARIAN commander in Ireland from 7 June 1647. By the time Cromwell reached Ireland in 1649 Jones had already turned the tide of the war there, with the victory at RATHMINES over the ROYALIST forces of ORMONDE. Jones died on active service 10 December 1649.

Joyce, George (Also known as Cornet Joyce)

A cornet (colour-bearer) in the NEW MODEL ARMY and an AGITATOR, he was sent by CROMWELL with 50 men to HOLDENBY HOUSE to take into his charge the person of the king, 3 June

1647. In 1648 he was a vocal advocate of bringing the king to trial, and acclaimed the HIGH COURT OF JUSTICE as the 'greatest work of righteousness'. A breach between Joyce and Cromwell developed afterwards.

Jubbes, John (d. 1658)

Lieutenant colonel in the NEW MODEL ARMY regiment of JOHN HEWSON. He was involved in the TRACT of 9 November 1647, *The Humble Remonstrance and Desires of Divers Officers and Soldiers in the Army under Colonel Hewson*, which denounced disbandment and service in Ireland. At the PUTNEY DEBATES Jubbes argued for the reinstatement of the king, with the proviso that the king accept responsibility for the civil war. He left the army in 1648, suspicious of its intentions, and devoted himself to legal and agricultural reforms. A bitter enemy of the LEVELLERS, he advocated the restoration of CHARLES II, and went into self-imposed exile in Jamaica.

Justices of the Peace

The immediate face of central GOVERNMENT in the counties of England and Wales; prominent local gentlemen who met four times a year (see QUARTER SESSIONS) to deal with matters as diverse as murder and riot, laws against ROMAN CATHOLICS, and the local implementation of government policies. GRAND JURIES could present matters to them for their judgement. In the summer of 1642 CHARLES I remodelled the Commissions for the Peace, as the boards of JPs were called, purging them of many JPs hostile to him, as PARLIAMENT had been quietly purging them of its opponents since 1640. During the peace negotiations of 1643 the restoration of those purged by Charles was on the agenda.

Juxon, William   See London, Bishop of

K

Kemys, Nicholas (d. 1648)

ROYALIST governor of CHEPSTOW CASTLE in the SECOND CIVIL WAR, having slipped away from Bath to South Wales. On the grounds that he had broken his parole, given after his active royalism in the FIRST CIVIL WAR, Kemys was shot to death when Chepstow fell.

Kentford Heath

A general rendezvous of the NEW MODEL ARMY was held on Kentford Heath in Suffolk 4–5 June 1647, before the army advanced on LONDON. A PETITION against the PRESBYTERIANS in PARLIAMENT was drawn up and the army undertook not to disband (see *ENGAGEMENT*) until its grievances, mostly to do with arrears of pay, were met. CROMWELL was present at the deliberations, which marked the politicizing of the New Model Army – a major political development in post-civil war England.

Kentish Petition

A PETITION drawn up at the ASSIZES at MAIDSTONE in March 1642, almost wholly due to the energy of SIR EDWARD DERING, urging PARLIAMENT to reach a compromise with the king. The leaders of the petition movement were arrested and the petition burnt by the common hangman.

Kilkenny

Centre and base in Ireland of the IRISH CATHOLIC CONFEDERACY and, in 1648–9, headquarters of the army of the ROYALIST leader, ORMONDE. CROMWELL took the town 27 March 1650.

Kilmeadan Castle

A castle in County Waterford, Ireland. It was captured 2 December 1649 by CROMWELL as he marched from Waterford to Kilmacthomas. The castle's governor was hanged.

Kilsyth, Battle of (15 August 1645)

Defeat of a COVENANTER army, with the loss of more than 6,000 men, by MONTROSE. News of this battle forced the SCOTTISH ARMY to abandon the siege of HEREFORD and to move back north towards the Scottish border.

In 1650 Kilsyth Castle resisted CROMWELL.

King and Parliament

A fiction of importance to the PARLIAMENT in the early years of civil war, namely that its soldiers were fighting for king and Parliament, and CHARLES I was beguiled and misled by traitors and CAVALIERS. See also SOVEREIGNTY.

King, James (1589–1652)

Scottish professional soldier who, at the entreaty of HENRIETTA MARIA, left service in Europe to become commander of the FOOT in the army of the EARL OF NEWCASTLE. He was raised to the peerage as Lord Eythin in 1643. His strategic equivocation in 1644 materially contributed to the ROYALIST disaster on MARSTON MOOR, whereupon he returned to Europe.

P.R. Newman, *The Battle of Marston Moor* (Chichester 1981).

King's Bench, Court of

Part of the machinery of central GOVERNMENT, headed by a Lord Chief Justice who might also sit on the PRIVY COUNCIL, and with seniority over the COURT OF COMMON PLEAS. Under the COMMONWEALTH it was known as the Upper Bench.

King's Lynn

Originally just 'Lynn', this was a PARLIAMENTARIAN garrison port in Norfolk, visited by CROMWELL in March 1643 to investigate rumours of a ROYALIST plot to seize it. On 13 August the governor, Sir Hamon L'Estrange, declared for the king. The EARL OF MANCHESTER recovered the port 16 September.

Kingston, Robert Pierrepoint Earl of (1584–1643)

A powerful Lincolnshire nobleman who, for several months after the outbreak of war, hesitated before declaring himself for the king. He was captured in March 1643 and killed by ROYALISTS during their attempt to release him.

Kingston upon Thames

In July 1648 the EARL OF HOLLAND with a ROYALIST army mustered at Kingston before advancing deeper into Surrey. He fell back on the town where he was defeated by NEW MODEL ARMY cavalry, 7 July.

Knockanoss, Battle of (13 November 1647)

Defeat of a rebel Irish army (see IRISH REBELLION) under Lord Taafe by parliamentary forces commanded by LORD INCHIQUIN, in which ALASTER MACDONALD was killed.

L

Laggan Army

Formed in September 1647 by the PARLIAMENT, and sent into Ireland under MONCK. It was a fusion of parliamentary troops under CHARLES COOTE and Scots under ROBERT MONRO, neither of whom acknowledged Monck's authority.

Lambert, John (1619–84)

Officer in his native Yorkshire under FERDINANDO LORD FAIRFAX. He became a commander in the NEW MODEL ARMY and in 1647 was connected with the AGITATORS and with the HEADS OF THE PROPOSALS. He denounced the TREATY OF NEWPORT but kept away from the trial and execution of the king. He fought at DUNBAR and shared authority in Scotland 1650–2. A contemporary described him as 'An unfathomed man ... the more to be feared'. His period of greatest influence was during the Protectorate of CROMWELL, and he was gaoled for life at the restoration of CHARLES II.

W.H. Dawson, *Cromwell's Understudy* (London 1938).

Lambe, Thomas (d. 1673)

BAPTIST preacher with LEVELLER associations, active in Wiltshire 1642–6. He was responsible for distribution of material critical of the EARLS OF ESSEX and MANCHESTER. His TRACT *The Fountains of Free Grace Opened* (1648) criticized doctrinaire CALVINISM, and paved the way for disagreements with fellow Baptists on the issue of laying on of hands in baptism.

Langdale, Sir Marmaduke (1598–1661)

A Yorkshireman with extensive military experience in Europe, who in 1642 engineered the replacement of the EARL OF CUMBERLAND with the EARL OF NEWCASTLE as commander for the king in Yorkshire. A subordinate commander under GORING to 1644, after MARSTON MOOR he commanded the NORTHERN HORSE. In arms in 1648, he fled into exile. Langdale was one of the king's finest cavalry commanders (see PONTEFRACT) and a man who commanded ungrudging respect from either side, despite his advocacy of Irish alliance and Spanish help after 1649. He was described by a contemporary as 'A faithful and indefatigable commander'.

F.H. Sunderland, *Marmaduke Lord Langdale of Holme on Spalding Moor* (London 1926).

Langport, Battle of (10 July 1645)

GORING, laying siege to TAUNTON, Somerset, was forced to abandon it by the approach of the NEW MODEL

ARMY under SIR THOMAS FAIRFAX and to make a tactical withdrawal towards BRIDGWATER, but was worsted in a sudden attack.

Lansdown, Battle of (5 July 1643)

A successful attack by Lord Hopton (see SIR RALPH HOPTON) on SIR WILLIAM WALLER's parliamentary troops near Bath, Somerset, was marred by the death in action of SIR BEVIL GRENVILLE and Hopton's own injuries from an explosion. The ROYALISTS fell back upon DEVIZES, where Waller blockaded them.

Large Petition

The single most comprehensive statement of LEVELLER politics, appearing in March 1647. On 20 May the HOUSE OF COMMONS voted that it be burnt. The PETITION ignored the role of the NEW MODEL ARMY entirely and seems to have been the work of civilians based in LONDON.

Larner, William (d. 1659)

LONDON bookseller and publisher and associate of JOHN LILBURNE, whose LEVELLER views Larner shared. Arrested in May 1646, he was one of those whose release was demanded in the Leveller-inspired *A Remonstrance of Many Thousand Citizens*. The NEW MODEL ARMY's AGITATORS pressed for his release. Larner's periods of imprisonment earned him the role of martyr for the Leveller movement: the 'To the Commons'

PETITION of 19 January 1649 presented him as such.

Lathom House

A house in Lancashire, the principal residence of the EARL OF DERBY. It was garrisoned for the king in 1642 and held against SIR THOMAS FAIRFAX by the earl's wife, CHARLOTTE COUNTESS OF DERBY, in January 1644. The fruitless siege was abandoned 27 May on the advance of PRINCE RUPERT, who relieved the countess of her authority. It finally surrendered 2 December 1645 and was razed to the ground.

Laudians and Laudianism

The Laudians were those, usually clergy, associated with the religious policies of ARCHBISHOP LAUD during the 1630s. The fundamental tenets of Laudianism were uniformity in worship and discipline, using the PRAYER BOOK as the basis; a promotion of ceremonial and ritual, such as genuflection at the name of Christ; and the restoration of the altar to the east end of the church. Laudianism was effectively crushed by the LONG PARLIAMENT in 1641, but its doctrine and rituals re-emerged in 1660.

Laud, William (1573–1645)

Stigmatized by his political and religious enemies as the 'root and ground of all our miseries', Archbishop Laud, as privy councillor (see PRIVY COUNCIL), bishop of LONDON and, from 1633, archbishop of CANTERBURY, was closely associated with royal GOVERNMENT. His pressure for uniformity in the CHURCH OF ENGLAND created widespread animosity, even among future supporters of the king in the civil war. Much of the opprobrium in which he was held passed by association to the king and his advisors. Laud was impeached (see IMPEACHMENT) by the LONG PARLIAMENT in 1641, tried in 1644, and executed in 1645. See also LAUDIANISM.

Laugharne, Rowland (d. 1676)

A PARLIAMENTARIAN commander, and a successful one, in South Wales in the FIRST CIVIL WAR. In 1648 he declared for the king, but was defeated at ST FAGANS, was captured, and escaped execution on the throw of dice. It was JOHN POYER who lost that throw.

Launceston, Battle of (23 April 1643)

PARLIAMENTARIAN forces attacked SIR RALPH HOPTON at Launceston, Cornwall, but were driven off with heavy losses. Launceston Castle was not considered tenable by either side.

Law of Nature

A system of imperatives over and above mere human laws. The Law of Nature was ordinarily associated with a concept of natural rights that limited the power of monarchy, and regulated the relationships between people in a way quite distinct from the rules of any society to which people might belong. Those advocating the trial and punishment of

CHARLES I referred to this 'natural law'.

Leatherhead Mutiny

In February 1645 cavalry units of the army of the EARL OF ESSEX stationed at Leatherhead, Surrey, mutinied against being passed to the command of SIR WILLIAM WALLER, under whom they refused to serve, not even for 'all the money in England'. A similar mutiny occurred at Henley-on-Thames.

Lecturers

Usually PURITANS introduced into a parish by groups of the laity, financed from a fund of supporters' money, to give sermons on set days of the week. Lecturers might be imposed upon a non-Puritan clergyman by his Puritan flock.

P. Seaver, *The Puritan Lectureships, The Politics of Religious Dissent 1560–1662* (London 1970).

Ledbury, Battle of (22 April 1645)

Scene in Worcestershire of the defeat of EDWARD MASSEY by ROYALISTS under PRINCE RUPERT in street fighting.

Leicester

PARLIAMENTARIAN headquarters for Leicestershire from 1642. On 29 May 1645 the king's army laid siege, and the town was stormed with considerable bloodshed on 31 May. After the BATTLE OF NASEBY the town surrendered to SIR THOMAS FAIRFAX, 18 June 1645.

Leinster Army

Last field army of the IRISH CATHOLIC CONFEDERACY, commanded by the EARL OF CLANRICARDE, which surrendered to EDMUND LUDLOW May 1652.

Lenthall, William (1591–1662)

Speaker of the HOUSE OF COMMONS and MP for Woodstock in the SHORT and LONG PARLIAMENTS. When CHARLES I sought to arrest the FIVE MEMBERS in 1642, Lenthall described the role of Speaker as one entirely at the disposal of the Commons itself. An INDEPENDENT, much criticized by JOHN LILBURNE, Lenthall used his casting vote in 1647 against negotiations with the king. He desired a limited monarchy, not a REPUBLIC, and even urged the crown for CROMWELL in 1650.

Leslie, David (d. 1682)

Leslie commanded the cavalry in the SCOTTISH ARMY which invaded England in 1644, and fought at MARSTON MOOR in a subordinate role to CROMWELL. Returning to Scotland he routed MONTROSE at PHILIPHAUGH in 1645. He commanded the Scottish ROYALIST forces that backed CHARLES II in 1650 and, after out-manoeuvring Cromwell near EDINBURGH, was taken by surprise and beaten at

DUNBAR. He was gaoled in LONDON from 1651 to 1660.

Levellers

A radical political group, largely LONDON based, associated with the ideas of JOHN LILBURNE but not clearly led by him. The name 'Levellers' began to circulate in late 1647, the year of their main impact on national events. They were virtually spent by 1649, and were seeking rapprochement with the ROYALISTS. Their programme included an extended franchise, RELIGIOUS TOLERATION, and the abolition of the HOUSE OF LORDS. Considerable support came from the NEW MODEL ARMY, which gave the Levellers an illusion of potential achievement (see AGITATORS). The *AGREEMENT OF THE PEOPLE* is considered their manifesto, the LARGE PETITION the first published expression of their ideals.

H.N. Brailsford, *The Levellers and the English Revolution* (London 1961).

Leven, Alexander Leslie Earl of (1580–1661)

Leven was the cautious and competent commander of the SCOTTISH ARMY which invaded England in 1644. He commanded the allied army of the Scots and PARLIAMENTARIANS at MARSTON MOOR, and materially contributed to PARLIAMENT's eventual success in 1646, although distracted by MONTROSE in Scotland. Leven was captured fighting for CHARLES II in 1650 and gaoled in LONDON.

Leycester, John

Leycester was the poetic eulogist of JOHN HAMPDEN, and wrote (in 1646) *England's Miraculous Preservation* to celebrate PARLIAMENT's success.

Lichfield

A ROYALIST garrison was based around St Chad's cathedral in Lichfield, Staffordshire, in early 1643. In February LORD BROOKE laid siege, and was himself shot dead by marksmen on St Chad's day, which occasioned much ominous comment. On 20 April 1643 PRINCE RUPERT took back the town from the PARLIA-MENTARIANS, but it fell to them again 6 March 1646.

Lilburne, John (1615–57)

Nicknamed 'Honest John' and 'Free-born John', Lilburne was a major political writer and pamphleteer of the 1640s, whose ideas found expression in the demands of the LEVEL-LERS, although he did not lead them. A fighting soldier in PARLIAMENT's cause, serving under LORD BROOKE, the EARL OF ESSEX and the EARL OF MANCHESTER, his evolving political ideas found friends in the NEW MODEL ARMY. His fundamental doctrine was that of GOVERNMENT by consent of the governed, with extended franchise. An advocate of RELIGIOUS TOLERATION – his own beliefs were a curious mixture of ANTINOMIANISM and ARMINIANISM with CALVINISM – he turned his invective readily against Parliament. His TRACT (one of almost a hundred attributed to him), *Jonah's Cry from the Whale's Belly* (1647), denounced the 'unrighteous Parliament' and represented the notion of Natural Law (see LAW OF NATURE). It has been said that his attempt to unite Levellers and INDEPENDENTS proved destructive of the Levellers, and little that he sought was achieved.

Lilburne, Robert (1613–65)

Elder brother of JOHN LILBURNE and a serving colonel in the NEW MODEL ARMY. He was a BAPTIST, hostile to PRESBYTERIANISM and a close political associate of JOHN LAMBERT. It was his regiment that mutinied at CORKBUSH FIELD in November 1647, espousing the cause of the *AGREEMENT OF THE PEOPLE*. He sat on the HIGH COURT OF JUSTICE to try the king and signed the death warrant. He was gaoled in 1660.

Lilly, William (1602–81)

Astrologer and publisher of almanacks, as well as of prophetic and visionary works. His *The Starry Messenger*, which predicted a major victory for the PARLIAMENT, appeared on the day that the BATTLE OF NASEBY was fought. He was a supporter of the NEW MODEL ARMY. In his memoirs of his life and times, Lilly recorded one of the few first-hand accounts of the last stand of the royalist WHITECOATS at MARSTON MOOR.

K.M. Briggs (ed.), *Mr. William Lilly's History of His Life and Times* (London 1974).

Limerick

A major ROYALIST garrison in Ireland, which CROMWELL avoided in his campaigns but which was besieged 14 June 1651 by IRETON, and which fell to him 27 October. The civilian population was expelled to make way for colonists. Ireton died in Limerick 26 November, of the plague.

Lindsey, Robert Bertie Earl of (1582–1642)

Lieutenant General of the ROYALIST army on the eve of EDGEHILL in 1642, and denounced by PARLIAMENT as 'a disturber of the peace of the kingdom'. After an argument with PRINCE RUPERT he stepped down from command, and was killed in the battle as a volunteer.

Lines of communication

Some 18 miles (29 km) of earthen defences, with redoubts and scarping works, built around LONDON from February 1643. More than 20 forts were completed by May of that year. The lines were manned against the NEW MODEL ARMY in June 1647, but SIR THOMAS FAIRFAX took one of the forts by surrender, whereupon the rest capitulated. Demolition began in September 1647.

Lisle, John (1610–64)

MP for WINCHESTER in the SHORT and LONG PARLIAMENTS and a prime mover in the creation of the COMMITTEE FOR BOTH KINGDOMS. A supporter of the NEW MODEL ARMY, he advocated the king's trial and helped draft the death sentence. He was a member of the COUNCIL OF STATE. He was assassinated in Lausanne,

Switzerland, by an Irish ROYALIST in 1664.

Lisle, Sir George (d. 1648)

Commanded troops for the king from 1642 to 1646 and ended the war as Lieutenant General under HENRY HASTINGS. In arms in COLCHESTER in 1648, he was court martialled and shot to death on the orders of SIR THOMAS FAIRFAX, alongside SIR CHARLES LUCAS.

Lister, Joseph

Author of *An account of the Sore Calamities that befel Bradford (Yorkshire) in the time of the Civil War*. He was an eyewitness of the fighting of 1643.

Little Dean, Battle of (11 April 1643)

Following upon the battle at HIGHNAM, SIR WILLIAM WALLER advanced into Wales and PRINCE MAURICE moved to block his retreat. Waller's army was drawn into a full-scale engagement at Little Dean, Gloucestershire, and was defeated.

Littleton, Edward Lord (1589–1645)

Ennobled in 1641, he was Keeper of the GREAT SEAL when civil war broke out in 1642, and conveyed it to YORK. He was member of the PRIVY COUNCIL, commanded a regiment in

OXFORD from March 1645, and died in August 1645.

and was a chaplain to the NEW MODEL ARMY in 1651.

Liverpool

Crucial port town in Lancashire, facing Ireland. It was stormed and taken by PRINCE RUPERT 12 June 1644 after several days' bombardment, and was then a ROYALIST garrison until its surrender in November.

Lobsters

Nickname for the HORSE regiment of SIR ARTHUR HASELRIG, an allusion to their three-quarter armour (see CUIRASSIERS). This 'impenetrable' regiment was broken in action at ROUNDWAY DOWN.

Livesey, Sir Michael (1611–63)

A Kentish PARLIAMENTARIAN proclaimed a traitor by the king in 1642. Livesey fought without distinction at CROPREDY BRIDGE, and general complaints against him led him to withdraw his troops from SIR WILLIAM WALLER's army and to refuse to serve under SIR THOMAS FAIRFAX. He was RECRUITER MP for Queenborough, Kent, from 1645. He served on the HIGH COURT OF JUSTICE and signed the death warrant. Attainted (see ATTAINDER) in 1660, he fled to Holland.

Localism

A historiographical term describing an attitude of the civil war years best displayed by the CLUBMEN. Localism regarded the war as intrusive and the product of 'outsiders', but it need not be identified with the view of 'NEUTERS', for localism might also mean an attachment to local defence and local leadership within the framework of ROYALIST or PARLIAMENTARIAN war efforts. If so, it must be seen as a weakening factor, as when LUDLOW's Wiltshire forces refused to march into Hampshire.

Llwyd, Morgan (1619–59)

An INDEPENDENT minister whose verse

> The law was ever above Kings
> And Christ above the law
> Unhappy Charles provoked the Lamb
> To dust he must withdraw,

encapsulates the attitude of religious Independents towards CHARLES I. He worked for the COMMITTEE FOR THE PROPAGATION OF THE GOSPEL IN WALES

Local pacts

A historiographical term to cover all attempts, notably in the autumn of 1642, by gentlemen in various counties to reach an agreement not to fight. A good example is that for Yorkshire negotiated at Rothwell, near Leeds, 29 September 1642, by which both the MILITIA ORDINANCE and the COMMISSION OF ARRAY were rejected, there was to be no persecution of DELINQUENTS and the arms of the TRAINED BANDS were to go into store. Such pacts failed because they lacked sufficient support to make them work.

Lockyer, Robert (1626–49)

AGITATOR in the NEW MODEL ARMY regiment of Colonel Whalley. He was deeply involved in the CORKBUSH FIELD mutiny. In 1649 Lockyer led his comrades in resisting an order to suppress LEVELLERS in Essex, and was tried by court martial and shot 27 April. His funeral was the last major display of Leveller strength, the hundreds of mourners favouring the green ribbon badge of the movement.

London

The city of London was both the capital city of England and the pre-eminent centre for financial dealing and trade. It was also (see WESTMINSTER) adjacent to the seat of central GOVERNMENT. It remained a PARLIAMENTARIAN stronghold throughout the civil wars, although the volatile 'mob', which had pressured the LONG PARLIAMENT for reforms 1640–2, was not necessarily partisan. The Lord Mayor in 1642, SIR RICHARD GURNEY, actively championed the king. Seizure of London was crucial to ROYALIST war objectives, but it was only really threatened in November 1642, when its TRAINED BANDS stood firm. It remained the centre of political developments because of its association with government.

London, William Juxon Bishop of (1582–1663)

Lord Treasurer to CHARLES I 1638–41,

he advised the king to veto the execution of STRAFFORD. Bishop Juxon (appointed archbishop of CANTERBURY in 1660) attended the king in 1648 and was with him on the scaffold 30 January 1649.

Longford, Battle of (25 March 1644)

A relief column of PARLIAMENTARIAN troops en route to Lilleshall Abbey was destroyed in Shropshire by ROYALIST forces, who subsequently took Longford House 2 April 1644.

Long Parliament

First met 3 November 1640 and sat, without dissolution, until 16 March 1660. It rapidly succeeded the SHORT PARLIAMENT, and was petitioned for in August 1640 by 12 members of the HOUSE OF LORDS acting in concert with JOHN PYM. It impeached (see IMPEACHMENT) STRAFFORD, passed the TRIENNIAL ACT (see also ACTS OF PARLIAMENT), abolished SHIP MONEY and moved towards reform of the government of the church. It narrowly passed the GRAND REMONSTRANCE presented to the king in 1641, excluded bishops from the House of Lords (see BISHOPS' EXCLUSION BILL) and presented the NINETEEN PROPOSITIONS to the king. Diminished in numbers by royalist defections 1642–3, its numbers were swelled from 1645 onwards by the RECRUITER MPs. The NEW MODEL ARMY, with the connivance of some INDEPENDENT members, carried through PRIDE'S PURGE in 1648, and thereafter the Parliament was known derisively as the RUMP, which was expelled by CROMWELL in 1653. It next met in 1659.

Lords Commissioners

A committee set up by CHARLES I to supervise OXFORD and its use as a military base, and to make recommendations to the COUNCIL OF WAR.

Also, those entrusted by PARLIAMENT with its version of the GREAT SEAL.

Lords Lieutenant and Deputy Lieutenants

The Lord Lieutenant (of a county or group of counties) was a leading nobleman of substantial regional or court standing, appointed to oversee the TRAINED BANDS. In this he was assisted and advised by Deputies, men of social eminence within their county or county division. A Tudor innovation, the Lords Lieutenant in 1642 received the instructions from PARLIAMENT issued under the MILITIA ORDINANCE, whereas CHARLES I bypassed them with the COMMISSION OF ARRAY. Their allegiance to either side from 1642–3 was not crucial.

Lorraine, Duke of

Dispossessed of his French duchy in 1633, the duke was stationed in the Spanish Netherlands in 1650 with men and money at his disposal and was looked to by some Irish ROYALISTS as a leader. The EARL OF CLANRICARDE, Lord Deputy in Ireland by

appointment of CHARLES I, refused to countenance this alliance.

Lostwithiel

In August 1644 this was the Cornish headquarters of the EARL OF ESSEX, against which the king's army proceeded in a series of actions (see BEACON HILL and CASTLE DORE) which led to the capitulation of the entire parliamentary army at FOWEY and the flight of Essex.

Lovelace, Richard (1618–58)

A ROYALIST activist and poet. His 'To Lucasta, going to the warres' is perhaps one of the best-known of cavalier poems (see CAVALIER POETS), with its final lines 'I could not love thee, dear, so much / Lov'd I not Honour more'. Lovelace fought for CHARLES I to 1646, and again in 1648.

Love, Nicholas (1608–82)

RECRUITER MP for WINCHESTER from 1645 and a canon of Winchester Cathedral, Love sat on the HIGH COURT OF JUSTICE to try CHARLES I and was one of the subcommittee of seven charged with drafting the death sentence, from which he demurred. He fled to Switzerland in 1660.

Love plot

A conspiracy centred upon the Welsh PURITAN minister Christopher Love, who had become enmeshed in correspondence between PRESBYTERIANS and ROYALISTS in exile. Arrested 14 May 1650, he was sentenced by the HIGH COURT OF JUSTICE and executed 22 August 1651. James Gibbons, servant of DENZIL HOLLES, was also implicated and executed.

Lucas, Sir Charles (1613–48)

An energetic and competent ROYALIST cavalry commander, who shared the fate of SIR GEORGE LISLE after the fall of COLCHESTER in 1648. He was of 'a nature not to be lived with, of an ill understanding, of a rough and proud nature', thought EDWARD HYDE. Lucas served under PRINCE RUPERT and the EARL OF NEWCASTLE in the FIRST CIVIL WAR, and commanded royalist forces in Essex in 1648.

Ludlow, Edmund (1617–92)

A thorough-going COMMONWEALTHSMAN, soldier and RECRUITER MP for Wiltshire from 1646. He signed the *ENGAGEMENT* of the NEW MODEL ARMY in 1647, and sat upon the HIGH COURT OF JUSTICE and signed the king's death warrant in 1649. He became Commander-in-Chief in Ireland after the death of IRETON. He clashed bitterly with CROMWELL and denounced the abandonment of the principles for which they had fought. He fled to exile in 1660. A watered-down version of his memoirs appeared in Switzerland in 1698. They were largely a virulent attack upon Cromwell, but denied that Ireton was, as some believed at the time, able to manipulate him.

C.H. Firth (ed.), *Memoirs of Edmund Ludlow* 2 vols. (London 1894).

Luke, Sir Samuel (1603–70)

MP for Bedford in the SHORT and LONG PARLIAMENTS, he fought as a DRAGOON commander under the EARL OF ESSEX. He was a critic both of the EARL OF MANCHESTER and of the NEW MODEL ARMY, from whom his PRESBYTERIANISM distanced him. He was excluded from PARLIAMENT at PRIDE'S PURGE. It has been suggested that Luke was the model for Samuel Butler's Hudibras, the main character of a long satirical poem of the same name (1663–8). He himself left substantial letter books from his war service.

H.G. Tibbutt (ed.), *The Letterbooks of Sir Samuel Luke 1644–45* (London 1963).

Lunsford, Sir Thomas (1610–53)

According to one contemporary, 'a young outlaw who neither fears God nor man', a 'swaggering ruffian'. CHARLES I laid upon him the honour of the post of Lieutenant of the Tower (of LONDON) in 1641, an honour rapidly withdrawn after protests. His knighthood, however, reaffirmed royal favour. He commanded the guards that accompanied Charles I to arrest the FIVE MEMBERS. Lunsford fought until 1646, and died in America.

Lyme Regis

An important PARLIAMENTARIAN port in Dorset, besieged unsuccessfully by PRINCE MAURICE from 20 April 1644 to 15 June, when it was relieved by the EARL OF ESSEX. The siege was an example of the pointless employment of an army – Maurice's – which might have been better engaged elsewhere.

M

MacDonald (MacDonnell), Alaster (d. 1647)

A supporter of the IRISH REBELLION of 1641, MacDonald in 1644 was sent to Scotland with troops to support MONTROSE, in pursuit of a clan feud with the EARL OF ARGYLE, a COVE-NANTER. He died by treachery, in Ireland.

Macroom, Battle of (10 April 1651)

The last Irish ROYALIST force in the province of Munster was defeated by Lord Broghill. The royalist leader, the Catholic Boetius Egan, bishop of New Ross, was hanged.

Magna Carta

This ancient treaty, forced from King John by his nobility in the early 13th century, was part of the mythology of parliamentarianism. 'This is what we have fought for', declared SIR THOMAS FAIRFAX, 'and by God's help must maintain'. Fairfax's declaration was made after the NEW MODEL ARMY's occupation of LONDON in 1647.

Maidstone, Battle of (1 June 1648)

Maidstone, Kent, was occupied by 7,000 ROYALIST insurgents, against whom SIR THOMAS FAIRFAX, crossing the Medway at EAST FARLEIGH, advanced. The battle was fierce and raged through the town, but the royalists broke and fled, mostly into Essex (see COLCHESTER).

Malignants

A term of opprobrium, used of those who supported CHARLES I or CHARLES II in arms or by other means. The term implied a natural disposition towards treachery and enmity to the state. See also DELINQUENTS.

Malpas, Battle of (25 August 1644)

Malpas, Cheshire, was the scene of the defeat of ROYALIST cavalry (including the NORTHERN HORSE), retreating out of Yorkshire after MARSTON MOOR, by SIR WILLIAM BRERETON.

Manchester

A strongly pro-PARLIAMENTARIAN Lancashire town from 1642, where the supposed first casualty of the civil war (see RICHARD PERCEVAL) was killed in street fighting against the ROYALISTS, July 1642. The EARL OF DERBY failed to take Manchester by siege in September 1642 and never thereafter troubled it.

Manchester, Edward Montagu Earl of (1602–71)

Commander-in-Chief of the army of PARLIAMENT's EASTERN ASSOCIATION, with CROMWELL as commander of the cavalry. Cromwell's position in the army had less to do with Manchester (they detested each other) than with the favour of the EARL OF WARWICK. After MARSTON MOOR the criticism of Manchester by Cromwell contributed to the earl's disillusion with the whole war, and the SELF DENYING ORDINANCE enabled him to relinquish command. He opposed the king's execution.

Man of Blood

A term applied to King CHARLES I in the period preceding and during his TRIAL, January 1649. It conveyed the belief that he was responsible for the bloodshed of the civil war years, for which he was duly tried and executed.

Marcher Association

Association of the counties of Worcestershire, Shropshire, Staffordshire and Herefordshire, formed by 11 January 1645 on the initiative of the GRAND JURY of Worcestershire. It was intended to form a new ROYALIST army based on the POSSE COMITATUS, with its own officers (see LOCALISM) and own funds. The assent of the king was given 15 February, but the association was wrecked in the CLUBMEN risings and the reimposition of military controls by 'outsiders'.

Marlborough

On 5 December 1642 ROYALIST troops under HENRY WILMOT captured this Wiltshire town from the enemy and subjected it to systematic plunder before withdrawing.

Marshall's Elm, Battle of (4 August 1642)

An early civil war engagement in Somerset, when 80 ROYALIST cavalry routed an enemy force of 600 near Walton Hill, in an unlooked-for encounter.

Marshall, Stephen (1594–1655)

A PURITAN minister and friend of PYM, active in the ROOT AND BRANCH MOVEMENT, and a forthright preaching advocate of the parliamentary cause. He was involved in negotiation of the SOLEMN LEAGUE AND COVENANT and appointed chaplain to CHARLES I in 1647, whose execution in 1649 he vehemently opposed. An INDEPENDENT, he supported the NEW MODEL ARMY in its dealings with PARLIAMENT.

Marston Moor, Battle of (2 July 1644)

The single largest civil war battle (with more than 45,000 men engaged and over 4,000 dead), which saw the destruction of the ROYALIST army of the EARL OF NEWCASTLE. The royalist commander was PRINCE RUPERT. The army of the PARLIAMENT was allied at Marston Moor, Yorkshire, with that of the Scots, and overall command lay with the EARL OF LEVEN. A close-run thing, Parliament's victory was snatched from possible defeat by CROMWELL.

P.R. Newman, *The Battle of Marston Moor* (Chichester 1981).

Marten, Henry (1602–80)

MP for Berkshire in the SHORT and LONG PARLIAMENTS, and from an early date a forthright republican (see COMMONWEALTHSMAN). A bitter enemy of the Scottish alliance of 1643, and critical of the PRESBYTER-IANS, he was an early advocate of the king's trial: he was gaoled by PYM in 1643 for calling for the king's deposition. His religious beliefs were slim, but did embrace toleration for ROMAN CATHOLICS. He was critical of CROM-WELL, but served on the HIGH COURT OF JUSTICE and signed the king's death warrant in 1649. His kindness towards ROYALISTS saved him from execution in 1660, but he died in gaol at CHEPSTOW CASTLE in 1680.

Martin Marpriest

Pseudonym adopted by RICHARD OVERTON, deliberately recalling 'Martin Marprelate', the pen name used by the author or authors of a series of satirical Puritan TRACTS in the 16th century.

Marvell, Andrew (1621–78)

Poet and prose writer whose work flourished in the 1650s. He spent most of the civil war years, as did THOMAS HOBBES, in Europe. In 1649 he collaborated with MILTON on *Eikonoklastes*, a reply to EIKON BASILIKE,

and his 'Horatian Ode upon Crom-well's Return from Ireland' (1650) saw the king's execution as inevitable. He was tutor in the household of SIR THOMAS FAIRFAX.

J.D. Hunt, *Andrew Marvell: His Life and Writing* (London 1978).

Massey, Edward (d. 1674)

Edward Massey's parliamentarianism (see PARLIAMENTARIANS) was the result of his failing to secure service in the king's armies. As governor of GLOUCESTER and commander of the western army he distinguished himself, and was returned as RECRUITER MP for Gloucester in the LONG PARLIAMENT, retaining his command. Resentful of the NEW MODEL ARMY and strongly PRESBYTER-IAN, he was expelled at PRIDE'S PURGE, and joined the ROYALIST court in exile, fighting for CHARLES II in 1650–51. He was captured, but escaped from the Tower of LONDON and went to Europe.

Masterless men

The term applies to 'vagrants', but more strongly reflects the contemporary concern of society with those elements lacking settled residence, occupation and the control of an employer. The number of vagrants rose rapidly in England towards 1640 as the result of, among other things, demographic pressures. Masterless men were able and fit to work, but did not, and were casually employed or unemployed. They were seen as a threat to stable social conditions. How many of them found employment in the civil war armies cannot be determined, but Gough in his *History of Myddle* (Shropshire), in listing those villagers that enlisted under the king, demonstrated the masterless men's 'surplus' status in the community. See also CONSERVATISM, CUSTOM AND DEFERENCE.

Matchlock

By civil war standards a primitive but much employed musket, relying upon the application of a smouldering taper or waxed cord to gunpowder in the pan of the musket, thus igniting a charge in the barrel. It was dangerous in that the taper had to be kept permanently lit in the event of action, and unreliable in that it was susceptible to heavy rain. The flintlock (see FLINTLOCK) and the wheellock gradually replaced it.

Maurice, Prince (1620–52)

Younger brother of PRINCE RUPERT and nephew to CHARLES I, whom he served in arms from 1642 to 1646, latterly as commander in South Wales. Much in his brother's shadow, Maurice was nonetheless a competent general. He died at sea serving under Prince Rupert in 1652.

Maynard, John (1602–90)

MP for Totnes, Devon, in the SHORT and LONG PARLIAMENTS. As a lawyer, he framed the IMPEACHMENT of STRAFFORD. He served on the WESTMINSTER ASSEMBLY, and later denounced the trial (see TRIAL OF CHARLES I) and execution of the king. He was

gaoled in 1655 for regarding CROMWELL's rule as usurpation, but was crown prosecutor after 1660.

May, Thomas (1595–1650)

Author of the 'official' work, *History of the Parliament begun in November 1640*, published in 1647 (when May was Secretary to the PARLIAMENT). The work was critical of the emphasis laid upon religion by Parliament, which he felt had alienated many from its cause.

Meldrum, Sir John (d. 1645)

A Scottish professional soldier with experience in Europe and Ulster, who took service with the PARLIAMENT in 1642 and played a crucial role in the defence of HULL in 1643. Humiliated by PRINCE RUPERT at NEWARK-ON-TRENT in March 1644, Meldrum was killed besieging SCARBOROUGH CASTLE.

Melton Mowbray

A PARLIAMENTARIAN garrison town in Leicestershire, attacked in November 1643 by ROYALIST raiders. In February 1645 it was the scene of an encounter between the NORTHERN HORSE and local parliamentarian units, which were defeated by the royalists.

Mercurius Aulicus

Published from Oriel College, OXFORD, between January 1643 and September 1645, this was the 'official' NEWSBOOK of the ROYALISTS, and appeared weekly. Its first editor was PETER HEYLYN and its second Sir John Berkenhead (1617–79), assisted by GEORGE DIGBY.

P.W. Thomas, *Sir John Berkenhead* (Oxford 1969).

Mercurius Militaris

A newssheet, published in 1648 and 1649, that may be considered the mouthpiece of the AGITATORS of the NEW MODEL ARMY and generally in support of the LEVELLERS. It was written mainly by JOHN HARRIS.

Mercurius Pragmaticus

A pro-ROYALIST record of affairs in PARLIAMENT, begun in September 1647 by MARCHAMONT NEEDHAM, and notable for its anti-Scottish invective.

Middlewich, Battles of (13 March and 26 December 1643)

In the action of March at Middlewich, Cheshire, SIR WILLIAM BRERETON completed the destruction of the ROYALIST forces of SIR THOMAS ASTON. In the engagement in December JOHN BYRON defeated Brereton and forced PARLIAMENT to send troops into Cheshire from Lincolnshire under SIR THOMAS FAIRFAX.

Middling sort

A contemporary term, to be equated not with 'middle classes' but rather with 'the people' – that is, freeholders, craftsmen, masters of men, heads of households, independent men. One contemporary thought the term meant 'the true and best citizens', distinguished from the gentry and the lowest sort of people. RICHARD BAXTER equated active PARLIAMENTARIANS with the middling sort, godly and sober opponents of a corrupt gentry and a mercenary poor.

Mildmay, Sir Henry (1593–1664)

MP for Maldon, Essex, in the SHORT and LONG PARLIAMENTS, an early supporter of STRAFFORD who moved towards opposition to the court from religious principles. In 1647 a pro-LEVELLER, he was believed to have been planning the IMPEACHMENT of CROMWELL. He sat on the HIGH COURT OF JUSTICE in 1649 but declined to sign the death warrant. He served on the COUNCIL OF STATE and was allowed to go into exile in 1660.

Military manuals

Many of the inexperienced army commanders of the civil war years relied not only upon professional soldiers but upon manuals of the art of war. The most widely read were William Bariffe's *Military Discipline* (1635), Henry Hexham's *Principles of the Art Military* (1637), Gerrard Barry's *Discourse of Military Discipline* (1634) and William Eldred's *Gunner's Glasse* (1646). On the eve of EDGEHILL in 1642, the ROYALIST high command was split over whether to employ Swedish or Dutch tactics in the battle.

Military rank and precedence

The king, as commander-in-chief of his own armies, usually held the rank of captain general, which in contemporary terms was superior to that of lord general, held by ROYALIST and PARLIAMENTARIAN commanders such as the EARLS OF ESSEX, MANCHESTER, NEWCASTLE and FORTH. Armies being divided into HORSE and FOOT, there were lieutenant generals over each, assisted by major generals, rather as lieutenant colonels of regiments had (sergeant) majors immediately subordinate to them. The rank of field marshal general is also met with at this time (see JOHN BYRON), and seems to have combined control of horse and foot beneath the lord general. The same rank structures applied to the artillery. The rank of colonel general (held by GLEMHAM under Newcastle) might apply to control of a county or grouping thereof in military terms, or to authority beneath the lieutenant general over the foot of an army. Ranks such as provost marshal general or scoutmaster general might be held (with additional pay) by inferior officers, sometime of the rank of captain. See also DRAGOONS.

Militia   See Trained Bands

Militia Bill

First proposed 19 July 1941, this became important in the wake of the IRISH REBELLION of that year. In December SIR ARTHUR HASELRIG introduced a Militia Bill demanding the transfer of control of the armed forces from the crown to a lord general, to be appointed by the PARLIAMENT. It was a direct challenge to the ROYAL PREROGATIVE, and the first reading of the bill passed by only 158 to 125 votes.

Militia Ordinance

New LORDS LIEUTENANT were proposed in PARLIAMENT 31 January 1642, in a move towards control of the armed forces that were to be raised to quell the IRISH REBELLION. King CHARLES I's rejection of the MILITIA BILL – 'You have asked that of me in this never asked of a king' – led to an ORDINANCE of 5 May by which Parliament assumed sovereign (see SOVEREIGNTY) powers. This move has since been called 'the bedrock of parliamentary policy' henceforth.

Millenarianism

The belief that the Millennium (Christ's 1,000-year reign upon earth) would begin in the 6,001st year after the creation, which had been computed as taking place in 4004 BC. It would be heralded by the destruction of Antichrist (the pope), the rule of the SAINTS and the conversion of the Jews. Millenarianism inspired much of the sectarianism (see SECTARIES AND SEPARATISTS) of the civil war years.

B. Capp, 'Popular Millenarianism, The Fifth Monarchists', in J.F. McGregor and B. Reay (eds), *Radical Religion in the English Revolution* (London 1984).

Milton, John (1608–74)

A PURITAN of remarkable heterodoxy, Secretary for Foreign Tongues to the COUNCIL OF STATE, poet, publicist and polemicist. Milton's early works (the poems 'Comus' of 1634 and 'Lycidas' of 1638) made him less famous than his five TRACTS of 1641–2 attacking EPISCOPACY. In 1644 he urged popular mass education (*Of Education*) and went on to denounce CENSORSHIP in his *Areopagitica*. He justified the execution of the king in *The Tenure of Kings and Magistrates* (1649) and his *Eikonoklastes* was a direct response to the *EIKON BASILIKE*. Staunch COMMON-WEALTHSMAN and champion of CROMWELL, his works *Paradise Lost* (1667), *Paradise Regained* (1671) and *Samson Agonistes* (1671) reflect, among other things, the dark view he took of the restoration of CHARLES II.

E.M. Tilyard, *Milton* (London 1949).

Modbury, Battles of (6 December 1642, 21 February 1643)

In the first encounter at Modbury, Devonshire, of December 1642, SIR RALPH HOPTON's newly raised ROYALIST troops were attacked and beaten by local PARLIAMENTARIAN forces. In February 1643 a stubborn royalist defence of the town was fought, which ended in defeat and the abandonment of the royalist advance into Devonshire.

Monck, George (1608–70)

George Monck's crucial role in the restoration of CHARLES II 1659–60, when he commanded the army, and for which he was created Duke of Albermarle by the king, was the last act in a long military career. He fought in the BISHOPS' WARS and against the Irish from 1641. In 1643 he

joined the ROYALIST forces in England, was captured, and was employed by PARLIAMENT as a commander, again in Ireland. CROMWELL came to rely heavily upon him and showed him favour, hence his influence in 1659.

Monckton, Philip (1622–79)

A calvary commander under the EARL OF NEWCASTLE after previous service in the TRAINED BANDS. He also served with the NORTHERN HORSE. He chose exile from 1649. His memoirs are self-laudatory but useful.

E. Peacock (ed.), *The Monckton Papers* (Philobiblon Society 1884).

Monro, Robert (d. 1680)

A Scottish veteran of the Swedish army, Monro was appointed commander of an expeditionary force sent from Scotland to Ulster in 1642 to combat the IRISH REBELLION. In 1648 Monro went over to the ROYALISTS, was arrested by MONCK and was incarcerated in England until 1654.

Montgomery Castle

This castle in Montgomeryshire was secured for the king in 1642 by LORD HERBERT OF CHERBURY but abandoned to the PARLIAMENTARIANS 7 September 1644. The resulting siege by JOHN BYRON led to the single most important battle in North Wales, fought upon 18 September, which saw the destruction of the king's IRISH TROOPS. The consequences were reversed briefly when the king advanced up the border and Montgomery went over to the royalists; then the king turned against the midlands, April 1645.

Montrose, James Graham Marquess of (1612–50)

Commanded troops for the COVENANTERS from 1638 and served against the king in the BISHOPS' WARS. He fell foul of ARGYLE, went over to the king, and from 1644 waged a ruthless and brilliant war against the Covenanters in Scotland, which ended with the BATTLE OF PHILIPHAUGH. Active for CHARLES II in Scotland, he was betrayed to the Covenanters and executed in EDINBURGH, 1650.

Moore, John (1599–1650)

MP for LIVERPOOL in the LONG PARLIAMENT and a diarist of events in the HOUSE OF COMMONS. A colonel first in LONDON in 1642 and then in Lancashire, he was driven from the county by PRINCE RUPERT in 1644. A soldier in Ireland, a supporter of PRIDE's PURGE and a member of the HIGH COURT OF JUSTICE to try CHARLES I, Moore signed the death warrant. Back in Ireland he was the victor of the BATTLE OF BAGGOT-RATH 2 August 1649 and became Governor of Dublin. He died on service.

Morpeth Castle

Lying to the north of NEWCASTLE UPON TYNE, it was seized by the SCOTTISH ARMY in January 1644, retaken by local ROYALISTS, taken again by the Scots in March, and then stormed and taken by MONTROSE 30 May 1644.

Morris, John (1620–49)

ROYALIST governor of PONTEFRACT, Yorkshire, during the 1648 fighting, having previously fought for the PARLIAMENT but been denied a command in the NEW MODEL ARMY. He was held responsible for the (from the New Model Army's viewpoint, convenient) murder of THOMAS RAINSBOROUGH, and after Pontefract fell he was apprehended, tried and executed at YORK.

Mortalism

A doctrine to be found in various religious sects (see SECTARIES AND SEPARATISTS) of the civil war period, and also known as 'annihilationism', denying the resurrection of the body and the afterlife whether in heaven or in hell. It was a doctrine that influenced GERRARD WINSTANLEY and RICHARD OVERTON.

My One Flesh

A RANTER group in LONDON. See also Lawrence Clarkson.

N

Nags Head Tavern

On 15 November 1648 JOHN LIL-BURNE, JOHN WILDMAN and other INDEPENDENTS met at the Nags Head Tavern, LONDON, to iron out a constitutional settlement proposal.

Nalson, John (1638–86)

Nalson's importance lies in his *Impartial Collection of the Great Affairs of State, from the beginning of the Scotch Rebellion in the year 1639, to the Murder of Charles I*, a useful compendium of documentation which, as its title implies, was pro-ROYALIST and an alternative to the *Historical Collections* of JOHN RUSHWORTH. It was published in 1682 and 1683.

Nantwich, Battles of (28 January 1643, 25 January 1644)

In the action of January 1643, at Nantwich, Cheshire, SIR WILLIAM BRERETON's defeat of ROYALIST forces under THOMAS ASTON forced the neutrals (see NEUTERS) in the county to side with PARLIAMENT. The action in January 1644 was fought between JOHN BYRON's royalists and SIR THOMAS FAIRFAX. The royalists were defeated, throwing North Wales wide open to resurgent parliamentary activity.

Naseby, Battle of (14 June 1645)

This decisive engagement between the field army of the king and the NEW MODEL ARMY took place in Northamptonshire shortly after the fall of LEICESTER to the ROYALISTS. The New Model was sent, under SIR THOMAS FAIRFAX, to force an engagement which, although it hung in the balance, was won for PARLIA-MENT by CROMWELL's decisive action. The defeated royalists, depleted of infantry, did not recover from this defeat, although at a COUNCIL OF WAR, 23 June 1645, it was resolved to recruit 10,000 infantrymen in Wales and its borders.

National Oath

An oath imposed, from 5 April 1645, upon all those previously dwelling in areas controlled by ROYALIST forces, to the effect that the persons taking it had in no way assisted the royalist war effort.

Natural Law   See Law of Nature

Navy

By 1642 the naval establishment had been improved as a result of the SHIP MONEY levies. It consisted of three 1st rates, thirteen 2nd rates, ten 3rd rates and fourteen other vessels. The oldest ship available was a 3rd rate of

34 guns built in 1601, and the majority of 1st to 3rd rates were at least seven years old and nine of them more than 20. The fleet was ordinarily supplemented by armed merchantmen, and employed on summer or winter guards of the coastline. In July 1642 four ships declared for the king but were overcome by a fleet decidedly PARLIA-MENTARIAN in sympathy (see EARL OF WARWICK). The ROYALISTS impro-vised, using privateers and with the assistance of Frederick Henry, the Stadtholder of Orange (see FOREIGN AID), who issued letters of marque licensing Dunkirk privateers to attack pro-Parliament ships. In March 1644 the Earl of Warwick reckoned roya-list naval strength at 250 ships of between 50 and 600 tons.

Navy Commissioners

Set up by PARLIAMENT in July 1642 to replace the Principal Officers of the old board, and consisting of 12 members headed by SIR HENRY VANE (THE YOUNGER).

A Committee for the Navy was set up by Parliament in November 1642 with 18 members from the two houses of Parliament.

Needham, March(a)mont (1620–78)

The bitterly anti-ROYALIST writer of the journal *Mercurius Britannicus* from 1643, Needham was arrested by PARLIAMENT for his attacks on the king. He swung over to support of the king by September 1647 and his new journal, MERCURIUS PRAGMATI-CUS, espoused the side of the roya-lists. Arrested again, he eventually took the ENGAGEMENT and became a propagandist on behalf of CROMWELL. His belated but virulent republica-nism (see COMMONWEALTHSMEN) obliged him to flee to Europe in 1660, but he was pardoned and returned home.

Neuters

A contemporary term for 'neutrals', those that desired (from whatever reason) to keep aloof from the war or the effects of the war. The CLUBMEN phenomenon of 1644–45 had its roots in some form of neutralism, but was essentially responsive to events, whereas early neuters endeavoured to prevent hostilities from breaking out in their areas (see also LOCALISM). Armed neuters in Cheshire in June 1642 championed a form of dual obedience to king and PARLIAMENT, but in December 1642 overran their county and forced the dominant ROYALIST party there to negotiation and demilitarization.

Newark Castle

A fortress on the Anglo-Scottish border where, in September 1645 after the BATTLE AT PHILIPHAUGH, 200 Irish prisoners of war were syste-matically slaughtered by COVE-NANTER troops.

Newark-on-Trent

A major and very powerful ROYALIST fortress controlling the Great North Road and crossings of the River Trent in Nottinghamshire. It resisted major siege attempts in 1643 and in March 1644, when MELDRUM was defeated and humiliated by PRINCE RUPERT's relief march, 21 March. A siege begun in November 1645 by a Scottish and PARLIAMENTARIAN army proved ineffective: Newark surrendered by order of the king 6 May 1646.

Newbury, Battles of (19–20 September 1643, 27 October 1644)

In the battle of September 1643 ROYALISTS holding Newbury, Berkshire, attempted to block the EARL OF ESSEX's march from GLOUCESTER to LONDON, but the action was abandoned. In October 1644 a royalist army under the king's command, moving to relieve DONNINGTON CASTLE, dealt effectively with EASTERN ASSOCIATION troops under a hesitant EARL OF MANCHESTER and a slothful CROMWELL.

Newcastle Emlyn, Battle of (23 April 1645)

A decisive victory for CHARLES GERARD over ROWLAND LAUGHARNE's PARLIAMENTARIANS, who had laid siege to the castle. Gerard's victory enabled him to take Haverfordwest, and to thrust the enemy out of Pembrokeshire.

Newcastle Propositions

Draft proposals for negotiated peace communicated to the king (then in Scottish hands) 14 July 1646 by commissioners from PARLIAMENT. The proposals included a demand for the king to swear to sustain the SOLEMN LEAGUE AND COVENANT, to recognize PRESBYTERIANISM, concede control of armed forces to Parliament for 20 years, and to accept punitive measures against leading ROYALISTS. These proposals were wholly unacceptable to the king, although Parliament continued to see them as viable well into 1647. The Scots handed the king back to Parliament February 1647.

Newcastle Upon Tyne

Major port on the north-east coast of England, secured for the king in summer 1642 by the EARL OF NEWCASTLE. Garrisoned by Sir John Marley, it resisted the SCOTTISH ARMY in February 1644 and withstood siege until 19 October, when it was stormed with considerable slaughter.

Roger Howell, *Newcastle upon Tyne and the Puritan Revolution* (Oxford 1967).

Newcastle, William Cavendish Earl of (1593–1676)

CHARLES I's Commander-in-Chief in the counties of northern England from 1642 until 1644 when, after MARSTON MOOR, he resigned his command and went into exile. For a brief time in the summer of 1643 (see ADWALTON MOOR) he was paramount, and his success so worried the PARLIAMENT that it pushed rapidly forward with its Scottish alliance (see SOLEMN LEAGUE AND COVENANT). Newcastle remained in exile until 1660.

New impost   See Excise

Newmarket

CHARLES I was lodged in a royal palace in Newmarket, Suffolk, 7–24 June 1647 as prisoner of the NEW MODEL ARMY, which mustered at nearby KENTFORD HEATH.

New Model Army

Dissatisfaction with existing parliamentary armies developed in 1644, and 'new modelling' of the forces was proposed in November. The HOUSE OF LORDS, in the wake of the SELF DENYING ORDINANCE, agreed to an ORDINANCE of 17 February 1645 to create a new army of 22,000 men (to be paid for by a special additional monthly levy of £53,500) and to be based largely upon the EASTERN ASSOCIATION, although intended to swallow up the forces of the EARL OF ESSEX and SIR WILLIAM WALLER. SIR THOMAS FAIRFAX was to be Commander-in-Chief in a command structure not at all radical in personnel. 'Never', observed one contemporary, 'did hardly any army go forth to war with less confidence of their own side, or more contempt of their enemies', although the victory at NASEBY remedied that. By 1646 the New Model accounted for less than half of the PARLIAMENT's forces: the army of the NORTHERN ASSOCIATION was itself 20,000 strong. Petitions for the New Model's disbandment were frequent in 1646–7 because of the financial burden on the eastern counties. Increased radicalism in the ranks has been seen as a response to moves for disbandment and plans to send regiments into Ireland.

M. Kishlansky, *The Rise of the New Model Army* (Cambridge 1979).

New Noddle

A derisive term for the NEW MODEL ARMY, and by no means exclusively ROYALIST in origin.

Newnham, Battle of (8 May 1644)

A ROYALIST garrison town controlling links between Gloucestershire and South Wales, stormed and taken by EDWARD MASSEY from the royalists under SIR JOHN WINTOUR.

Newport, Treaty of

A series of negotiations held, at an inn in Newport, Isle of Wight, between CHARLES I and commissioners sent from PARLIAMENT. They commenced 18 September 1648. Parliament's terms were a resurrection of the NEWCASTLE PROPOSITIONS, but efforts failed again in view of the king's determined attitude to the CHURCH OF ENGLAND. Even so, the HOUSE OF COMMONS felt after the negotiations, by 129 votes to 83, that there was room for progress.

New Ross

A town in County Wexford, Ireland, garrisoned in 1649 by ROYALIST forces under Lucas Taafe. CROMWELL lay siege 17 October; it fell 19 October, and thereafter became a base for NEW MODEL ARMY operations.

Newsbooks

The importance of propaganda to the war effort was recognized by PARLIAMENT 4 June 1642, when a committee was appointed to regularize distribution of published materials. The king, when he came to YORK in March 1642, set up a printer there to produce copies of royal declarations and proposals. Throughout the civil war consecutively numbered weekly or bi-weekly newsbooks appeared from both sides chronicling events with commentary. The most successful of these was the ROYALIST *MERCURIUS AULICUS*. From 1649 Parliament officially sanctioned only two such publications in its interest. See also TRACTS.

Nicholas, Sir Edward (1593–1669)

Secretary of State to both CHARLES I and CHARLES II from 1641, and thus close to Charles I during the years 1642–6. A negotiator at UXBRIDGE in 1645, he was excluded from the counsels of Charles II until 1654 by the influence of QUEEN HENRIETTA MARIA and was pensioned off in 1662. He left at his death an extensive series of papers. He was very much the loyal civil servant.

Nineteen Propositions

Proposals sent from PARLIAMENT to the king at YORK 1 June 1642. Virtually an ultimatum, although somewhat modified by the PEACE GROUP in Parliament, who regarded them merely as an agenda. Parliament anticipated royal rejection of terms that included control of all executive activity, rigid enforcement of anti-Catholic legislation and the subjection of ministerial appointments to parliamentary scrutiny and approval.

Norfolk Rising

On 5 December 1650 a localized and ineffective ROYALIST uprising occurred in Norfolk, which was easily suppressed. The COUNCIL OF STATE, however, saw it as the false start of a more widespread insurrection involving armed invasion from Europe under the EARL OF NEWCASTLE. Nothing came of it.

Northampton

The town was seized and occupied by LEVELLERS under WILLIAM THOMPSON in May 1649. On 17 May NEW MODEL ARMY units attacked and retook it, killing Thompson and several others.

Northcote, Sir John (1599–1676)

MP for Ashburton, Devonshire, in the LONG PARLIAMENT and a PRESBYTERIAN, excluded at PRIDE'S PURGE. He left a notebook, useful to historians, which was published in 1887.

Northern Association

PARLIAMENT's grouping of the north-eastern counties. In reality, Parliamentary efforts were confined to Yorkshire, where the association's military commanders were, in turn, FERDINAND LORD FAIRFAX, JOHN LAMBERT and SYDENHAM POYNTZ. The army of the association was 20,000 strong in 1646, but was largely demobilized between December 1647 and February 1648 in a general demobilization policy aimed at surviving provincial armies. Poyntz, a hard-line PRESBYTERIAN and suspicious of the NEW MODEL ARMY, was for a time seen by Presbyterians in Parliament as a possible weapon against the New Model.

Northern Horse

Collective name for the HORSE regiments of the EARL OF NEWCASTLE's army after its disbandment in the wake of MARSTON MOOR. The cavalry regiments (commanded successively by GEORGE GORING, SIR MARMADUKE LANGDALE and GEORGE DIGBY) fought throughout 1644–5 as a distinct unit with other ROYALIST armies. They achieved the brilliantly executed relief of PONTEFRACT in 1645, but were mauled at NASEBY and fought their last fight near CARLISLE October 1645.

Norton, Richard (1615–91)

Nicknamed 'Idle Dick' and 'the great incendiary' of Hampshire in 1643. A PRESBYTERIAN and commander of the HAMBLETON BOYS, Norton served in the EASTERN ASSOCIATION army under CROMWELL. He was returned as RECRUITER MP for Hampshire in 1645, was an irregular attender at the HOUSE OF COMMONS and opposed PRIDE'S PURGE and the king's execution. He was the son-in-law of, consecutively, SIR WALTER EARLE and LORD SAYE AND SELE.

Norwich

Scene in Norfolk of an outbreak of pro-ROYALIST rioting in May 1648, which was suppressed by regular troops. More than half a dozen ringleaders were executed 2 January 1649.

Norwich, George Goring Earl of (1583–1663)

Created Earl of Norwich in 1644 by CHARLES I (a peerage not recognized by PARLIAMENT), and acted as his representative in France. Parliament impeached (see IMPEACHMENT) him of treason. In 1648, captured at COLCHESTER, Norwich was sentenced to death, but the casting vote in the HOUSE OF COMMONS reprieved him.

Norwich, Joseph Hall Bishop of (1574–1656)

A notable champion of EPISCOPACY in the HOUSE OF LORDS, and the author of works directed at separatists (see SECTARIES AND SEPARATISTS) and PRESBYTERIANS. He was impeached (see IMPEACHMENT) and gaoled in 1642, although he was not a LAUDIAN.

Nottingham

On 22 August 1642 King CHARLES I raised his standard at Nottingham and thus began the civil wars. EDWARD HYDE referred to a 'general air of sadness' that covered the town. Late in the year Colonel Hutchinson (see MRS LUCY HUTCHINSON) seized the town for PARLIAMENT. It fell to JOHN BYRON in September 1643, but Hutchinson clung on to the castle.

Null and Void Ordinance

The HOUSE OF COMMONS voted 20 August 1648 to regard as null and void all votes taken in the House between 26 July (when the INDEPENDENT members fled to the NEW MODEL ARMY) and 6 August, the date of the army's occupation of LONDON.

Nye, Philip (1596–1672)

INDEPENDENT minister, protégé of the EARL OF MANCHESTER and member of the WESTMINSTER ASSEMBLY. Nye was instrumental in getting Independents into the Assembly, and had already assisted SIR HENRY VANE in mitigating the full intentions of the Scots in the SOLEMN LEAGUE AND COVENANT. An opponent of the LEVELLERS and chaplain to CROMWELL, he was reckoned as a future archbishop of CANTERBURY in the event of Cromwell accepting the crown.

O

Office of Addresses

Proposed to PARLIAMENT by the reformer SAMUEL HARTLIB and intended as a centrally funded body to coordinate reforms in commerce, trade, industry and agriculture. Parliament's approval of the principle in 1646 came to nothing.

Oglander, Sir John (1585–1655)

SHERIFF of Hampshire in 1642–3 and a committed ROYALIST. His 'diary' survives and was published in 1888.

W.H. Long (ed.), *The Oglander Memoirs* (London 1888).

Okey, John (1606–62)

A brewer's drayman, he rose to become a colonel in the NEW MODEL ARMY. He served on the HIGH COURT OF JUSTICE, signed the king's death warrant, and sat on the subcomittee which ordered the manner of the king's execution, in 1649. He was arrested in Holland in 1662 and executed in LONDON.

Old English and New English

Two groups of English settlers in Ireland. The Old English were descended from pre-Elizabethan settlers there, and were largely Catholic, while the New English were 17th-century colonists and were predominantly Protestant. See also IRISH REBELLION.

Old Horse

Cavalry regiments of HENRY WIL-MOT's brigade of the king's main field army. Wilmot was arrested 8 August 1644 for entering into direct talks with the EARL OF ESSEX and was replaced by GEORGE GORING. Wilmot's cavalry, nicknamed 'The Old Horse', refused to serve under their new commander and petitioned the king to express their 'great amazement' at what had happened.

Old Ironsides

Nickname for OLIVER CROMWELL.

Old Loyalty   See Basing House.

Old Service

A term coined by a PARLIAMENTARIAN major general in the 1650s to describe the royalism (see ROYALISTS) in arms of the 1640s.

Old Subtlety

Nickname of LORD SAYE AND SELE.

O'More, Rory (d. c.1652)

O'More (Anglicized as Moore) was prominent in the IRISH REBELLION and won a crucial battle at Julianstown in 1641. He worked for an alliance between the IRISH CATHOLIC CONFEDERACY and the EARL OF ORMONDE's ROYALISTS, and appears to have died c.1652 somewhere in Ireland.

One and All

After the second BATTLE OF NEWBURY in October 1644, local ROYALISTS in Somerset (see LOCALISM) sought to remove royalist troops from their county in favour of local forces. Their slogan 'One and All' reflected a general enthusiasm for peace, but they were also nicknamed 'the third party' and 'the new COVENANTERS' by their critics. Their intentions surfaced again in CLUBMEN movements in 1645, and may be traced to origins in the attempts of 1642, both in Somerset and elsewhere, to limit the impact of the war.

O'Neill, Hugh (d. c.1661)

Arrived in Ireland in 1642 as a commander for the IRISH CATHOLIC CONFEDERACY and from 1646 to 1649 commander in Ulster. He defied CROMWELL from CLONMEL, but surrendered LIMERICK to IRETON in 1651. His Spanish citizenship saved him from execution.

O'Neill, Owen Roe (1590–1649)

The nephew of the Earl of Tyrone driven from Ulster 40 years before, Owen Roe landed in Donegal in July 1642 to head the IRISH REBELLION. Representative of the dispossessed Gaelic element, and High Chief of Ulster, he had military experience in the Spanish armies. He led the Irish forces until his death, 6 November 1649, at Cloughoughter, County Cavan, and was succeeded as Commander-in-Chief by Eamon MacMahon, bishop of Clogher.

Ordinances

Legislation passed through PARLIAMENT but lacking royal assent. Ordinances were always intended to be temporary expedients, but a clause to that effect in the MILITIA ORDINANCE of 1642 was withdrawn. Theoretically akin to royal PROCLAMATIONS, the standing of Ordinances depended upon Parliament's ability to enforce them. They were, if used to push through legislation against the wishes of the king, a direct attack on the ROYAL PREROGATIVE. See also ACTS OF PARLIAMENT.

Ormonde, James Butler Earl of (1610–88)

Irish peer of English extraction, and a convert to Protestantism, Ormonde was appointed 10 November 1641 by CHARLES I to resist the IRISH REBELLION. In November 1643 he was commissioned to enter England to replace LORD CAPEL in North Wales, but the authority was vested in JOHN BYRON in Ormonde's absence. The earl never made the journey, though by concluding peace with the Irish rebels he was able to ship regiments over to help the king. His office of Lord Lieutenant in Ireland was superseded briefly by the EARL OF GLAMORGAN in 1645. Ormonde made his peace with PARLIAMENT in 1647, but in 1648 returned to Ireland, again as a ROYALIST commander, made peace with the Irish rebels, and in 1649 proclaimed CHARLES II. CROMWELL effectively destroyed the Irish–royalist forces and Ormonde went into exile in 1650.

Ormonde Peace

A treaty arrived at in March 1646 between the ROYALIST commander ORMONDE and the IRISH CATHOLIC CONFEDERACY at KILKENNY, giving to the rebels a general pardon. The peace was condemned by the papal nuncio, RINUCCINI, and was rejected by a General Assembly of the Confederacy's Supreme Council in January 1647.

Ormskirk, Battle of (25 August 1644)

A defeat sustained in Lancashire by the NORTHERN HORSE at the hands of MELDRUM during their march south after the battle of MARSTON MOOR.

Overton, Richard (d. 1664)

A LEVELLER writer of TRACTS specializing in invective, and probable author of *THE HUNTING OF THE FOXES* of March 1649. Overton was a virulent anti-Catholic and anti-EPISCOPACY writer in 1642, and in 1644 he collided with PRESBYTERIANISM in his tract *Mans Mortalitie*, which denied the immortality of the soul. Using the pseudonym MARTIN MARPRELATE, he continued attacks on Presbyterianism and became involved in the Leveller unrest of 1647–9. He was an early (1646) advocate of the abolition of monarchy.

Owen, John (1616–83)

Although classed as an INDEPENDENT, Owen gradually shifted away from PRESBYTERIANISM until, by 1646, he was an outright supporter of congregationalism and GATHERED CHURCHES. Chaplain to SIR THOMAS FAIRFAX in 1648, his sermon on the day after the execution of the king in 1649 demonstrated clear MILLENARIANISM.

Owen, Sir John (1600–66)

A prominent North Wales ROYALIST commander who served the king throughout the 1642–6 war, and, as Major General under PRINCE MAURICE, held out in CONWAY CASTLE to 18 November 1646. In arms again in 1648, he was taken at Y DALAR HIR and sentenced to death in LONDON in 1649 with LORD CAPEL, but was reprieved. He remained in goal until 1655.

Oxford

This university city was occupied, in September 1642, by royalist troops under JOHN BYRON, who then withdrew. It became the headquarters of the king shortly afterwards, however, and did not fall into parliamentary hands until 13 July 1646, when it was surrendered, on royal orders, by SIR THOMAS GLEMHAM. It was for most of the war the chief royalist arsenal, with large-scale sword manufacture at nearby Wolvercote. Originally seen as the base for an advance upon LONDON by the king that never materialized, it underwent desultory sieges in 1644 and again in 1645.

Oxford Army

That army, attached to the king's person, which was based upon the city of OXFORD, wherever it operated in the midlands and west and south-west.

Oxford Parliament

King CHARLES I summoned MPs and peers loyal to him to meet at OXFORD, from January 1644, to demonstrate his endorsement of the role of PARLIAMENT. The last session of the Oxford Parliament (November 1644 to March 1645) was rife with dissatisfaction at the war effort and talk of a compromise settlement, which caused the king to dissolve it as a 'mongrel parliament'. Nevertheless it attracted large numbers to its sittings and was, in those terms, a successful propaganda exercise at least.

Oxford Proposals

In January and March 1643 eight commissioners (including BULSTRODE WHITELOCKE) were sent by PARLIAMENT to the king at OXFORD to try to reach peace, but without success.

P

Pale (English)

The area of Ireland subdued in the 12th century and comprising Meath, Louth, Trim, Dublin, Kildare, Kilkenny, Waterford, Wexford and Tipperary by the late 14th century. By 1495 this area had shrunk to a strip of land around Dublin, when a great defensive fence or 'pale' was mooted. By the time of the IRISH REBELLION of 1641 it was the operations base for GOVERNMENT troops, but was weakened by the defection of the OLD ENGLISH to the rebel cause.

Palmer, Geoffrey

MP for Stamford, Lincolnshire, in the LONG PARLIAMENT. Upon the narrow passage of the GRAND REMONSTRANCE in November 1641, he denounced the supporters of it as 'a Rabble of inconsiderable Persons, set on by a juggling junto'. This description of the king's opponents in PARLIAMENT reflected the prevalent view that they were inconsequential men bent upon feathering their own nests from national discord, a view met with frequently in ROYALIST propaganda.

Papists and church papists

Terms of abuse levelled at open and covert ROMAN CATHOLICS. Anti-Catholicism was a fundamental ingredient of PARLIAMENTARIAN politics and beliefs. The terms associated all Catholics with papal pretensions and ambitions. It was rumoured in 1642 that many 'papists' resorted to the services of the CHURCH OF ENGLAND in order to qualify themselves to bear arms for the king, hence 'church papists'.

Pardon and Oblivion, Act of

Passed by PARLIAMENT 1 December 1651, this was an attempt to reassure opinion by discharging from SEQUESTRATION proceedings all those whose property was not actually sequestrated.

Parker, Henry (1604–52)

Probably the most able champion of the PARLIAMENTARIAN cause, drawing down upon him much ROYALIST polemic. He espoused the theory of GOVERNMENT by consent of the governed and looked toward a limited and mixed monarchy. His *Observations upon some of His Majesty's late Answers and Expresses* 1642, which followed the NINETEEN PROPOSITIONS, aroused strong royalist response. In *Jus Populi* (1644) he described Parliament as 'the soveraigne antidote of publike mischiefs'. He served as secretary to the HOUSE OF COMMONS.

Parliament

The English Parliament consisted of

three estates, the peers (temporal and spiritual) in the HOUSE OF LORDS and the commons in the HOUSE OF COMMONS. The NINETEEN PROPOSITIONS appeared to regard the king as a fourth estate, meaning he was integral to the structure of Parliament just as Parliament was integral to royal SOVEREIGNTY. The king's response to the Propositions seemed to concede this point. Scotland also had its own Parliament along similar structural lines: but see also COMMITTEE OF THE ESTATES.

Parliamentarians

A collective term for all those who supported, in arms or otherwise, the cause of the PARLIAMENT during the civil wars.

Peaceable Army

Some 4,000 men recruited in Glamorganshire and reviewed by CHARLES I, 29 July 1645, at Cardiff. Led by local gentry (see LOCALISM), this army was nevertheless an intervention in the war by the ordinary people of the county. Their attitude to the ROYALISTS was varyingly hostile despite their pretensions of loyalty to the Crown, and in September 1645 SIR MARMADUKE LANGDALE enforced the army's disbandment. The subsequent loss of BRISTOL by the king led to the army reforming and declaring for PARLIAMENT, but in February 1646 it mutinied rather than go against the royalist forces in RAGLAN CASTLE.

Peace Group

A grouping of MPs in PARLIAMENT,

noticeable in 1642–3 and again in 1646, but without recognizable 'party' structure, who favoured negotiation and a 'soft' approach to the king. In 1642 this group was best represented, but was not led, by SIMOND D'EWES. By 1646 'peace' politics and PRESBYTERIANISM came to be associated together, not least by thorough-going INDEPENDENTS suspicious of the SOLEMN LEAGUE AND COVENANT.

Pelham's Parliament (30 July– 5 August 1647)

A name applied to the sittings of the LONG PARLIAMENT after the flight of Speaker LENTHALL and 57 MPs to the safety of the NEW MODEL ARMY. With Henry Pelham in the Speaker's chair, the HOUSE OF COMMONS, dominated by the PRESBYTERIANS, reactivated the COMMITTEE OF SAFETY, recalled the ELEVEN MEMBERS and put LONDON on a defensive footing (see LINES OF COMMUNICATION). Their resolve weakened at the approach of the New Model.

Pembroke

From 1642 a solidly PARLIAMENTARIAN stronghold in South Wales which yielded, without a fight, to the ROYALIST forces of the EARL OF CARBERY in October 1643. JOHN POYER engineered the retrieval of the town for parliament soon afterwards. In March 1648 a group of former parliamentarians including ROWLAND LAUGHARNE and Poyer declared Pembroke for the king. Poyer defeated a parliamentarian force at Pwllcrochan 29 March 1648, but after the BATTLE

OF ST FAGANS siege was laid, and CROMWELL took the surrender 11 July.

Pembroke, Philip Herbert Earl of (1584–1650)

Although a favourite of both King James I and of CHARLES I, Pembroke was a strenuous opponent of STRAFFORD and was gaoled in the Tower of LONDON briefly for his intemperance in this respect. His political radicalism hardened, he was dismissed as Lord Chamberlain of the Royal Household. His active committee work for PARLIAMENT led to the demand that he be given a dukedom in the course of peace talks in 1645. In September 1648 Pembroke acted as a Commissioner, waiting upon the king during the TREATY OF NEWPORT talks. When the HOUSE OF LORDS was abolished Pembroke became an MP, and served on the COUNCIL OF STATE.

Pendennis Castle

A ROYALIST garrison in Cornwall from 1642, which SIR THOMAS FAIRFAX advanced against in March 1646. The royalist governor, Sir John Arundell, refused to surrender, but the garrison was starved out by 17 August.

Pennington, Isaac (1587–1660)

MP for LONDON in the SHORT and LONG PARLIAMENTS, a political rival of SIR RICHARD GURNEY and a thoroughgoing PURITAN. He played a major part in raising finance for the PARLIAMENT, and served on the HIGH COURT OF JUSTICE to try CHARLES I in

1649, but did not sign the death warrant. He was imprisoned in 1660.

Pensy-Pound

On 11 July 1645 CLUBMEN of Somerset, led by Humphrey Willis, entered into a formal alliance with the NEW MODEL ARMY at Pensy-Pound, Somerset.

Perceval, Richard

A linen weaver of MANCHESTER who was reputed by contemporaries to be the first fatal casualty of the civil war. He was killed in a street fight with ROYALIST supporters, and the EARL OF DERBY was charged with Perceval's death at his own trial in 1651.

Perfect Diurnal, The

A NEWSBOOK published in LONDON, edited from 1647 by Samuel Peeke using material supplied by JOHN RUSHWORTH. The *Diurnal* was revived in 1649 under Rushworth's direct editorship.

Perpetual Parliament Act

SIR ROGER TWYSDEN's description of the statute against the dissolution, prorogation and adjournment of PARLIAMENT (1641). The weight of the statute – that Parliament should itself consent to its own dissolution – was seen by many as a direct attack upon the king's PREROGATIVE.

Personal rule

On 2 March 1629 King CHARLES I dissolved PARLIAMENT (see also PER-PETUAL PARLIAMENT ACT) and did not summon it to meet again until 1640 (see SHORT PARLIAMENT). His action was taken in the light of severe difficulties with the Parliaments of 1625, 1626 and 1628–9. During this 11-year period of personal rule England enjoyed peace abroad, but was subjected to what some regarded as arbitrary and innovative means of raising revenue, including SHIP MONEY, distraint of knighthood (involving a fine on persons of standing), and the sale of monopolies and titles.

Peters, Hugh (1598–1660)

A minister at Salem, Massachusetts, on the eve of the civil war, where his strict CALVINIST belief in the separation of ministry and magistracy revealed itself in his preaching. Chaplain in the parliamentary armies from 1642, and prolific writer of accounts of actions which he saw, Peters was a strong INDEPENDENT whose preaching drew recruits to the cause. He was chaplain to the COUNCIL OF STATE from 1650 and was with CROMWELL at WORCESTER. He was executed in 1660.

Petition of Right

First drafted in the PARLIAMENT of 1628–9 by Sir Edward Coke and phrased as a supplication to the king, calling upon him to do right in a wide number of national grievances, particularly forced billeting of soldiers (see FREE QUARTER). The king assented to the content, but nothing came of the PETITION, although its provisions underlay much parliamentary reform of 1641–2.

Petition of the Officers and Soldiers of the (New Model) Army

Brought to the attention of the HOUSE OF COMMONS 27 March 1647. It was drafted at SAFFRON WALDEN in Essex and represented to the Commons the neglect of the army's pay and conditions, and the abandonment of the liberties for which it had fought. It called forth from the Commons the *DECLARATION OF DISLIKE* in response.

Petition of Women

This PETITION of 5 May 1649, presented to the RUMP PARLIAMENT, was occasioned by the trial and execution of ROBERT LOCKYER, the LEVELLER soldier. Its contents hearkened back to the PETITION OF RIGHT of 1628–9, particularly in denouncing the use of martial law (by which Lockyer was sentenced) in time of peace.

Petitions

A means of exerting pressure upon PARLIAMENT by the 'people'. Petitions could be delivered to the HOUSE OF COMMONS – accompanied, a ROYALIST noted, by 'irregular and tumultuous assemblies of people' – which could then either read and ignore them, or read and condemn them and proceed against their originators. Petitions were effective propaganda for the reformers of the LONG PARLIAMENT and were used cleverly by JOHN PYM to speed up measures, but they could also conflict; for example, pro- and anti-EPISCOPACY petitions sent in from various counties in 1641–2. Pro-episcopacy petitions were produced by 22 English counties in September–March 1641–2, often originating in the GRAND JURIES, and numerous petitions for peace circulated in mid 1642. LONDON petitions, mob-accompanied, had the most immediate impact upon Parliament.

Philiphaugh, Battle of (13 September 1645)

The decisive defeat of MONTROSE and his ROYALISTS by DAVID LESLIE and a COVENANTER army. See also NEWARK CASTLE.

Picture of the Council of State

A LEVELLER lampoon of the COUNCIL OF STATE, published in 1649.

Piercebridge, Battle of (16 December 1642)

First battle of the ROYALIST army of the EARL OF NEWCASTLE, which defeated Yorkshire PARLIAMENTARIAN troops in Durham as it advanced towards YORK.

Plundered Ministers, Committee for

Established by PARLIAMENT in 1645, to augment the incomes of a neighbouring or local minister or clergyman from the sequestered (see SEQUESTRATION) rectories, tithes and estates of DELINQUENT ROYALISTS.

Pluralities Bill

The HOUSE OF COMMONS introduced a bill against clergymen holding two or more benefices 25 February 1641. The measure constantly met royal obstruction and then veto.

Plymouth

On 30 September 1643 PRINCE MAURICE laid siege to this important PARLIAMENTARIAN port in Devonshire, but was forced to abandon it 22 December 1643. A ROYALIST blockade was maintained, ineffectually, to 1645. JOHN LAMBERT was imprisoned in Plymouth from 1670.

Poll Tax

A personal tax levied on men and women in 1222 to finance a Crusade, and levied according to means. It was used again in 1641 as an alternative to SHIP MONEY, with gradations according to wealth and status. It appeared again in 1660–61 and in 1689, but fell into disuse until 1989, when it was levied first in Scotland.

Pontefract

A garrison town and castle of strategic importance lying on routes north and south through Yorkshire. Garrisoned for the king in 1642, it was closely besieged August 1644 to 21 July 1645, when it surrendered. The NORTHERN HORSE under SIR MARMADUKE LANGDALE carried out a brilliant relief raid on 1 March 1645. On 8 June 1648 the castle was seized for the king by Colonel JOHN MORRIS and endured nine months of siege. On 10 August CROMWELL took the town, but the castle did not yield until 22 March 1649.

Porter, Endymion (1587–1649)

Close associate of the royal court and an expert in Spanish affairs, and in works of art, in the acquisition of which CHARLES I employed him. A courtier, he was returned as MP for Droitwich, Staffordshire, in the LONG PARLIAMENT, and voted against the ATTAINDER of STRAFFORD. The HOUSE OF COMMONS expelled him from their deliberations, and he was one of the ROYALISTS excluded from pardon by them. He fled to Europe in 1645.

Portsmouth

As early as 2 August 1642 GEORGE GORING, governor of this important south-coast port in Hampshire, declared for the king, but he surrendered to SIR WILLIAM WALLER 7 September. Thereafter it remained a vitally important PARLIAMENTARIAN base.

Posse comitatus

All abled-bodied men between 15 and 60 years of age, liable to be called up in arms by the SHERIFF of a county. In February 1642 an attempt to raise the Berkshire posse to guard the king at Windsor failed through lack of enthusiasm, as happened in Dorset in 1643, where an attempt was made to raise the posse against ENCLOSURE rioters. The posse was raised in Cornwall in September 1642 to seize local PARLIAMENTARIANS indicted as disturbers of the peace before the JUSTICES OF THE PEACE. SIR RALPH HOPTON reviewed 3,000 of the posse in Cornwall 4 October 1642, and found them well armed. The posse was placed under the power of the COMMISSIONERS OF ARRAY by the king in mid 1642. Like the TRAINED BANDS it was unreliable.

Powell, Vavasor (1617–70)

A Welsh preacher who, after working in LONDON 1642–6, returned to Wales as a leading figure in the evangelization of that country (see COMMITTEE FOR THE PROPAGATION OF THE GOSPEL). He moved towards the INDEPENDENTS and the BAPTISTS, and became a critic of CROMWELL. His itinerant mode of life perhaps inspired George Fox, the Quaker, but his preaching alarmed the GOVERNMENT, which constantly harried and imprisoned him from 1660 at least.

Powick Bridge, Battle of (23 September 1642)

The first real action of the civil wars, occasioned by PRINCE RUPERT attempting to cover a ROYALIST withdrawal from WORCESTER and colliding with advance elements of the army of the EARL OF ESSEX. Essex was routed.

Poyer, John (d. 1648)

In 1642 Mayor of Pembroke in South Wales. He secured the town and castle for the PARLIAMENT, and held on to it thereafter. This 'diligent officer' (as a contemporary described him), denied reimbursement for his considerable outlay in Parliament's behalf, declared for the king in 1648. Captured, he was executed in London in 1649.

Poyntz, Sydenham

A runaway LONDON apprentice who, after service in the Imperial army in Europe, joined that of the PARLIAMENT in 1645. As commander of the NORTHERN ASSOCIATION he won the BATTLE OF ROWTON HEATH. Considered a likely commander to challenge the NEW MODEL ARMY on behalf of Parliament, he was seized by his own men. After a brief association with anti-army politics in London, he fled to Europe. His *Vindication* was published in 1646.

Prayer Book

The Book of Common Prayer of the CHURCH OF ENGLAND was devised by Archbishop Cranmer in 1537, and appeared, revised, in 1549. It went into various new editions, the last prior to the civil wars in 1625. Its ritual was a particular target of reformers, and it was abolished by PARLIAMENT in 1640 (with private use forbidden in 1655). Not until 1645 was it superseded by the PRESBYTERIAN *DIRECTORY FOR PUBLIC WORSHIP*. In 1643 the king put on record his determination to see the Prayer Book given statutory protection. It was reintroduced in 1662.

Prerogative, Royal

Rights, privileges and powers vested in the monarch in virtue of the office of monarchy, which the LONG PARLIAMENT successfully sought to define and to limit by enactment of statute law. The MILITIA ORDINANCE was a direct attack upon one of the prerogatives of the crown.

Presbyterians and Presbyterianism

In a strictly religious sense, those who accepted and supported the government of the church by presbyters of equal rank, disowning EPISCOPACY and other 'popish' survivals of the pre-Reformation church. In 1646–8 Presbyterians might also have been those seeking negotiated settlement with the king, and politically *personae non gratae* with developing INDEPENDENCY. The Scottish church was most fully Presbyterian, founded on CALVINISM as presented in the works of John Knox (such as *Booke of Discipline* and *Booke of Common Order*), but even so, still had bishops. Presbyterianism as a form of national worship was clearly represented in the Westminster Confession of Faith of 1647, reflecting PARLIAMENT's agreement in the SOLEMN LEAGUE AND COVENANT to impose the system upon England. This was brought to nothing by the self-assertion of the NEW MODEL ARMY and its Independent spokesmen and leaders.

Preston, Battles of (20 March 1643, 17 August 1648)

The March 1643 engagement was a ROYALIST victory led by the EARL OF

DERBY against the diminished PARLIA-MENTARIAN garrison of Preston, Lancashire. In August 1648 the royalist invasion army of the DUKE OF HAMILTON was decisively beaten in fierce fighting between Wigan and Preston by CROMWELL, which effectively destroyed the royalist–Scottish army (see SCOTTISH ARMY).

Preston, Thomas (1585–1655)

An exile in Europe who returned to his native Ireland in 1642 to take up a command in the IRISH REBELLION. He was a rival of OWEN ROE O'NEILL, and their disputes hampered the war effort. Defeated at NEW ROSS by ORMONDE in 1643, he commanded in Leinster in 1646 and was decisively beaten at DANGAN HILL in 1649 by MICHAEL JONES. He fled to Europe, where CHARLES II created him Viscount Tara.

Pride's Purge

Colonel THOMAS PRIDE (later a signatory of the king's death warrant), aided by LORD GREY OF GROBY and EDMUND LUDLOW MP, on 6 December 1648 turned away from the HOUSE OF COMMONS about 140 MPs considered antagonistic to the army. What remained of the Commons thereafter became known as the RUMP. This action put paid to further negotiations between PARLIAMENT and the king, and was a prelude to the latter's trial.

D. Underdown, *Pride's Purge* (London 1971).

Pride, Thomas (d. 1658)

The officer of the NEW MODEL ARMY who gave his name to the purge of PARLIAMENT in 1648 (see PRIDE'S PURGE). He served on the HIGH COURT OF JUSTICE and signed the king's death warrant in 1649.

Prisoners of war

Where the bulk of the rank and file of either army was concerned, neither king nor PARLIAMENT had the means or resources for keeping them prisoner once captured. They were ordinarily paroled to return home, minus their weapons, or merely released (as at LOSTWITHIEL). Officers of all ranks might be held until a suitable EXCHANGE OF PRISONERS could be arranged, and there is some evidence of ransoming of prisoners; in March 1644 LORD DIGBY had a royal grant entitling him to all ransoms of enemy prisoners within the area of PRINCE RUPERT's command. Parliament made an exception with officers and men captured in England from the forces in Ireland (see IRISH TROOPS).

Privy Council

A small group of advisors to the monarch which had evolved from the King's Council of the middle ages, and consisted of the chief officers of the state and royal household. It met according to the will of the reigning monarch, and had powers of arrest and imprisonment without trial. King CHARLES I had a separate and distinct Privy Council for his kingdom of Scotland. PARLIAMENT sought to regulate the powers of the Council in 1641, especially its judicial functions. The COUNCIL OF STATE may be seen as a replacement of the Privy Council.

Privy Seal Letters

The OXFORD PARLIAMENT in 1644 authorized the issue of Privy Seal Letters to leading ROYALIST gentry, to give them authority to raise and to forward to OXFORD specified sums of money – a variation on FORCED LOANS. In the event, half the income went to PRINCE RUPERT as Commander-in-Chief and President of Wales.

Proclamations

Essentially, public notices issued by the monarch which served to supplement statute law or remedy defects prior to new legislation. The COURT OF STAR CHAMBER was used to enforce proclamations by James I and by CHARLES I, and critics regarded this as an attack upon the Common Law. Proclamations bore some similarity to ORDINANCES, and were also resorted to by PARLIAMENT. On 6 June 1642 Parliament issued a proclamation arrogating to itself SOVEREIGNTY, arguing the king's unfitness to govern.

Propositions for Money and Plate

A scheme introduced by PARLIAMENT in June 1642 to raise finance for its war effort by subscription. The propositions were to be enforced by MPs in their localities, but the

response was slow. Local committees were established to proceed, but most money was actually spent in the localities themselves. See also ADVENTURERS.

Protestation of the Lords and Commons

Issued in May 1642, this combined announcement presented the view that princes (in this case CHARLES I) erred in believing that their kingdoms existed for them, rather than they for their kingdoms.

Protestation Returns

A national oath of loyalty, at first applied to MPs of the LONG PARLIAMENT in 1641, to maintain the king, PARLIAMENT and the Protestant religion. It was intended to isolate PAPISTS and MALIGNANTS, but many papists signed it anyway. A clergyman described it as a 'Covenant', and its similarity to the SCOTTISH NATIONAL COVENANT is clear. The signatures were collected on a parochial basis nationwide. The CLUBMEN of Wiltshire and Dorset in their declaration of 25 May 1645 showed similar sentiments, particularly anti-Catholicism, to those of the Protestation of 1641.

Prynne, William (1600–69)

A victim of the COURT OF STAR CHAMBER, whose ears were cut off in 1634 for his pamphlet *Histriomastix*, which vilified CHARLES I and his queen. The LONG PARLIAMENT in 1640 declared the sentence (and a second) illegal. An ERASTIAN, intolerant of EPISCOPACY, PRESBYTERIANISM and the INDEPENDENTS, Prynne was equally hostile to the NEW MODEL ARMY. His motion in the HOUSE OF COMMONS of 2 December 1648 to continue negotiations with the king, which passed by 129 to 83 votes, was a deliberate defiance of the army. The motion hastened PRIDE'S PURGE. An inveterate, articulate and prolific critic of the REPUBLIC and of CROMWELL, Prynne ushered in the restoration of CHARLES II with an eloquence that earned him the title 'the Cato of the age'.

Puritans and Puritanism

More properly described as an attitude of mind or an outlook than as a body of doctrine, Puritanism is a blanket term for extreme Protestants and may encapsulate PRESBYTERIANS and INDEPENDENTS. The emphasis was upon individual responsibility in worship, and opposition to ARMINIANISM and ROMAN CATHOLICISM. JOHN PYM in 1640 described the term Puritan as 'an odious and factious name' used to create social dissent. RICHARD BAXTER called them 'precisians, religious persons, that used to talk of God'. Puritanism was socially conservative and a reaction to disorder, real or perceived; hence its attacks upon customary observances and traditions popular with the common people. But it was also dynamically reforming in matters of ritual and worship, raising preaching and exposition of the scriptures above emphasis upon ritual and liturgy.

Putney Debates

Held in Putney Church, Surrey, in October and November 1647 to discuss the issues raised by the *AGREEMENT OF THE PEOPLE*. The records of the debates have been seen as revelatory of the radical and PURITAN thinking of the time. SIR THOMAS FAIRFAX absented himself, but CROMWELL chaired the debates and IRETON championed the anti-AGITATOR case. William Clarke took down the text of the discussions and transcribed them. The chief purpose of the debates seems to have been, from the point of view of GRANDEES like Cromwell, to preserve the unity of the NEW MODEL ARMY.

Pym, John (1584–1643)

Pym has since been described as 'the middle man', who 'walked alone [but] sometimes in conjunction with a few close allies'. He was nicknamed 'King Pym' by ROYALISTS, in derisive allusion to his signature 'Pym' on an order of PARLIAMENT of August 1641. (The king's signature was simply 'Charles', but others signed their full names.) MP for Tavistock in all Parliaments from 1625, his name was made in committee work where his endurance and anti-Catholicism marked him out, and his industrious attention to procedure and his resolute pursuit of STRAFFORD and LAUD gave him considerable, if not absolute, power over fellow MPs. Prominent in the drafting of the GRAND REMONSTRANCE, and one of the FIVE MEMBERS whom CHARLES I sought to arrest in 1642, Pym directed the early war effort of Parliament, and was behind the introduction of the EXCISE. He also urged the SOLEMN LEAGUE

AND COVENANT upon Parliament. His influence was at first partly dependent upon close allies in the HOUSE OF LORDS, but by 1642–3, and the departure of royalist MPs to join the king, his integrity was inviolate.

Q

Quarles, Francis (1592–1644)

Chronologer to the City of LONDON from 1638, three years after the publication of his famous book *Emblems*, which went into many editions. A ROYALIST, his 1644 TRACT *The Loyall Convert* attacked CROMWELL as a sacrilegious defacer of churches. In the course of the war many of his papers were wantonly destroyed.

Quarter and petty sessions

The JUSTICES OF THE PEACE met four times annually – in quarter sessions – at Epiphany, Easter, Trinity and Michaelmas. The justices heard presentments from a jury, and dealt with matters ranging from crimes to economic and social regulations and problems. From 1631 the royal Book of Orders required justices to meet monthly in petty sessions, and subjected these meetings to the overview of the judges of assize (see ASSIZES).

Queen's Pocket Pistol

A siege CANNON some 5,700 lb (2,586 kg) in weight firing a 36-lb (16.3-kg) ball. It was taken from the ROYALISTS 11 October 1643 outside HULL and, rechristened 'Sweet Lips', was used against NEWARK until recaptured by the royalists in March 1644. It was lost again at MARSTON MOOR in July, and the parliamentary forces carted it south to use against BASING HOUSE.

R

Raglan Castle

The palatial fortress of the Somerset family in South Wales, and base for their massive war effort on behalf of the king (see EARL OF WORCESTER and EARL OF GLAMORGAN.) It was besieged in the spring of 1646 and fell 19 August. PARLIAMENT ordered a day of thanksgiving upon news of its fall.

Rain(s)borough (Rainborow), Thomas (d. 1648)

A colonel in the NEW MODEL ARMY who, at the PUTNEY DEBATES, opposed both CROMWELL and IRETON. 'I do think', he said, 'that the poorest man in England is not at all bound in a strict sense to that government he hath not had a voice to put himself under'. A republican (see COMMON-WEALTHSMAN) of considerable charisma, his death on 29 October 1648 at Doncaster, contrived by ROYALISTS out of PONTEFRACT, was a relief to some of the New Model GRANDEES, but was very probably the result of a bungled kidnap attempt.

Rank and precedent in civilian life

England had a hierarchically structured society, dominated in terms of status and privilege (subject to the crown) by the peers or nobility (dukes, marquesses, earls, viscounts and lords). James I introduced the rank of baronet in 1611 to provide revenue from aspirants, and to bridge the gap between lords and knights, the next rung in the social ladder. Knights made on the field of battle, however, continued to enjoy precedence over baronets. Beneath the knight stood the esquire and then the gentleman, but in reality someone entitled to the rank of esquire (for example, the son of a peer) might well enjoy precedence over a knight or, indeed, a baronet.

Army command in 1642 reflected social rank as much as military skills (see MILITARY RANK AND PRECEDENCE): PARLIAMENT (with generals such as the EARLS OF ESSEX, STAMFORD and MANCHESTER) was as much concerned with social considerations as the king (with generals such as the EARLS OF NEWCASTLE and FORTHE and the MAR-QUESS OF HERTFORD). As the war progressed, social distinctions mattered less than military prowess, although that was often rewarded (on the king's side) by admission into the ranks of social and civilian importance. The SELF DENYING ORD-INANCE of 1645 did rid Parliament's armies of peer commanders, and they were replaced by men who belonged to the lower ranks of a clearly defined order of social precedence, and their politics reflected that.

Ranters

A small but vocal religious sect (see SECTARIES AND SEPARATISTS) whose beliefs enshrined ANTINOMIANISM and pantheism, and who denied the necessity of obedience to the laws of God. They were considered by some to be descendants (in doctrine) of the Familists, who laid emphasis on the teaching of 'love'. RICHARD BAXTER denounced their 'horrid oaths and curses, and blasphemy'. It is impossible to estimate their real numbers.

J. Friedman, *Blasphemy, Immorality and Anarchy: The Ranters and the English Revolution* (Ohio 1987).

Rathmines, Battle of (2 August 1649)

The scene in Ireland of a decisive defeat inflicted upon the Irish ROYALISTS of the EARLS OF ORMONDE and INCHIQUIN by MICHAEL JONES, which made Dublin secure. The battle provoked OWEN ROE O'NEILL to declare for King CHARLES II.

Reading

Important strategic town in Berkshire, situated between LONDON and OXFORD. Reading was seized for the king in November 1642 but surrendered to the EARL OF SUSSEX the following April. ROYALISTS reoccupied the town after the first BATTLE OF NEWBURY, but abandoned it again. The headquarters of the NEW MODEL ARMY removed to Reading in June 1647, and debates as to future actions took place there 15 July.

Recruiter MPs and elections

The term 'Recruiter' was applied by ROYALISTS to those elections held to replace members of the LONG PARLIAMENT who were with the king – to 'recruit' or make up the numbers. The elections were essential to maintain numbers in the HOUSE OF COMMONS. Among those elected on a Recruiter ticket were IRETON, LUDLOW, RAINBOROUGH and PRYNNE.

Red Hill, Battle of   See Isle of Anglesey

Red Marley, Battle of (4 August 1644)

ROYALISTS encamped around Red Marley in Gloucestershire were attacked by MASSEY before they could advance against GLOUCESTER, and were beaten in a running fight. The victory of the PARLIAMENTARIANS threw HEREFORD open to attack.

Red Men of the Dusk

A local and pejorative term for the ROYALIST soldiers of HEREFORD garrison. The original Red Men of the Dusk had been thieves and brigands in mid Wales in the Tudor period.

Reformadoes

A broad term applied to officers on full or half pay, lacking actual command of troops. In 1641 many reformadoes arrived in LONDON from the army sent against the Scots, and from them SIR THOMAS LUNSFORD formed a following for the king. During the civil war years, troops composed of reformadoes appeared on both sides.

Regicides

The 49 signatories of the death warrant of CHARLES I and the two executioners employed to do the job. ROYALIST vengeance-seekers applied the same term of opprobrium to functionaries of the HIGH COURT OF JUSTICE such as ISAAC DORISLAUS.

Religious toleration

One of the favourite themes of the demands of INDEPENDENTS in their struggle against PRESBYTERIANISM, but almost always and wholly dismissive of toleration for ROMAN CATHOLICS.

Reliquae Sacrae Carolinae

A compilation, in 1650, of various speeches, papers and letters of King CHARLES I together with the *EIKON BASILIKE*, put together to feed the wide demand for information respecting the dead king. It was part of the effective propaganda war waged by ROYALISTS against the COMMONWEALTH.

Remonstrance of the (New Model) Army of 16th November 1648

This document was drafted by IRETON at Windsor in the wake of meetings of the GENERAL COUNCIL OF THE ARMY, held in October and early November. The COUNCIL OF OFFICERS had hesitated at demands for the trial of the king, causing Ireton to seek friendly relations with the LEVELLERS at the NAGS HEAD TAVERN. The *Remonstrance* relied heavily upon arguments based upon the LAW OF NATURE and was accepted by SIR THOMAS FAIRFAX and the General Council for presentation to PARLIAMENT 20 November. Parliament postponed consideration of the 25,000-word document. See also REMONSTRANCES OF THE NEW MODEL ARMY.

Remonstrances of the New Model Army

Issued 23 June, 18 August, 14 November 1647 and 16 November 1648 (see REMONSTRANCE OF THE NEW MODEL ARMY OF 16TH NOVEMBER 1648). That of June 1647 sought a response to the DECLARATION (OF 14TH JUNE 1647), seeking the suspension of the ELEVEN MEMBERS. That of 18 August was issued by the GENERAL COUNCIL OF THE ARMY, seeking movement from the king on the HEADS OF THE PROPOSALS. The Committee of the COUNCIL OF WAR, headed by CROMWELL and IRETON, issued that of 14 November attacking 'new AGENTS' and LEVELLERS.

Remonstrants

Those COVENANTERS who, after the BATTLE OF DUNBAR, in 1650 opposed the alliance with CHARLES II on grounds of suspicion of his intent towards the Covenant. Their opponents were known as Resolutionists and were led by ARGYLE who, in the

COMMITTEE OF THE ESTATES, denounced the Remonstrants.

Republic

The English Republic was created by PARLIAMENT 19 May 1649, following the execution of the king and the abolition of monarchy and of the HOUSE OF LORDS. Contemporaries preferred the term COMMONWEALTH and republicans tended to be described as COMMONWEALTHSMEN.

Requests, Court of

A PREROGATIVE court known also as 'The Court of Poor Men's Cases', which had sat at Westminster since the early 16th century offering cheap and speedy redress. It was regarded with hostility by common lawyers, who saw it slip into disuse from 1641.

Ricraft, Josiah (d. *c*.1680)

A PRESBYTERIAN writer with ROYALIST leanings, who produced a eulogy of the EARL OF ESSEX entitled *A perfect List of the many Victories obtained (through the Blessing of God) by the Parliament's Forces under the Command of his Excellence the Earl of Essex* (1645). This coincided with Essex's fall and the SELF DENYING ORDINANCE. In 1646 he made up for that with a similar eulogy of SIR THOMAS FAIRFAX and the NEW MODEL ARMY. *A Survey of England's Champions and Truthe's Faithfull Patriots* was a 1647 picture-book of PARLIAMENTARIAN and Scottish commanders, with explanatory text.

Rinuccini, Giovanni Battista

The archbishop of Ferma and nuncio of Pope Innocent X (1644–55) to the IRISH CATHOLIC CONFEDERACY. Pope Innocent's accession to the papal throne encouraged CHARLES I to seek Irish help (see GLAMORGAN'S TREATIES), but Rinuccini was adamant in refusing to compromise the position of the Catholic hierarchy and church in Ireland.

Ripple Field, Battle of (13 April 1643)

Parliamentary troops under SIR WILLIAM WALLER advancing from Tewkesbury, Gloucestershire, were badly beaten by forces under PRINCE MAURICE. Waller's infantry were scattered and his prestige as a general was badly dented.

Rob-Carrier

A nickname applied to the ROYALIST commander HENRY HASTINGS and also to the royalist governors of LICHFIELD and DUDLEY, who robbed carriers or traders on the roads.

Robin Hog

A derisory nickname applied by the SCOTTISH ARMY to the countrymen of northern England, upon whom the Scots subsisted at FREE QUARTER.

Roman Catholics   See Catholic Recusants and Papists and Church Papists.

Root and Branch Movement

A negative and ERASTIAN pressure for the abolition of EPISCOPACY in the CHURCH OF ENGLAND. There seems to have been a widespread belief that the government of the church required reform in the face of LAUDIANISM, and the LONG PARLIAMENT both engineered and responded to county PETITIONS calling for the rooting out of episcopacy. The PURITAN clergy of LONDON sent up a petition in December 1640 to abolish episcopacy 'root and branch'. A BISHOPS' EXCLUSION bill had been thrown out of the HOUSE OF LORDS 8 June 1641. A bill to abolish episcopacy was introduced into the HOUSE OF COMMONS 27 May, and extended to Deans and Chapters. The motives of the Root and Branchers were suspect: DIGBY observed 'instead of every Bishop wee put downe in a Diocese wee shall set up a Pope in every Parish', and the division of opinion over the future of church government hardened attitudes prior to the civil war.

Rosworm, Joh(a)n (d. *c.*1660)

A professional military engineer from Germany who, in 1642, undertook to fortify and defend MANCHESTER against the ROYALIST forces of the EARL OF DERBY. He became engineer-general in England and Wales in 1651. His account of his service at Manchester, published in 1649, was essentially a complaint against his employers, but is useful.

Roundheads

A derogatory term applied to PARLIAMENTARIANS of all shades of opinion. The term first appears to have been used of LONDON apprentices rioting in 1641, but it was also, in 1642 at least, a nickname for a type of club used by soldiers of the POSSE COMITATUS. Certainly the term did not acquire the same degree of self-application as did 'CAVALIERS' for the ROYALISTS.

Roundway Down, Battle of (13 July 1643)

The army of SIR WILLIAM WALLER was drawn away from the siege of DEVIZES', Wiltshire, by advancing ROYALIST troops under HENRY WILMOT. In the ensuing battle Wilmot broke Waller's army comprehensively, killing 600 men and seeing the rest off. Waller's army never recovered.

Rous, Francis (1579–1659)

A long-serving MP sitting for Truro, Devonshire, in the SHORT and LONG PARLIAMENTS. He was half-brother to JOHN PYM, and had been a writer of semi-theologial TRACTS. He shifted towards the INDEPENDENTS by 1649 and was an advocate of a 'preaching ministry'. He was to be Speaker of the PARLIAMENT during the COMMONWEALTH.

Rowton Heath (Moor), Battle of (24 September 1645)

A series of running fights between ROYALIST cavalry under SIR MARMADUKE LANGDALE and PARLIAMENTARIAN troops under MICHAEL JONES beneath the walls of CHESTER, which the king had just entered with a relief army. Jones won a sweeping victory.

Royalists

Supporters, whether in arms or otherwise, of CHARLES I and CHARLES II. In 1648 some former PARLIAMENTA-RIANS, changing sides, became roya-lists, but it is impossible to define an ideology of royalism that would unite the various types of royalist.

Rudyerd, Sir Benjamin (1572–1658)

MP for Wilton in the SHORT and LONG PARLIAMENTS. In the 'ROOT AND BRANCH debates in 1641, Rudyerd neatly summed up the constitutional implication: 'a popular Democraticall Government of the Church [will not be] suitable or acceptable to a Royall, Monarchicall Government of the State'.

Rump (Parliament)

What was left of the membership of the HOUSE OF COMMONS after PRIDE'S PURGE in December 1648, and seen even by the initiators of the purge as a 'stop-gap' and 'mere expedient'. The average attendance was about 80 MPs present in the house at any one time. CROMWELL in 1653 rejected even those, but the Rump sat again May 1659. MONCK, in the prelimina-ries to the Restoration, recalled the members excluded in 1648.

Blair Worden, *The Rump Parliament* (Cambridge 1974).

Rupert, Prince (1619–82)

The second son of CHARLES I's sister Elizabeth, by her marriage to Frederick, Elector Palatine. PARLIA-MENTARIANS played upon his half-German origins. His youth was spent in war, and in 1642 he joined Charles I as General of the HORSE, winning the first ROYALIST victory at POWICK BRIDGE. His military achievements (CIRENCESTER, the taking of BRISTOL, CHALGROVE FIELD and NEWARK) created a legend around him of con-siderable potency. The relative ease of his relief march to YORK in 1644 was due to the fear of him felt by parlia-mentarian commanders en route. Defeated at MARSTON MOOR, he later tried to urge his uncle to make peace, was reluctant to fight at NASEBY and was cashiered after surrendering Bris-tol September 1645. From 1648 he commanded fleets against the PARLIA-MENT, although decisively defeated in 1650. He used innovatory tactics in the field, and introduced mining against besieged towns and for-tresses. A sober, gifted cavalry leader, if not a truly competent general.

Patrick Morrah, *Prince Rupert of the Rhine* (London 1976).

Rushworth, John (1612–90)

Although Rushworth has been called a historian, his *Historical Collections* (covering the years to 1648), published between 1659 and 1701, were in fact a PARLIAMENTARIAN work which NALSON sought to answer. Rushworth had been secretary to the NEW MODEL ARMY, and in 1650 to CROMWELL, so his 'Collections' are of enormous histor-ical importance, if selective.

Historical Collections of Private Passages of State, 7 vols. (1659–1701).

S

Sabbatarians

Sabbatarians believed that the observation of the Sabbath Day was
enjoined upon Christians, and in
1595 a PURITAN *Book of the Sabbath*
challenged the position of the episcopal (see EPISCOPACY) church. *THE
BOOK OF SPORTS* created a lot of
Sabbatarian opposition, notably in
the Traskites or Seventh Day Men.
They (and later Theophilus Bradburn
in his *Defence of the Sabbath Day*)
maintained the Lord's Day to be a
working day, and the seventh day,
Saturday, to be the day for observance. The COURT OF HIGH COMMIS-
SION forced a retraction.

Safety, Committee of

First established by PARLIAMENT 4
July 1642 to liaise between Parliament
and its army commanders, but superseded in 1643 by the COMMITTEE OF
BOTH KINGDOMS. In June 1647 a
Committee of Safety was revived to
defend 'Kingdom, Parliament and
the City' (of LONDON) against the
manoeuvres of the NEW MODEL ARMY.
In January 1648 a Committee for
Safety, evolving from the Committee
for Both Kingdoms, took over control
of the executive arm of GOVERNMENT.

Saffron Walden

Location in Essex for a series of
meetings of officers of the NEW
MODEL ARMY between 21 March and

16 May 1647. Parliamentary commissioners were present at deliberations
15 April. The size of the meeting on
15–16 May can be seen as a forerunner of the GENERAL COUNCIL OF THE
ARMY.

St Fagans, Battle of (8 May 1648)

Scene in Glamorganshire of the
defeat of the ROYALIST insurgent
forces of ROWLAND LAUGHARNE by
NEW MODEL ARMY units, which put
paid to the 1648 rising in South
Wales.

St John, Oliver (1598–1673)

An eminent lawyer, one of JOHN
HAMPDEN's counsel, and MP for
Totnes, Devonshire, in the LONG
PARLIAMENT. He led the attack on
SHIP MONEY and, as solicitor-general,
drew up the IMPEACHMENT of STRAF-
FORD. He sided with the NEW MODEL
ARMY in 1647 and became Chief
Justice of the COURT OF COMMON
PLEAS in 1648, but stood aloof from
the trial of the king in 1649, although
he had to publish a vindication of
himself. He was disabled from
holding office after 1660.

St Neots

ROYALIST fugitives out of Surrey took
refuge in St Neots Huntingdonshire,
in July 1648. They were attacked by

Colonel Adrian Scrope and dispersed 9 July. The royalist leader, the EARL OF HOLLAND, was taken.

rendezvous of mutinous LEVELLER troops on the eve of their march to BURFORD.

St Peter's Church

A public service at St Peter's Church, Paul's Wharf, LONDON, was broken up 9 September 1649 by NEW MODEL ARMY troops, upon report that the PRAYER BOOK was being used. The incident was highlighted in a TRACT, *An Appeal to Heaven*.

Saints

Speaking of the civil war, CROMWELL observed, 'Religion was not the thing at first contested for, but God brought it to that issue at last'. It became *the* issue, arguably, in the confrontation between the INDEPEN-DENTS and the orthodox PRESBYTER-IANS, turning upon the question of toleration (see RELIGIOUS TOLER-ATION) for 'tender consciences'. The idea of the 'saints', meaning the 'elect', was fundamental to CALVINIST theology. In civil war terms, the identification of the NEW MODEL ARMY with God's cause implied the equa-tion of the soldiery with the saints.

Salisbury

In early December 1644 the cathedral close of Salisbury, Wiltshire, was seized by troops under EDMUND LUDLOW and fortified. The royalist NORTHERN HORSE attacked and drove them out, and then established camp around Salisbury, prior to their relief ride to PONTEFRACT. In May 1649 Salisbury was the scene of the

Salisbury, William Cecil Earl of (1591–1668)

One of CHARLES I's PRIVY COUNCIL and a negotiator during the Treaty of Ripon in 1640, he abandoned the king in 1642 and went over to PARLIAMENT. According to one histor-ian it was a matter of conscience. The earl was present at the TREATY OF NEWPORT in 1648 but opposed the trial of the king. He served neverthe-less on the COUNCIL OF STATE and sat as an MP (for KING'S LYNN) in the HOUSE OF COMMONS after the abolition of the HOUSE OF LORDS.

Saltpetre-men

Functionaries of the royal monopoly on saltpetre (potassium nitrate), a crucial ingredient of gunpowder. They enjoyed unrestricted right of entry to all premises to excavate the material. This right was abolished in 1641 but Parliamentary attempts to resurrect it (balked in 1642 by SIMOND D'EWES) restored the powers of the saltpetre-men in 1643.

Savile, Thomas Lord (1590–1658)

Savile's role in the events of the years 1639–43 remains decidedly equivocal. He seems to have offered help to the Scots (see BISHOPS' WARS) on behalf of himself and other peers, including the EARL OF ESSEX, LORD BROOKE and the EARL OF WARWICK. Although a member of the PRIVY COUNCIL from 1641, the ROYALISTS mistrusted him, and the EARL OF NEWCASTLE arrested him and confined him in NEWARK. The king pardoned him in 1643 and created him Earl of Sussex in 1644, but in 1645, accused of treachery towards the king, he went over to the PARLIAMENT (whose protection had been offered him in 1642). Savile may have seen himself as a mediator, but his actions remain confused.

Saye and Sele, William Fiennes Viscount

Nicknamed 'Old Subtlety', Saye and Sele was a thorough-going ERASTIAN with a long history of opposition to the royal GOVERNMENT, such as his endorsement of the PETITION OF RIGHT. PRIVY COUNCILLOR and Master of the COURT OF WARDS AND LIVERIES in 1641, he supported the ROOT AND BRANCH MOVEMENT and the NINETEEN PROPOSITIONS of June 1642. He introduced into the HOUSE OF LORDS the ORDINANCE to set up the COMMITTEE OF BOTH KINGDOMS, and was critical in carrying the proposals for the NEW MODEL ARMY. Hostile to the INDEPEN-DENTS, Saye and Sele sought agreement with the king through the TREATY OF NEWPORT, and retired from public life after the king's execution, a convinced enemy of the REPUBLIC.

Scarborough Castle

A castle in Yorkshire, held for the PARLIAMENT from December 1642 by SIR HUGH CHOLMELEY, who then defected to the ROYALISTS in March 1643 and held the castle for them. Scarborough was besieged from mid 1644 until its surrender after fierce bombardment 22 July 1645. The parliamentarian commander MEL-DRUM was killed outside its walls. After MARSTON MOOR the EARL OF NEWCASTLE and his staff sailed from Scarborough to Hamburg. In 1648 the then governor, Colonel Boynton, declared for the king and the castle did not surrender until 19 December 1648.

Scarrifhollis, Battle of (June 1650)

The bishop of Clogher, Commander-in-Chief of the Irish ROYALIST forces after the death of OWEN ROE O'NEILL, was defeated at Scarrifhollis, County Donegal, near Letterkenny. The bishop himself was captured and hanged in Londonderry.

Scottish Affairs, Committee for (Also known as Goldsmiths Hall Committee)

The committee arose from the negotiations between PARLIAMENT and the Scots for a military alliance in 1643 (see SOLEMN LEAGUE AND COVE-NANT). Its task was to raise money to pay the Scots; those responsible for raising money were known as the Goldsmiths Hall Committee, and those for distributing the money as the Committee for Scottish Affairs. The Goldsmiths Hall Committee became merged in the COMMITTEE FOR COMPOUNDING WITH DELIN-QUENTS from 1644.

Scottish Army

When the Scottish army invaded northern England in January 1644, in line with the alliance mapped out in the SOLEMN LEAGUE AND COVENANT, it was 21,000 strong and commanded by the EARL OF LEVEN. It contributed materially to PARLIAMENT's eventual victory, although it was accused of dilatoriness by political enemies in Parliament and the NEW MODEL ARMY. The Scots quit England 30 January 1647, but in the spring there were plans to bring back 6,000 of them to tackle the New Model Army, which was seen as mutinous and rebellious. These came to nothing. The alliance between CHARLES I and the Scots split the Scottish forces, and a projected invasion force of 40,000 was never realized. The army fought under DAVID LESLIE with some flair in 1650 but was worsted at DUNBAR. In 1651, 13,000 strong and commanded by Leslie, it launched CHARLES II's invasion of England, which met with disaster at WORCESTER.

Scottish National Covenant

A highly organized but nevertheless spontaneous outburst of Scottish national feeling in the face of attempts by CHARLES I to impose church reforms of a LAUDIAN nature in Scotland. The Covenant was first subscribed in Edinburgh in 1638 by an assembly of noblemen, clergy and leading citizens, and then was distributed nationwide for support 'in defence of the true reformed religion and our liberties, laws and estates'. See also COVENANTS.

Scott, Thomas (d. 1660)

RECRUITER MP for Aylesbury, Buckinghamshire, from 1645. On 24 May 1648 he supported the VOTE OF NO ADDRESSES, saying '[the king] should be brought to his trial and drawn, hanged and quartered ... he being the only cause of all the bloodshed'. Scott signed the king's death warrant. He was seized in Brussels in 1660, and executed in England.

Seacroft Moor, Battle of (30 March 1643)

Conclusion in Yorkshire of a running fight between PARLIAMENTARIAN troops under FERDINANDO LORD FAIRFAX and ROYALISTS under GEORGE GORING, which ended with the complete destruction of the parliamentarian infantry.

Sectaries and Separatists

These terms were, like that of PURITAN, abusive labels flung at INDEPENDENTS of more or less exotic religious ideas by their enemies. The terms implied 'rebel', and hinted at dissolution and undermining of society.

Seekers

A PURITAN sect (see SECTARIES AND SEPARATISTS) later absorbed into the Quakers. According to RICHARD BAXTER they regarded the scriptures as 'uncertain', and therefore believed there was a need to 'seek' to find the true scriptures and ordinances for the ministry of the church.

Selby, Battle of (11 April 1644)

A decisive defeat was inflicted on the Yorkshire ROYALISTS commanded by JOHN BELASYSE, by forces under FERDINANDO LORD FAIRFAX and his son SIR THOMAS FAIRFAX. The battle opened the way to YORK, and forced the EARL OF NEWCASTLE to abandon his Durham campaign against the SCOTTISH ARMY.

Selden, John (1584–1654)

An eminent jurist, whose work *History of Tythes* (1617) was suppressed as offensive to the church. MP for OXFORD University in the LONG PARLIAMENT, Selden was involved in the IMPEACHMENT of WILLIAM LAUD. Between 1640 and 1642 he published *De Jure Naturali, Judicature in Parliament* and *Privileges of Baronage*. He served on the WESTMINSTER ASSEMBLY, but at the king's execution withdrew from public life. His secretary compiled the *Table Talk* which is easily the most accessible of Selden's thought.

Self Denying Ordinance

Dissatisfaction with the way in which the PARLIAMENT's war effort was being conducted led to the introduction on 9 December 1644, in the HOUSE OF COMMONS, of a bill to enact that 'no member of either House ... should during the war enjoy or execute any office or command, military or civil, and that an ordinance be brought in to that effect'.

The HOUSE OF LORDS hesitated, and modified the wording, and the ORDINANCE was passed 3 April 1645. It disposed at once of the EARLS OF ESSEX and MANCHESTER and prepared the way for the NEW MODEL ARMY. RECRUITER MPs were exempt from the ordinance.

Sequestration

PARLIAMENT, 27 March 1643, passed an ORDINANCE for the sequestration (seizure) of the estates of ROYALISTS, and the diversion of revenues therefrom to its war effort. The royalists, in a piecemeal fashion, followed a similar process in areas under their control. As early as December 1642 in Cornwall such a process was already under way, and Parliament merely systematized it. The king endeavoured to preserve to himself the power of sanctioning sequestrations, but in practice it fell to local initiative. See also COMMITTEE FOR COMPOUNDING WITH DELINQUENTS, COMMITTEE FOR ADVANCE OF MONEY and COMMITTEE FOR SEQUESTRATIONS.

Sequestrations, Committee for

Set up by PARLIAMENT to implement the provisions of its ordinance of March 1643 (see SEQUESTRATION), with county subcommittees acting upon information. From a sequestered estate one fifth was set aside for the family support of the DELINQUENT concerned, or one third if the owner was a CATHOLIC RECUSANT not involved in support of the king. The system encouraged venality and deceit, particularly in the use of informers.

Sexby, Edward (d. 1658)

An officer of the NEW MODEL ARMY serving under CROMWELL who imbibed LEVELLER ideas during the crises of 1647. Cashiered in 1651, he became implicated in ROYALIST plots against the life of Cromwell, and was author of *Killing No Murder*, which appeared in 1657. He died in gaol the same year.

Shepherd, Thomas

An AGITATOR from the NEW MODEL ARMY. Shepherd, EDWARD SEXBY and WILLIAM ALLEN presented, 29 April 1647, a letter to the HOUSE OF COMMONS listing the grievances of the army.

Sherburn In Elmet, Battles of (15 October 1645)

The NORTHERN HORSE, commanded by LORD DIGBY, surprised the town of Sherburn, Yorkshire, and captured it and its parliamentary garrison, but were themselves attacked and driven out by fresh troops under Colonel Copley.

Sheriff

An office of considerable antiquity which by the 17th century, in response to changes in administration of counties, had lost much prestige and power. The sheriff was chosen by central government and held office for a year. The policies of CHARLES I's PERSONAL RULE revitalized the post, especially in the collection of SHIP MONEY where the failure to meet prescribed income fell upon the sheriff himself. Thus many opposed to Ship Money nevertheless, as sheriffs, enforced its collection. The COMMISSION OF ARRAY was issued to sheriffs rather than to LORDS LIEUTENANT and so gave to the office-holders a crucial role in the development of ROYALIST forces.

Sheringham, Robert (1602–78)

A Latin and Hebraic scholar of OXFORD University who championed the ROYALIST cause. His *The King's Supremacy Asserted* was a direct response to the TREATISE OF MONARCHY, and denounced mixed monarchy as an absurdity.

Ship Money

Conceived of originally as an occasional tax imposed upon ports and coastal counties to finance shipping in time of emergency. Plans for naval rearmament in 1634 led CHARLES I to extend the levy to all counties in 1635, and by 1637 it had become a semi-permanent source of revenue. Although an equitable and efficient tax (the means of collection were later copied by PARLIAMENT during the civil war – see ASSESSMENTS), opponents of the royal government seized upon it as a major issue. The HAMPDEN CASE brought against a defaulter (see JOHN HAMPDEN) went in the king's favour, seven of twelve judges declaring for the king, but the narrowness of the judgement inspired opponents further. The LONG PARLIAMENT abolished Ship Money 5 July 1641, but the efficiency of its collection (producing around 90 per cent of the anticipated sums) recommended revitalization of the machinery of collection when it was found necessary to finance a war effort against the king.

Short Parliament

The first PARLIAMENT to meet since 1628–9. Writs to summon it went out in March 1640, a course forced upon the king by the BISHOPS' WARS. It met 13 April, resisted demands for confirming TUNNAGE AND POUNDAGE back to 1625 (the king had collected that levy without parliamentary consent), and sought to press home the grievances felt against royal GOVERNMENT. CHARLES I dissolved the Parliament 5 May.

Shrawardine Castle

A castle in Shropshire garrisoned for the king in 1644 by SIR WILLIAM VAUGHAN, and a base for operations against local PARLIAMENTARIANS. The castle fell after a long siege 29 June 1645.

Shrewsbury

CHARLES I came to Shrewsbury, Shropshire in September 1642, and it became the major ROYALIST base on the Welsh border, firmly in the hands of royalist sympathizers. PRINCE RUPERT used it as an operational base from 1644. The town fell 22 February 1645. Its loss was a critical blow to royalist morale and to communications down the border, and may have been due to internal treachery.

Skippon, Philip (d. 1660)

Skippon had experience of soldiering in Europe when appointed commander of the TRAINED BANDS in LONDON, 1642. He turned back the ROYALIST advance on London at TURNHAM GREEN. An active and competent field commander under the EARL OF ESSEX, he was crucial in bringing Essex's infantry into the NEW MODEL ARMY in 1645. As RECRUITER MP for Barnstaple, Devonshire, Skippon sided with the AGITATORS but otherwise adopted a moderate stance. He was a soldier's soldier, trusted by CROMWELL and by CHARLES II.

Skipton Castle

A castle in Yorkshire garrisoned for the king in 1642 by the EARL OF CUMBERLAND, and held by Sir John Mallory until 21 December 1645, when it fell to JOHN LAMBERT.

Slingsby, Sir Henry (1602–58)

A ROYALIST infantry colonel from 1642, having quit the PARLIAMENT where he sat as MP for Knaresborough, Yorkshire. He compiled a self-effacing 'diary' of events between 1642 and 1646 which he witnessed at first hand. Refusing to come to terms with the victorious Parliament, he was eventually (1658) tried on a trumped-up charge and executed in London.

D. Parsons (ed.), *The Diary of Sir Henry Slingsby* (London 1836).

Smith, John (d. 1644)

A ROYALIST colonel and most probably the man who retrieved the royal standard when it was captured at EDGEHILL in October 1642. He was knighted, and later killed in action at ALRESFORD.

Socinianism

An Italian anti-trinitarian doctrine that took root in Poland, where Faustus Socinus developed the writings of his uncle Laelius Socinus, early in the 16th century. Calvin himself had clashed with them (see CALVINISM). They termed themselves 'Unitarians', as believing God was one person and not a trinity, and a *Catechism or Confession of the Unitarians* appeared in England in 1609 with a dedication to James I. Two Socinians were burnt in 1612 for heresy – denial of God's divinity – but a small congregation developed during the 1640s under JOHN BIDDLE in Gloucestershire. It came to very little.

Solemn League and Covenant

The expression of the alliance formed between PARLIAMENT and the Scottish COVENANTERS in September 1643 in face of doubts as to Parliament's ability to win the civil war single-handed. On 5 February 1644 an ORDINANCE imposed the League and Covenant upon everyone in England and Wales, and taking of the Covenant became essential for holding command under the Parliament. Parliament had agreed to pay to the Scots £30,000 a month as subsidy and to enforce PRESBYTERIANISM upon England and Wales. On 19 August 1645 the first Ordinance to enforce that provision was passed, with another 14 March 1646. The INDEPENDENTS, the NEW MODEL ARMY and CHARLES I's successful attempts to win the Scots over to his side by 1648 effectively put paid to wholesale Presbyterianism south of the Anglo-Scottish border.

Sourton Down, Battle of (25–6 April 1643)

ROYALIST forces under HOPTON were defeated as they advanced on Okehampton, Devonshire, although after the fighting both sides withdrew.

Sovereignty

Perhaps the most crucial constitutional issue at stake in the civil war. The PARLIAMENTARIAN Henry Ludlow said in the HOUSE OF COMMONS in February 1642 that 'the king is derivative from the parliament and not the parliament from the king'. The question of where ultimate authority lay was already an issue by 1629, and only the defeat and execution of the king in 1649 appeared to resolve the matter. Nevertheless, the establishment of the republic or COMMONWEALTH was a poor alternative to the more widely desired 'mixed' or 'limited' monarchy that even some ROYALIST thinkers leaned towards. The king's resolution in the matter of his PREROGATIVE was partly the nature of the man, and partly a concern to pass on intact to his heir that which he had come by likewise intact. See also KING AND PARLIAMENT.

Spelman, Sir John (1594–1643)

A noted writer and political theorist who wrote on behalf of the king in 1642, arguing that English GOVERNMENT was, anyway, a 'limited' monarchy where the king was the pre-eminent partner. It was, Spelman wrote, 'a body mysticall governed by one man'.

Sprigg(e), Joshua (1618–84)

Compiled the eulogistic *Anglia Rediviva* (1647) chronicling the successes of the NEW MODEL ARMY under SIR THOMAS FAIRFAX, whom, clearly, he fiercely admired, and under whom he served. He was opposed, like his master, to the king's execution in 1649.

Anglia Rediviva, editions 1647, Oxford 1854, and 1984.

Stamford, Henry Grey Earl of (1599–1673)

Commanded for PARLIAMENT in the west country from 1642, subordinated to the EARL OF ESSEX, and was beaten at STRATTON in 1643. He surrendered EXETER to PRINCE MAURICE the same year. Articles of IMPEACHMENT were moved against

him in 1645 for a violent assault on SIR ARTHUR HASELRIG.

Stapleton (Stapilton), Sir Philip (1603–47)

MP for Boroughbridge, Yorkshire, in the LONG PARLIAMENT and served from 1642 in the army of the EARL OF ESSEX as well as on the COMMITTEE OF SAFETY. He later sat upon the COMMITTEE OF BOTH KINGDOMS. He was opposed to the SELF DENYING ORDINANCE and was one of the ELEVEN MEMBERS against whom the army moved in 1647.

Star Chamber, Court of

A court of law taking its name from the Star Chamber at Westminster, where it convened. The powers and jurisdictions of the court made it swift and effective in hearing petitions and in trying offences against the crown. It comprised a' Privy Councillors (see PRIVY COUNCIL), the Lord Chief Justice of the COURT OF KING'S BENCH, the Chief Justice of the COURT OF COMMON PLEAS and the Attorney General, who acted as the crown's representative. The LONG PARLIAMENT saw it as an instrument used by CHARLES I to harry his enemies, and abolished it in 1640.

Stow-on-the-Wold, Battle of (23 March 1646)

The last engagement of the ROYALIST army under Lord Astley (see SIR JACOB ASTLEY), which was attacked at Stow, Gloucestershire, by a vastly superior NEW MODEL ARMY. Bitter fighting forced Astley to surrender.

Stow was also the place where, 8 May 1645, the king's army was split into two parts, one to go with GEORGE GORING into the west country, the rest to follow the king. It was a serious weakening of the field army a little more than a month before NASEBY.

Strafford, Thomas Wentworth Earl of (1593–1641)

The first great victim of the LONG PARLIAMENT, largely for the reason that he had been the foremost and, for a time, the most influential of the advisors of CHARLES I. President of the COUNCIL OF THE NORTH and then Lord Deputy in Ireland, Strafford fell because of his failure to strike first against his political enemies in PARLIAMENT, who proceeded with his IMPEACHMENT on the grounds that he intended to create arbitrary GOVERNMENT by introducing an Irish army into England to serve the king. Condemned to die, Strafford failed to incite the king to exercise his power of veto, and so went to his death – 'Put not your trust in princes' was his resigned response to the royal inaction.

C.V. Wedgwood, *Thomas Wentworth First earl of Strafford: A Revaluation* (London 1961).

Stratford-upon-Avon

A town in Warwickshire of strategic importance, on road routes from Wales to GLOUCESTER and OXFORD. PARLIAMENTARIAN forces under LORD BROOKE took it 25 February 1642 and it remained in their hands.

Stratton, Battle of (15 May 1643)

ROYALISTS commanded by HOPTON halted and threw back, at Stratton, a PARLIAMENTARIAN advance into Cornwall, inflicting heavy losses.

Strode, William (1599–1645)

MP in the LONG PARLIAMENT, known as 'the martyr' for his previous tribulations under the COURT OF STAR CHAMBER. He proceeded vigorously against STRAFFORD in 1641, and was one of the FIVE MEMBERS against whom CHARLES I moved in 1642.

Sturminster Newton, Battle of (29 June 1645)

Scene in Dorset of an encounter between Dorset CLUBMEN, with ROYALIST assistance, and PARLIAMENTARIAN troops under EDWARD MASSEY, who retreated.

Subsidies

Grants made to the crown by PARLIAMENT over and above existing sources of revenue. CHARLES I was granted a subsidy of 4s. 8d. in the pound on real property and 2s. 8d. on personal property, for example. ROMAN CATHOLICS had to pay double.

Suckling, Sir John (1609–42)

CAVALIER POET, playwright, ROYALIST and courtier, reputedly (for he was known as a gamester) inventor of the game of cribbage. His play *The Discontented Colonel* dealt with the unrest in Scotland in 1640. Certainly implicated in the first of the ARMY PLOTS if not its contriver, he fled precipitately to Europe, where he may have committed suicide.

Symonds, Richard (1617–92)

A ROYALIST soldier and an inveterate observer and antiquary. He kept a diary of events in which he was involved that remains a useful source for the study of the royalist war effort.

C.E. Long (ed.), *The Diary of the Marches of the Royal Army During the Great Civil War kept by Richard Symonds* (Camden Society 1859).

T

Tables

An association of four committees (of the nobility, clergy, gentry and burgesses of Scotland) formed in 1637, and from whose deliberations emerged the SCOTTISH NATIONAL COVENANT. The members of the Tables were representatives of regions of the country based upon local PRESBYTERIAN church organization.

Taking the Accounts of the Kingdom, Committee for

A committee of PARLIAMENT formed 22 February 1644, and consisting of 25 members. Their exclusive concern lay with the activities of persons collecting and handling revenues due to the Parliament, from whatever source. From 1645 various subcommittees were established answerable to the main body.

Tate, Zouch (1606–50)

MP and political ally of CROMWELL who moved the SELF DENYING ORDINANCE in the HOUSE OF COMMONS.

Taunton

Held by the ROYALISTS from 5 June 1643, Taunton, Somerset, fell unexpectedly 10 July 1644. Repeated attempts to recapture it failed, and 8 May 1645 royalists under SIR RICHARD GRENVILLE stormed it. They withdrew upon the approach of a relief column, and a subsequent attempt on the town by GEORGE GORING failed as well.

Taxation   See Assessments, Excise and Subsidies

Taylor, Jeremy (1613–67)

A notable ROYALIST divine, sometime chaplain to WILLIAM LAUD and to CHARLES I. He was taken prisoner in South Wales in 1645. In seclusion he produced the devotional manuals *Holy Living* and *Holy Dying* in 1650 and 1651. Charles I gave to Taylor his watch and jewels shortly before his execution in 1649.

Taylor, John (1580–1653)

Nicknamed the 'water poet' in reference to his career as a Thames waterman. He wrote vigorously in the interests of King CHARLES I. In 1645 his *The General Complaint of the … oppressed distressed Commons of England … Crying out upon the Tyranny of the perpetuall Parliament at Westminster* condemned unwarranted change – 'the nature of an Englishman is, not to knowe when things are well'. In August 1649 a warrant was issued to seize his books and papers by the COUNCIL OF STATE, which had detected him in correspondence with ROYALIST exiles.

Ten Propositions

Drafted by JOHN PYM and passed by the HOUSE OF COMMONS 24 June 1641, these were an attempt to dissuade CHARLES I from journeying to Scotland. They failed, but represented another attack upon his freedom of manoeuvre.

Thomason, George (d. 1666)

A London bookseller who kept examples of all TRACTS and other publications that came his way during the civil war years. These are now intact in the British Library, and the Thomason Collection is the largest and most important of its kind. See also HAILSTONE TRACTS.

Thompson, ('Captain') William

A leading figure in the LEVELLER movement and the mutinies of May 1649. His writings included *England's Standard Advanced* (1649) and *England's Freedom, Soldiers' Rights* (1647), the latter inspired by the execution of RICHARD ARNOLD. Thompson was killed resisting arrest at Wellingborough, Northamptonshire.

Thriplow Heath

Scene in Cambridgeshire of the rendezvous of the NEW MODEL ARMY in June 1647.

Thurloe, John (1616–68)

Known as CROMWELL's master-spy. The civil servant's career that he pursued under the COMMONWEALTH began in 1652 when he became secretary to the COUNCIL OF STATE. He was a protégé of OLIVER ST JOHN. The collection of his *State Papers* (published in 1742) is important.

D.L. Hobman, *Cromwell's Master-Spy* (London 1961).

Tippermuir, Battle of (1 September 1644)

Scene in Scotland of a decisive victory by MONTROSE over a COVENANTER army more than twice as numerous as his own.

Tonbridge, Battle of (23 July 1643)

The last attempt by ROYALIST sympathizers in Kent to turn the county against PARLIAMENT was broken at Tonbridge after failure by the royalists to hold Sevenoaks.

Torrington, Battle of (16 February 1646)

Hopton, taking over command of ROYALIST forces previously under GEORGE GORING, occupied Torrington, Devonshire, to try to relieve pressure on EXETER, which was under siege. The NEW MODEL ARMY attacked Torrington and, despite losses, scattered the royalists.

Tracts

Unlike NEWSBOOKS, these were often the polemical offerings of individuals (see, for example, JOHN LILBURNE and GERRARD WINSTANLEY), printed cheaply and as often as not given away rather than sold. They were not purely religious by any means: woodcuts from them often adorned the walls of public houses.

Trained bands

Accurately described by LORD CAPEL as 'soldiers of place', the trained bands were a form of citizenry in arms organized on a county basis and controlled by the LORDS LIEUTENANT of counties. They differed from the POSSE COMITATUS in that only men of standing were eligible to serve (which omitted ROMAN CATHOLICS). The outbreak of civil war obliged both sides to try to rely upon such bands as they could raise, but the king rapidly disarmed many of them in favour of volunteer regiments. See also COMMISSIONS OF ARRAY and MILITIA ORDINANCE.

Trapham, Thomas

Surgeon to OLIVER CROMWELL, Trapham embalmed the body of CHARLES I after execution on 30 January 1649, and sewed back the severed head.

Treason Act

On 14 May 1649 PARLIAMENT, by act, transferred to itself those protections against treason which had been enjoyed by the (now abolished) monarchy, adding the clause that civilian incitement to mutiny in the army was also treason. That clause reflected both general insecurity and a response to renewed LEVELLER agitation.

Treatise of Monarchy, A

An important work of 1643 by PHILIP HUNTON, a PRESBYTERIAN, who argued for limited and mixed monarchy, saying that the sovereign power of the monarch (legislative authority) could not be exercised independently of PARLIAMENT. His views, more or less the opposite of those of THOMAS HOBBES, expressed the moderate parliamentarian concept of 'corporate SOVEREIGNTY'. He was answered by HENRY FERNE, SIR ROBERT FILMER and ROBERT SHERINGHAM's *The King's Supremacy Asserted*.

Tresillian Bridge

On 10 March 1646 HOPTON agreed at Tresillian Bridge, Cornwall, to the surrender of his army and to the cessation of hostilities. Talks continued at nearby Truro until 21 March.

Trial of Charles I

Commenced 21 January 1649 before the HIGH COURT OF JUSTICE convened for the purpose. CHARLES I chose to defend himself, but the sentence of death passed 26 January was a foregone conclusion. His execution, 30 January, was postponed to 2 p.m. in order that the RUMP might have time to pass an ACT abolishing the succession.

Triennial Act

A measure, proposed by the HOUSE OF COMMONS and consented to by

CHARLES I, to ensure a parliamentary sitting of at least 50 days every three years. The king regarded it as contrary to his PREROGATIVE, and it was intended as a direct restraint upon royal GOVERNMENT. It was not resorted to until 1660 and was repealed in 1664.

Tuam, John Maxwell Archbishop of (1590–1647)

A Scottish episcopalian and advisor to WILLIAM LAUD in the 1630s who, as bishop of Ross, introduced the new liturgy into his own services 1637–8. Driven from Scotland, in 1640 he became bishop of Killala in Ireland, but was forced from there by the IRISH REBELLION, returning to Dublin in 1645 as archbishop of Tuam. His more important writings were *Episcopacy not Abjured in his Majesties realm of Scotland* (1641) and *Sacro-Sancta Regum Majestas: or, the Sacred and Royall Prerogative of Christian Kings* (1644) which attacked theories of consent as legitimizing political power. Maxwell appears to have died of shock in 1647 after CHARLES I was handed over to the PARLIAMENT by the Scots.

Tullie, Isaac

A soldier in the ROYALIST garrison of CARLISLE and author of a *Narrative of the Siege*, first published in book form in 1840. It bears comparison with the royalist NATHAN DRAKE's similar account of the sieges of PONTEFRACT Castle, as strongly atmospheric of life under siege.

Tunnage (tonnage) and poundage

This source of royal revenue arose from two distinct SUBSIDIES, which by the late 14th century were treated as one and granted by PARLIAMENT to the crown. They were, respectively, a tax upon wine and a custom duty on imports and exports. In 1625 Parliament refused to make the conventional grant for life, but CHARLES I levied them anyway. They were given a statutory basis in 1641 but made subject to frequent parliamentary authorization.

Turnham Green, Battle of (13 November 1642)

Although not strictly a battle, this confrontation in Middlesex between the ROYALIST army and the TRAINED BANDS of LONDON under PHILIP SKIPPON was a major setback for the royalists, who had just taken BRENTFORD. They withdrew to Hounslow after a day of waiting for action.

Twysden, Sir Roger (1597–1672)

MP for Kent in the SHORT PARLIAMENT. He was a moderate ROYALIST and antiquary who fell foul of the HOUSE OF COMMONS in 1642 for signing the KENTISH PETITION (see also SIR EDWARD DERING) and was summoned before the House as a DELINQUENT. His *Historiae Anglicanae Scriptores Decem* (1652) was a major contribution to the study of the middle ages.

Tyldesley, Sir Thomas (1596–1651)

A ROMAN CATHOLIC and the backbone of ROYALIST activity in Lancashire in 1642 – 'a man much esteemed in the country', 'a noble generous minded gentleman', according to contemporary observation. He fought long and hard in all theatres of the civil war, refused to seek his COMPOSITION, was captured in arms in 1648 (see SECOND CIVIL WAR) and was shot dead at WIGAN LANE in 1651.

Tynemouth Castle

An important outlying garrison of NEWCASTLE UPON TYNE in Northumberland from 1642 to 1644, Tynemouth was thereafter garrisoned by parliamentary troops. In 1648 the PARLIAMENTARIAN governor, Henry Lilburne, declared for the king. SIR ARTHUR HASELRIG stormed Tynemouth and killed Henry Lilburne and most of his men.

U

Unitarianism   See Socinianism.

Upton upon Severn, Battle of

An engagement fought in Worcestershire on the eve of the BATTLE OF WORCESTER (3 September 1651), by which CROMWELL gained access to the west bank of the Severn. The ROYALIST commander, EDWARD MASSEY, was taken prisoner.

Urry (Hurry), Sir John (d. 1650)

A Scottish professional soldier. He was behind the revelation of the INCIDENT in 1641, fought for PARLIAMENT, went over to the king in 1643 and became Major General under PRINCE RUPERT. After MARSTON MOOR he defected to the Parliament, went to Scotland and fought against MONTROSE, but was defeated at AULDEARN. Taking the king's side again, he was captured in 1650 and executed in EDINBURGH by the COVENANTERS.

Ussher, James   See Armagh, Archbishop of

Uxbridge Propositions

From January to 22 February 1645 ROYALIST and PARLIAMENTARIAN commissioners met at Uxbridge to discuss peace, on terms largely Scottish in origin. The stumbling blocks remained the proscription of leading royalists, the requirement that the king take the SOLEMN LEAGUE AND COVENANT and the introduction of PRESBYTERIANISM. The talks foundered.

V

Vane, Sir Henry (the younger) (1613–62)

Of PURITAN persuasion, and governor of Massachusetts 1636–7. MP for HULL in the LONG PARLIAMENT, he used his father's private papers to bring down STRAFFORD (Vane's father, as Secretary of State, had access to the private correspondence of the king). He was prominent in the talks leading to the SOLEMN LEAGUE AND CONVENANT and from 1643 was for a time the most influential MP in the HOUSE OF COMMONS, but his sympathies were not with the PRESBYTERIANS, nor with the LEVELLERS. He dissociated himself from the TRIAL OF CHARLES I but flourished in affairs of state during the COMMONWEALTH. He was executed in 1662.

J.K. Adamson and H.F. Folland, *Sir Harry Vane* (London 1973).
V.A. Rowe, *Sir Henry Vane the Younger* (London 1970).

Vaughan, Sir William (d. 1649)

Returned from service in Ireland against the Irish rebels (see IRISH REBELLION) to serve the king. In 1644, as governor of SHRAWARDINE CASTLE, he earned the doubtful nickname 'The Devil of Shrawardine'. In 1648 he joined the ROYALIST forces in Ireland and was killed fighting at RATHMINES in 1649.

Veritie Victor

Pseudonym of the radical pamphleteer JOHN JUBBES, adopted briefly in 1648.

Verney, Sir Edmund (1590–1642)

MP for Chipping Wycombe in the LONG PARLIAMENT and associated with opposition to the court, but died as the royal standard bearer at the BATTLE OF EDGEHILL (1642). His son, also Edmund, was killed during the massacre at DROGHEDA in 1649.

Vicars, John (1580–1652)

A firm PRESBYTERIAN and critic of the INDEPENDENTS. His chronicle of the course of the FIRST CIVIL WAR, known popularly as *Parliamentary Chronicles*, assiduously sought to demonstrate the intervention of God as crucial to PARLIAMENTARIAN success. The first part, *Jehovah Jireh*, was published in 1644.

Vote of No Addresses

At the PUTNEY DEBATES, November 1647, THOMAS RAINSBOROUGH secured a vote against further talks with the king. This followed an unsuccessful attempt to move such a bill in the HOUSE OF COMMONS in September. On 3 January 1648 the Commons voted 191 to 42 against further addresses to the king, with which the HOUSE OF LORDS concurred, in the light of CHARLES I's alliance with the Scots. This vote notwithstanding, in May 1648 the Commons voted to reopen talks on the basis of the FOUR BILLS, and the Vote was rescinded 24 August 1648.

W

Wakefield, Battle of (21 May 1643)

The capture of Wakefield by SIR THOMAS FAIRFAX was the result of a desperate surprise attack which he launched against the ROYALIST-held town in response to pressure from neighbouring areas. The royalist cavalry commander GEORGE GORING was taken prisoner.

Walker, Clement (d. 1651)

A committed PRESBYTERIAN and MP for Wells, Somerset, from 1645. Expelled at PRIDE'S PURGE, his denunciation of the INDEPENDENTS, *History of Independency* (published in three parts between 1648 and 1651), led to his imprisonment, and his death in prison.

Walker, Sir Edward (1612–77)

Secretary at War to CHARLES I and to the king's PRIVY COUNCIL from 1644, serving later in a similar capacity to CHARLES II in exile. His *Historical Discourses Upon Several Occasions* (published in 1705) were less memoirs than informed commentary upon the events of the civil war years, with narratives.

Waller, Sir Hardress (1604–66)

A New English (see OLD ENGLISH AND NEW ENGLISH) landowner in Ireland and commander against the rebels there from 1641. He subsequently fought in England for PARLIAMENT from 1645, sat upon the HIGH COURT OF JUSTICE and signed the king's death warrant, and was imprisoned for life in 1660.

Waller, Sir William (1597–1668)

MP for Andover, Hampshire, in the LONG PARLIAMENT, a colonel under the EARL OF ESSEX for the PARLIAMENT and, from late 1642, architect of a series of important triumphs in the south and south-west that earned him the nickname of William the Conqueror. He was stopped decisively at ROUNDWAY DOWN by HENRY WILMOT. The SELF DENYING ORDINANCE put an end to his military career. A member of the COMMITTEE FOR BOTH KINGDOMS and supporter of the SOLEMN LEAGUE AND COVENANT, Waller rapidly fell foul of the NEW MODEL ARMY, was one of the ELEVEN MEMBERS and was gaoled for three years after PRIDE'S PURGE. Waller wrote his own *Vindication*, first published in 1793.

Waller's Plot

This plot, to betray LONDON to CHARLES I in May 1643, centred upon Edmund Waller (1606–87), a poet and MP for St Ives, Huntingdonshire, in the LONG PARLIAMENT. Such as the plot was, Waller himself betrayed it. He was expelled from the HOUSE OF

COMMONS, gaoled, and then banished. CROMWELL arranged his return in 1650, whereupon he became an enthusiastic supporter of the regime. His only consistent stance was as a promoter of RELIGIOUS TOLERATION.

Walwyn, William

A convinced LEVELLER and prolific pamphleteer, with a masterly use of irony in his work. He was prominent in the drafting of the *AGREEMENT OF THE PEOPLE* and also in inciting the NEW MODEL ARMY to mutiny against the GRANDEES, for which he was arrested in March 1649. There followed a flurry of publications by Walwyn, JOHN LILBURNE and others justifying their political positions, and he was released at the end of the year and disappeared from public life. He championed the causes of RELIGIOUS TOLERATION and the human rights of Irishmen, the latter certainly unpopular in England in the 1640s.

Wardour Castle

A castle in Wiltshire held for the king by less than 30 men during a siege of April–8 May 1643, which fell when mined. It fell again in the same way to the ROYALISTS in February 1644 when EDMUND LUDLOW surrendered.

Wards and Liveries, Court of

A court developed in the 16th century to enforce the rights of the crown against heirs of lands held in chief of (directly from) the crown. The Master of the Court (LORD SAYE AND SELE 1641–6) was also a Privy Councillor (see PRIVY COUNCIL), and permanent officers of the court, the 'feodaries', were appointed in every county. PARLIAMENT maintained the court until 1646 as a source of revenue, and a rival court was set up in OXFORD by the king.

Ware Mutiny   See Corkbush Field

Warwick Castle

A major base in Warwickshire for PARLIAMENTARIAN operations in the west midlands, originally garrisoned by LORD BROOKE. It endured a brief siege by the ROYALISTS under the Earl of Northampton.

Warwick, Philip (1609–83)

Sat in the LONG PARLIAMENT as MP for Radnor, where he opposed the ATTAINDER of STRAFFORD, and from which he was expelled in 1644. He served in the OXFORD PARLIAMENT and was secretary to CHARLES I in 1647 and 1648. His valuable *Memoires* were published in 1701.

Warwick, Robert Rich Earl of (1587–1658)

A powerful, influential peer with maritime and colonial interests in America, a convinced PURITAN and patron of CROMWELL, for whose meteoric rise Warwick was largely responsible. Lord High Admiral for the PARLIAMENT from 1642, he resigned 28 April 1645 in the wake of the

SELF DENYING ORDINANCE, when the admiralship was put into commission. Warwick was recalled in 1648 when the NAVY threatened to turn ROYALIST, but lost place and influence after 1649.

Waterford

A major ROYALIST stronghold in Ireland against which CROMWELL marched in November 1649, but which had to be blockaded until August 1650, when it finally surrendered to IRETON.

Western Association

Formed 11 February 1643 out of Gloucestershire, Wiltshire and Somerset (see COUNTY ASSOCIATIONS). The army of the association, commanded by EDWARD MASSEY, survived the creation of the NEW MODEL ARMY and was demobilized in October 1946. See also NORTHERN ASSOCIATION.

Westminster and Westminster Palace

The permanent seat of GOVERNMENT in England at the time of the civil war, but no longer a royal palace (see WHITEHALL). The HOUSE OF COMMONS met in St Stephen's Chapel and the law courts met in Westminster Hall, where CHARLES I was tried in 1649.

Westminster Assembly of Divines

The idea for such a group to determine the future of the CHURCH OF ENGLAND was first mooted in 1641.

The assembly set up in 1643 (its first meeting was 1 July) lacked representatives of EPISCOPACY and became dominated by PRESBYTERIANS. It consisted of 30 laymen and 120 clergymen, who drew up the CALVINIST *Confession of Faith* and prepared the DIRECTORY OF PUBLIC WORSHIP to replace the PRAYER BOOK. The Scots regarded the assembly as weak, the INDEPENDENTS were suspicious of it, and PARLIAMENT itself adopted a distinctly ERASTIAN attitude to its thorough-going Presbyterianism.

W.M. Hetherington, *History of the Westminster Assembly of Divines* (London 1843).

Wexford

A major ROYALIST base in Ireland commanded by Colonel David Synott, against which, October 1649, CROMWELL moved with 10,000 men. Bombardment led to negotiations, but in the midst of these, Cromwell launched an assault which took the town. More than 2,000 men were slaughtered in the massacre that followed, which Cromwell attributed to 'an unexpected Providence'.

Whalley, Battles of (20 April 1643)

Two engagements fought at Read Bank or Read Hall and then at Lango Green, all in Lancashire, are known as the Battle of Whalley (where the royalist EARL OF DERBY had his headquarters). It was a decisive defeat for the ROYALISTS and ensured PARLIAMENTARIAN domination of the county.

Whiggamore Raid

When news of the ROYALIST defeat at PRESTON in 1648 came to Scotland, the EARL OF LEVEN led an attempt to overthrow the Engagers (see *ENGAGEMENT*) in EDINBURGH, but was dispersed near Stirling. On 12 September troops under ARGYLE were routed at Linlithgow.

Whitecoats

A ROYALIST infantry regiment, that of the EARL OF NEWCASTLE, which perished almost to a man at MARSTON MOOR 2 July 1644, although given opportunity to surrender. Their self-sacrifice was remarkable for the time, since surrender would have led to release very rapidly.

Whitehall Palace

The chief royal residence in London, ever since Henry VIII had given up the use of WESTMINSTER PALACE. During the civil war the Whitehall Palace was used as lodgings for MPs. On a scaffold outside the banqueting hall CHARLES I was beheaded 30 January 1649.

Whitelocke, Bulstrode (1605–76)

Whitelocke's importance lies in his *Memorials of English Affairs 1625–1660* (first published in four volumes in 1853), which is a largely secondary compilation rather than memoirs. Whitelocke was MP for Marlow, Buckinghamshire, in the LONG PARLIAMENT and chaired the committee prosecuting STRAFFORD. He later saw himself as a mediator for peace between king and PARLIAMENT, and dissembled over his role in the passage of the SELF DENYING ORDINANCE. He carefully cultivated his friendship with CROMWELL and avoided exclusion at PRIDE'S PURGE, but kept his distance from the actual trial and execution of the king (see TRIAL OF CHARLES I).

Whitford, Walter

A former ROYALIST officer who had been taken at NASEBY in 1645. He was named as one of the assassins of ISAAC DORISLAUS in 1649.

Wigan Lane, Battle of (25 August 1651)

Wigan, Lancashire, was long reputed a ROYALIST town during the FIRST CIVIL WAR. On 18 August 1648 Scottish troops were driven in retreat through the town by CROMWELL. On 25 August 1651 a royalist army under the EARL OF DERBY was ambushed near Wigan and defeated.

Wildman, John (1621–93)

Briefly a soldier in the NEW MODEL ARMY, Wildman emerged in 1647 as the spokesman of the soldiers' 'new AGENTS' at the PUTNEY DEBATES. He was the author of *THE CASE OF THE ARMY TRULY STATED*. Imprisoned January to August 1648 by order of the HOUSE OF COMMONS, he and JOHN LILBURNE were both present at the NAGS HEAD TAVERN after their release, where a new *AGREEMENT OF THE PEOPLE* was drafted. After that Wildman abandoned political agitation. He became a soldier again, and a speculator in the forfeited estates of ROYALISTS.

Williams, John See York, Archbishop of

Willoughby on the Wolds, Battle of (5 July 1648)

Scene in Nottinghamshire of the defeat of ROYALIST troops out of Yorkshire by local PARLIAMENTARIAN units, during the SECOND CIVIL WAR.

Wilmot, Henry (1613–58)

MP for Tamworth, Staffordshire, in the LONG PARLIAMENT. He was implicated in the ARMY PLOTS of 1641 and expelled from the HOUSE OF COMMONS. 'A man proud and ambitious and incapable of being contented', as one contemporary saw him, he was Lieutenant General of HORSE to the king in 1643 and elevated to the peerage. A more than competent commander, he won ROUNDWAY DOWN, but was arrested in 1644 for corresponding with the EARL OF ESSEX (see also the OLD HORSE). He was a bitter enemy of PRINCE RUPERT. He was later instrumental in the escape of CHARLES II after the battle of WORCESTER. He died in exile.

Winceby, Battle of (11 October 1643)

A major defeat inflicted upon ROYALIST troops in Lincolnshire by forces of the EASTERN ASSOCIATION and Yorkshire parliamentarians under SIR THOMAS FAIRFAX. CROMWELL was unhorsed and almost killed by the royalist Ingram Hopton. GAINSBOROUGH and Lincoln fell soon after, and the royalists laying siege to HULL abandoned that too.

Winchester

A ROYALIST garrison town in Hampshire which held out against SIR WILLIAM WALLER in May 1643 but fell to CROMWELL 6 October 1645.

Winchester, John Paulet Marquess of (1598–1675)

Known as 'the great loyalist' in respect of his spirited defence of BASING HOUSE, which fell to CROMWELL in 1645. Heavily in debt, therefore unable to make his COMPOSITION, he spent the following years in one gaol or another.

Windebank, Francis (1613–45)

The son of CHARLES I's Secretary of State, and in the household of the PRINCE OF WALES. In April 1645 he surrendered BLETCHINGDON HOUSE to CROMWELL without offering resistance. He was tried by court martial and shot at OXFORD, the king refusing to reprieve him.

Windsor

The NEW MODEL ARMY in the presence of CROMWELL held a three-day prayer session at Windsor, Berkshire, from 29 April 1648, after which it was resolved to call 'CHARLES STUART' to 'an account'.

Winstanley, Gerrard

The effective leader, or spokesman, of the DIGGERS. He saw himself as a true LEVELLER, advocating abolition of private property in his TRACT *The True Leveller's Standard Advanced*. He believed that a state of perfection, such as had prevailed before the Fall, could be achieved by abandoning wage labour, technology and private property rights. Some have seen him as the original Quaker.

T. Wilson Hayes, *Winstanley the Digger* (London 1979).

Wintour, Sir John (1600–62)

Secretary to QUEEN HENRIETTA MARIA 1638–42, and called by Parliamentarian polemicists 'the Court-Papist' (see PAPISTS) and 'the Queen's whiteboy'. He acquired extensive land interests in Gloucestershire, which he used as a base for his military actions against GLOUCESTER, a PARLIAMENTARIAN stronghold. Driven from the Forest of Dean by 1645, he went into hiding, and was exempted from pardon and sentenced to banishment. He was arrested in LONDON in 1649 and named for trial before the HIGH COURT OF JUSTICE, but the proceedings went no further. He remained in prison until 1659.

Winwick, Battle of (19 August 1648)

Scene in Cheshire of a bitter encounter between CROMWELL and Scottish ROYALIST troops, in which the latter were routed.

Witchcraft

Not itself a phenomenon of great occurrence in England, as compared with Europe, but the conditions of the civil war created 'epidemics' of accusations, especially in Essex in 1644–5. Witchcraft, with its astrological, soothsaying features, has been seen as filling a vacuum left in popular religion after the reformation. Scholars have shown that accusations arose from inter-familial or inter-communal tensions.

Woodhouse, Michael

A ROYALIST colonel, sent over from Ireland by ORMONDE early in 1643, he earned himself the soubriquet 'the bloody butcher' for his treatment of the garrison of HOPTON CASTLE. RICHARD SYMONDS noted in his journal that Woodhouse had been in the household of the DUKE OF HAMILTON. Woodhouse had a fierce reputation as a plunderer, but faded from notice after his surrender in 1646.

Woodstock Devil

The story of the Woodstock Devil was popular, and not only amongst ROYALISTS, in 1649 in England. It concerned the supernatural afflictions suffered by PARLIAMENT's commissioners who, in October 1649, went to the royal manor of Woodstock to dispose of its contents. The author of the disturbances was Joseph Collins, employed by the commissioners under an assumed name, but known, apparently, as 'funny Joe' in the area.

Worcester

A ROYALIST garrison city in Worcestershire, and base for operations from 1642 to its surrender 23 July 1646 after a two-month bombardment. On 22 August 1651 forces under CHARLES II occupied the city. On 3 September CROMWELL launched a massive attack against the royalist troops beneath the walls, and in the subsequent heavy fighting 3,000 royalists were killed and 10,000 captured. It was Cromwell's last military action, his 'crowning mercy'. Charles II fled into hiding and thence into exile.

Worcester, Henry Somerset Marquess of (1577–1646)

Reckoned by some to be the richest man in England in 1642, when he put his fortress of RAGLAN, his money, estates and family at the service of the king. His marquessate, bestowed in 1643, was an acknowledgement of his contribution to the war effort in South Wales and the border. He remained in Raglan until it fell to the PARLIAMENT in 1646, and was then imprisoned in LONDON, where he died.

Wortley, Sir Francis (1592–1652)

A reasonably obscure Yorkshire country gentleman who came to national prominence in May 1642, when he drew his sword in public in YORK and declared himself for the king. Denounced as a 'prime and pernicious' ROYALIST, he hurried to excuse his action by issuing *A Declaration from York by Sir Francis Wortley Knight and Baronet. In Vindication of himself from divers aspersions and rumours concerning the drawing of his sword*, which was simultaneously published in LONDON. Plans to impeach (see IMPEACHMENT) him of High Treason fell through and he faded from notoriety, but was taken prisoner in 1644 and sent to LONDON, where he died in the Tower in 1652.

Y

Y Dalar Hir, Battle of (5 June 1648)

A ROYALIST force under SIR JOHN OWEN was defeated at Y Dalar Hir, Caernarfonshire, between Aber and Bangor, by a small parliamentary column, in a decisive action involving little more than 500 men.

York

King CHARLES I set up his court at York from 19 March 1642 as a base to prepare for civil war and to gather supporters, far away from PARLIAMENT at WESTMINSTER. After his departure in July, York became a ROYALIST garrison and base. It was besieged April to June 1644 by a Scottish and PARLIAMENTARIAN army, but PRINCE RUPERT relieved the city 30 June. Following MARSTON MOOR, the city was again besieged and surrendered 16 July 1644.

York, John Williams Archbishop of (1582–1650)

As bishop of Lincoln, Williams played an equivocal role in the early years of the reign of CHARLES I, and was accused of betraying the confidentiality of the PRIVY COUNCIL in 1628. He was gaoled in the Tower of LONDON, for other offences, from 1637 to 1640, but was appointed archbishop of YORK in 1641. When war broke out he abandoned York and his fortified house at nearby Cawood, and fled to his native North Wales to garrison CONWAY CASTLE for the king. In 1645 he negotiated a cessation of hostilities with local PARLIAMENTARIAN commanders, but was deprived of Conway by SIR JOHN OWEN and denounced to the king.

The earliest life of the archbishop, written by John Hackett Bishop of Lichfield, was *Socrinia Reserata* (published 1692). Contemporaries reckoned him a double-dealer.

CHRONOLOGY

1640	13 April	Short Parliament meets
	15 May	Parliament dissolved
	26 October	Treaty of Ripon with Scots
	3 November	Long Parliament meets
1641	16 February	Triennial Act
	3 May	First Army Plot revealed
	10 May	Act of Attainder against Strafford
	12 May	Strafford executed
	24 June	Ten Propositions
	23 October	Irish Rebellion breaks out
	30 October	Second Army Plot revealed
	1 December	Grand Remonstrance presented to Charles I
1642	4 January	Attempt on the Five Members
	10 January	Charles I leaves London

1642	5 March	Militia Ordinance
	23 April	Hotham bars Hull to king
	1 June	Nineteen Propositions
	11 June	Commissions of Array
	4 July	Committee of Safety established
	11 July	Hotham again bars Hull to king
	15 July	Fighting in Manchester
	4 August	Battle of Marshall's Elm
	22 August	Royal standard raised at Nottingham
	22 September	Episcopacy suspended
	23 October	Battle of Edgehill
	12 November	Storm of Brentford
	13 November	Royalists turned back at Turnham Green
1643	1 February	Negotiations open at Oxford
	27 March	First Ordinance for Sequestration

1643	14 April	Oxford talks break down
	24 May	*Treatise of Monarchy* published
	24 June	Battle of Chalgrove Field
	30 June	Battle of Adwalton Moor
	1 July	Westminster Assembly of Divines meets
	5 July	Battle of Lansdown
	13 July	Battle of Roundway Down
	25 September	Solemn League and Covenant
	11 October	Battle of Winceby
	8 December	John Pym dies
1644	19 January	Scottish army invades England
	22 January	Oxford Parliament meets
	25 January	Battle of Nantwich
	25 January	Committee of Both Kingdoms set up
	29 March	Battle of Cheriton

1644	11 April	Battle of Selby
	29 June	Battle of Cropredy Bridge
	2 July	Battle of Marston Moor
	14 July	Queen Henrietta Maria leaves England
	16 July	Surrender of York
	1 September	Battle of Tippermuir
	2 September	Lostwithiel
	27 October	Second Battle of Newbury
1645	4 January	Ordinance for *Directory of Worship*
	10 January	Archbishop William Laud executed
	29 January	Uxbridge negotiations open
	17 February	New Model Army Ordinance
	3 April	Self Denying Ordinance
	30 May	Storm of Leicester
	14 June	Battle of Naseby

1645	10 July	Battle of Langport
	15 August	Battle of Kilsyth
	25 August	Glamorgan's Treaty with Irish
	10 September	Fall of Bristol
	13 September	Battle of Philiphaugh
	24 September	Battle of Rowton Heath
	20 December	Glamorgan's Second Treaty
1646	21 March	Astley surrenders at Stow-on-the-Wold
	5 May	King surrenders to Scots
	6 May	Surrender of Newark-on-Trent
	5 June	Battle of Benburb
	13 July	Oxford surrenders
	14 July	Newcastle Propositions
	9 October	Abolition of episcopacy
1647	30 January	Scots surrender king

1647	21 March	First Saffron Walden meeting of MPs and army officers
	15 April	Second Saffron Walden meeting
	28 April	Agitators address the House of Commons
	7 May	Third Saffron Walden meeting
	4 June	King removed to Newmarket
	5 June	*Solemn Engagement*
	14 June	*Declaration of the New Model Army*
	16 June	Army moves against Eleven Members
	23 July	Heads of Proposals submitted to king
	30 July	Speaker and Independent MPs flee to the army
	6 August	Army occupies London
	8 August	Battle of Dangan Hill
	20 August	Null and Void Ordinance
	7 September	Hampton Court Proposals

1647	15 October	*Case of the Army Truly Stated*
	28 October	*Agreement of the People*
	28 October	Putney Debates begin
	11 November	King escapes to Isle of Wight
	14 December	Four Bills
	24 December	Four Bills presented to king
	26 December	King and Scots enter into *The Engagement*
1648	3 January	Vote of No Addresses
	23 March	Laugharne's revolt in Wales
	8 May	Battle of St Fagans
	24 May	House of Commons votes to negotiate with king
	26 May	Kentish revolt fails
	27 May	Navy revolts against Parliament
	1 June	Battle of Maidstone
	8 June	Rising in Essex
	13 June	Colchester Castle seized
	10 July	Battle of St Neots

1648	17 August	Battle of Preston
	18 August	Batle of Wigan
	24 August	Repeal of Vote of No Addresses
	25 August	Duke of Hamilton surrenders
	27 August	Colchester Castle surrenders
	11 September	Levellers' *Humble Petition*
	18 September	Newport Treaty talks begin
	29 October	Assassination of Rainsborough
	16 November	*Remonstrance of the Army*
	2 December	Army occupies London
	6 December	Pride's Purge
1649	4 January	Assumption of full legislative power by House of Commons
	20 January	Trial of Charles I commences
	30 January	Execution of Charles I
	5 February	Charles II proclaimed in Scotland
	8 February	*Eikon Basilike* printed

1649	14 February	Council of State set up
	17 March	Abolition of monarchy
	19 March	Abolition of House of Lords
	27 April	Execution of Lockyer the mutineer
	15 May	Mutiny suppressed at Burford
	19 May	England proclaimed a Commonwealth
	2 August	Battle of Rathmines
	11 September	Drogheda slaughter
	11 October	Wexford slaughter
1650	2 January	Engagement Act
	27 April	Battle of Carbisdale
	21 May	Execution of Montrose
	26 May	Ireton takes over in Ireland
	11 June	Treaty of Heligoland
	26 June	Fairfax resigns his commission
	3 September	Battle of Dunbar

1651	1 January	Charles II crowned in Scotland
	15 July	English troops enter Scotland
	20 July	Battle of Inverkeithing
	1 August	Charles II sets off for England
	28 August	Scottish Committee of the Estates taken
	3 September	Battle of Worcester

SELECT BIBLIOGRAPHY

Adair, J., *Roundhead General: A Biography of Sir William Waller*, London 1969.

Adair, J., *Cheriton 1644 The Campaign and the Battle*, Kineton 1973.

Allen, J.W., *English Political Thought 1603–1644*, London 1938.

Ashton, R., *The English Civil War: Conservatism and Revolution 1603–1649*, London 1978.

Aylmer, G.E., *The Struggle for the Constitution*, London 1963.

Aylmer, G.E., *The King's Servants*, London 1973.

Aylmer, G.E., *Rebellion or Revolution*, Oxford 1986.

Bossy, J., *The English Catholic Community 1570–1850*, London 1975.

Bottigheimer, K.S., *English Money and Irish Land*, Oxford 1971.

Boynton, L., *The Elizabethan Militia 1558–1638*, London 1967.

Brunton, D., and Pennington, D.H., *Members of the Long Parliament*, London 1954.

Buchan, J., *Montrose*, London 1928.

Burne, A.H., and Young, P., *The Great Civil War: A Military History of the First Civil War 1642–1646*, London 1959.

Carlton, C., *Charles I: The Personal Monarch*, London 1983.

Cliffe, J.T., *The Puritan Gentry*, London 1984.

Davies, R.T., *Four Centuries of Witch Beliefs*, London 1947.

Dodd, A.H., *Studies in Stuart Wales*, Cardiff 1952.

Durston, C., *The Family in the English Revolution*, London 1989.

Eccleshall, R., *Order and Reason in Politics: Theories of Absolute and Limited Monarchy in Early Modern England*, Oxford 1978.

Eustace, T., ed., *Statesmen and Politicians of the Stuart Age*, London 1985.

Firth, C.H., *Cromwell's Army*, London 1902.

FitzPatrick, B., *Seventeenth Century Ireland: The War of Religions*, Dublin 1988.

Fletcher, A., *The Outbreak of the English Civil War*, London 1981.

Gardiner, S.R., *History of the Great Civil War 1642–1648*, London 1901.

Hardacre, P.H., *The Royalists during the Puritan Revolution*, London 1956.

Hexter, J.H., *The Reign of King Pym*, Harvard 1941.

Hill, C., *The World Turned Upside Down*, London 1972.

Hirst, D., *The Representative of the People? Voters and Voting in England under the Early Stuarts*, Cambridge 1975.

Hirst, D., *Authority and Conflict: England 1605–1658*, London 1986.

Hutton, R., *The Royalist War Effort, 1642–1646*, London 1982.

Keeler, M., *The Long Parliament 1640–1641*, Philadelphia 1954.

Kenyon, J.P., *The Stuart Constitution*, London 1966.

Kenyon, J.P., *The Civil Wars of England*, London 1988.

Lamont, W.M., *Godly Rule: Politics and Religion 1603–1660*, London 1969.

Lindley, K., *Fenland Riots and the English Revolution*, London 1982.

Loftis, J., ed., *The Memoirs of Anne Lady Halkett and Ann Lady Fanshawe*, Oxford 1979.

Lucas Philips, C.E., *Cromwell's Captains*, London 1938.

MacCurtain, M., *Tudor and Stuart Ireland*, Dublin 1972.

MacFarlane, A., *Witchcraft in Tudor and Stuart England*, London 1970.

McGregor, J.F., and Reay, B., *Radical Religion in the English Revolution*, Oxford 1984.

Manning, B., *The English People and the English Revolution 1640–1649*, London 1976.

Marchant, R.A., *The Church under the Law*, Cambridge 1969.

Moody, T.W., ed., *The New History of Ireland Volume 3, Early Modern Ireland 1534–1691*, Oxford 1976.

Morrill, J., *The Revolt of the Provinces*, rev. edn London 1980.

Newman, P.R., *Royalist Officers in England and Wales 1642–1660*, New York 1981.

Newman, P.R., *Atlas of the English Civil War*, London 1985.

Parry, R.H., *The English Civil War and After 1642–1658*, London 1970.

Pennington, D., and Thomas, K., eds, *Puritans and Revolutionaries*, London 1978.

Phillips, J.R., *Memorials of the Civil War in Wales and the Marches 1642–1649*, 2 vols, London 1874.

Powell, J.R., *The Navy in the English Civil War*, London 1962.

Richardson, R.C., *The Debate on the English Revolution*, London 1977.

Rogers, H.C.B., *Battles and Generals of the Civil Wars, 1642–1651*, London 1968.

Roots, I., *The Great Rebellion 1642–1660*, London 1966.

Russell, C., *The Crisis of Parliaments 1509–1660*, Oxford 1971.

Russell, C., ed., *The Origins of the English Civil War*, London 1973.

Shwoerer, L., *No Standing Armies! The Anti-Army Ideology in 17th Century England*, London 1974.

Shaw, W.A., *A History of the English Church during the Civil Wars and under the Commonwealth 1640–1660*, 2 vols, London 1900.

Spufford, M., *Contrasting Communities*, London 1974.

Stevenson, D., *The Scottish Revolution 1637–1644*, London n.d.

Stevenson, D., *Revolution and Counter-Revolution in Scotland, 1644–1651*, London 1977.

Thomas, K.V., *Religion and the Decline of Magic*, London 1971.

Trevor Roper, H.R., *Archbishop Laud*, 2nd edn, London 1962.

Underdown, D., *Royalist Conspiracy in England 1649–1660*, Yale 1960.

Underdown, D., *Pride's Purge*, Oxford 1971.

Underdown, D., *Revel, Riot and Rebellion*, Oxford 1985.

Wedgwood, C.V., *The King's Peace*, London 1955.

Wedgwood, C.V., *The King's War*, London 1958.

Woodhouse, A.S.P., *Puritanism and Liberty*, 2nd edn, London 1974.

Woolrych, A., *Battles of the English Civil War*, London 1961.

Woolrych, A., *Commonwealth to Protectorate*, Oxford 1982.

Woolrych, A., *Soldiers and Statesmen: The General Council of the Army and its Debates, 1647–1648*, Oxford 1987.

Wrightson, K., *English Society 1580–1680*, London 1982.

Young, P., and Holmes, R., *The English Civil War: A Military History of the Three Civil Wars*, London 1974.

MAPS

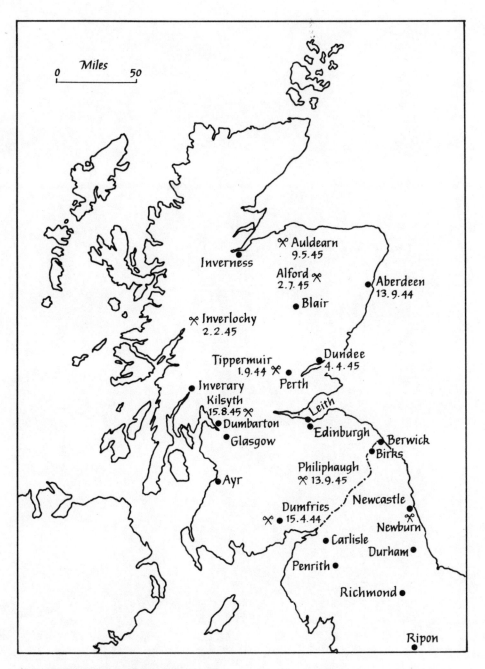

Miles
0   50

✗ Auldearn
  9.5.45

Alford ✗
2.7.45

● Aberdeen
  13.9.44

Inverness ●

● Blair

✗ Inverlochy
  2.2.45

Tippermuir
1.9.44 ✗

Dundee ✗
4.4.45

● Perth

✗ Inverary

Kilsyth
15.8.45 ✗

● Dumbarton

● Glasgow

Leith

● Edinburgh

● Berwick
● Birks

Philiphaugh
✗ 13.9.45

● Ayr

Dumfries
✗ ● 15.4.44

Newcastle ●

Newburn ✗

● Carlisle

Durham ●

Penrith ●

Richmond ●

Ripon ●

Civil War in Scotland 1644–45

Civil War in Ireland 1641–52

- ▲ Royalist garrison
- ■ Parliamentarian garrison
- ▨ Royalist controlled
- ⌐ ‑ ¬ Parliamentary controlled

Corbridge ✕
19.2.44
▲ Newcastle
▲ Carlisle

Marston Moor ✕
2.7.44
▲ York
■ Hull

Adwalton ✕
30.6.43

■ Manchester

Winceby 11.10.43

▲ Chester
▲ Newark

Nantwich ✕
25.1.44
■ Nottingham

Hopton Heath ✕
19.3.43
▲ Lichfield
■ Birmingham

Ripple Field ✕
13.4.43
Cropredy Bridge ✕
29.6.44

Gloucester ■
Oxford ▲
Chalgrove Field ✕ 10.6.43

Lansdown Hill ✕
5.7.43
■ LONDON

Bristol ▲
Newbury ✕
27.10.44 & 20.9.43

Roundway Down ✕
13.7.43
● Alton

Marshall's ✕
Elm 1642
▲ Wardour Castle

Stratton ✕
16.5.43
Sourton Down ✕
25.4.43
✕ Cheriton 29.3.44

Braddock Down ✕
19.1.43
Lostwithiel ✕ 31.8.44

0 Miles 50

Civil War Actions 1643–44

The Second Civil War 1648 – The Scottish Invasion

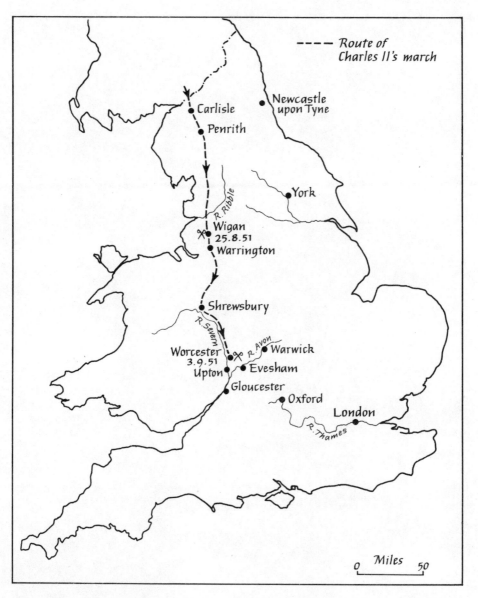

- - - - Route of
Charles II's march

Newcastle
upon Tyne

Carlisle
Penrith

York

R. Ribble

Wigan
25.8.51
Warrington

Shrewsbury

R. Severn

Worcester
3.9.51
Upton

R. Avon

Warwick

Evesham

Gloucester

Oxford

London

R. Thames

Miles
0   50

The 1651 Insurrection